Contents

For WILMUS

remembering big seas

The Field of Sighing

A Highland boyhood

by Donald Cameron

Birlinn

This edition published in 2003 by
Birlinn Limited
West Newington House
10 Newington Road
Edinburgh
EH9 1QS

www.birlinn.co.uk

First published in 1966 by Longmans

ISBN 1 84158 233 6

British Library Cataloguing-in-Publication Data
A catalogue record of this book is available
from the British Library

Printed and bound by Creative Print and Design, Ebbw Vale

Introduction

It's a quarter of a century since I first encountered *The Field of Sighing*. I read it with a sense of wonder and delight, and have re-read it with deepening pleasure several times since. The author has a wonderfully off-hand way with traditional knowledge – his mention at p. 185 of how the waders covered Our Lord with seaweed when the Roman soldiers came to arrest Him calls to mind how, in the version I know, Christ hides under some straw, the hen scratches it away, and the duck covers Him up again. He also has a remarkable talent for describing middle-aged and elderly women.

It's a classic of its kind, though what exactly its kind *is* is open to debate. The term 'poetic soap' doesn't do it justice – 'poetic family saga', perhaps, 'in a richly-described natural setting'. A book about human relationships written by a naturalist, at a universal level it goes much deeper than those classic works on Highland shepherding, Iain Thomson's *Isolation Shepherd* and John Barrington's *Red Sky at Night*.

It's a beautifully crafted book, moving gracefully in ten well-planned chapters through a young man's recollections of a Highland community in peace and in war from his birth at Blarosnich in April 1925 to his departure for the Merchant Navy in 1942 or 1943. The last chapter is full of surprises. There are touches of humour, as when the narrator's grandmother harangues the maid 'in the same way as she plagued her Maker on a Sunday morning about the foxes'. A plot-line runs through the book, but it's hard to know who or what is the real hero or heroine – the narcissistic young narrator? his grandmother? Blarosnich in all its moods? It's the embellishment that really counts, the description, the love of detail. Glance through *The Field of Sighing*, however, and look at the chapter endings. They're all perfect; and they're all about human relationships.

There's middle ground between wild nature and human relationships, but ask ten individuals what this middle ground contains and they'll give you ten different answers. Many of these answers are to be found scattered around the book. There's farming itself, of course – cattle and sheep and drains and hay-making. Hunting – the stags of autumn are lovingly described, we learn of the slaughter of gannets and puffins in Eilean a'Cathmara, the two farmers go duck-shooting once a week in autumn and winter, and our narrator is especially happy when going round the west shore and over to the island after seals. Spirituality – the enduring tension between Presbyterian righteousness and the attachment to charms, spells and amulets that lies at the interface between Primalism and Catholicism is much to the fore. There's sexuality, too, in its moody, uncertain teenage variety, expressed with a sublime combination of delicacy and honesty.

And food. Oh yes, food. If you love food, you'll love *The Field of Sighing*: it's surely the grandfather and grandmother of Scots cookery writing. Food is described with an affection close to passion.

> When the cattle crossed the ford I was free to return for breakfast. But often I went searching for mushrooms. They were not hard to find, for in the Earl's Park they seemed to have favourite places to grow in. Sometimes I arrived back at the house with my beret half full. By the time we had finished our porridge they would be welling with their own sweet juice on top of the stove, ready for succulent eating. Those mellow October mornings began with the taste of mushrooms and crispy bacon and the sweet tang of salt-sharp and wood-smoke air . . .

Donald Cameron wrote another book, *Sons of El Dorado: Venezuelan Adventure*, 1968, also published by Longmans. 'Of all the seas I have sailed,' he declares, 'not many come to mind. And I have sailed quite a few since leaving Blarosnich, my Highland sheep-farm home, as a boy of seventeen.' Writing 'for DAL / on weathering the storm / out of Rotterdam', he tells how the age-old lure of diamonds brings him to Venezuela, where the combination of his father's and mother's names turns him into Don Aldo con Merón y Campelo. Delayed by the rains, he spends several months teaching English in Caracas. He makes many friends and begins to write, until finally able to go prospecting. In the end he is driven from the country by an epidemic of yellow fever, the danger of impending revolution, and the murder of a popular young writer who is interested in translating his poetry. This man, nicknamed the *Enfant Terrible*, is killed with a red-hot poker in the same unspeakable manner as Edward II in 1327. Declaring his intention to head for the West Indies and on to Canada, the narrator moves on.

Though constructed just as carefully, *Sons of El Dorado* is *The Field of Sighing* in reverse. Cameron's greatest strength, as we've seen, lies in displaying human interreaction in the teeth of wild nature. *The Field of Sighing* contains nine chapters about Blarosnich, and one about a visit to London; *Sons of El Dorado* has seven chapters about Caracas and places like it, but only one about the Interior.

Let me introduce the 'Field of Sighing' and its people as succinctly as I can. It lies in the south-western corner of a West Highland peninsula bordered on three sides by turbulent seas and rocky, inaccessible coasts. The six-roomed farmhouse is out of sight and earshot of the sea, and enjoys a well-stocked orchard. A mile down to the west, by the shore, is a crofting township where about sixty people live in twenty houses. Up the road to the east is the Big House with its sporting tenants. Beyond the Big House is the estate's other farm, Sallachie – *Seileachaidh*, 'the Place of Willows'.

Blarosnich Farm lies in a 'narrow strath' (a contradiction in terms?) between two hills. To the north and west, towering above wooded lower slopes, is Craigclamhan – *Creag a' Chlamhain*, 'the Rock of the Peregrine Falcon'. To the north and east, behind Sallachie, is a lesser hill called Craighar – *Creag Shear*, 'Eastern Rock'? Stretching across half the moor between Craigclamhan and Craighar are the long, reedy arms of *Lochan Màthair Labharaig*, 'the Mother Lochan of Labharag', garlanded with yellow iris.

Labharag itself, 'the Noisy Little Female', spills over the immense rock-face which buttresses the moor and plunges through braes of grey scree to the valley bottom. The narrator's father builds a corn-mill to harness its power. Two other burns join it in its lower reaches; together they make a good-sized river which pounds over boulders and waterfalls, one of which tumbles 'like a tress of hair' into a deep churning basin – the Stag's Pool. On either side of Stag's Pool the slopes are clothed in thick woods of beech, oak, sycamore, pine, spruce and larch, while along the banks of Labharag grow alder, ash and birch.

As the patrimony of Sir Duncan Campbell of Glenorchy, who died at Flodden in 1513, Blarosnich became part of the vast estates of his successors the earls of Breadalbane. After the days of the great marquis in Prince Albert's era, the Breadalbane blood-line faltered and many of the estates were sold off. Now all that remains of Sir Duncan's lands to the family, just across the stepping-stones of Labharag from Blarosnich Farm, is a tiny parcel called the Earl's Park, which they have kept for the sole purpose of holding on to their ancient titles. An untamed wilderness full of birch, rowans and birdsong, it's completely enclosed by a stone dyke (as are the Blarosnich tack and the crofters' common pasture, both of whose marches come to meet it).

The flattest part of the peninsula is around the shores of Lochan Màthair Labharaig in the centre. It's known as *a' Mhìn Choiseachd*, 'the Easy Walking'. Where the path meets the sea on the north side, more than two hours walking and climbing from Blarosnich, is an idyllic spot known as Pitlobar – *Peit an Lobhair*, or *Baile an Lobhair* perhaps in modern Gaelic, 'the Leper's Township'.

There's only one house at Pitlobar nowadays. It faces across a treacherous 'kyle' or strait, on the other side of which lie the low southern cliffs of *Eilean a'Cathmara*. Better perhaps *Eilean a' Chath Mhara* ('the Isle of the Sea Battle'), it is 'the largest of three small islands on the other side of Craigclamhan mountain'.

To what battle its name refers we don't know, but before the famine of 1847–49 the island supported a sizeable population. On it are a deserted township, a larger ruin called St Mungo's Cell, and a rushy lochan. Behind its high northern cliffs lie eight miles of dangerous currents, where the broad mouth of a great sea-loch meets the Atlantic, until one reaches the mainland again on the other side.

Blarosnich farm has good land for cattle and sheep in three places – the far shore of Pitlobar, the Craigclamhan flanks, and the lochan moor. Sallachie, by contrast, with only a short stretch of coastline where it touches the northern shore a little east of Pitlobar, has just two small grass parks and hardly enough moor. It's a place full of stones, not willows – a difficult farm to work, despite having no great peak to compare with the magnificence of Craigclamhan. Blarosnich acts as a windbreak for Sallachie, shielding it from the Atlantic, but when the snow falls at Sallachie it seems deeper and more treacherous than at Blarosnich.

When the policeman comes to the Field of Sighing he has ten miles to travel. There are roads in the peninsula, coursed by pony-traps, cars, lorries, tractors, motorbikes and bicycles, but the way out is by sea. You go down to the pier by the coastguard station, the ferryman brings you to the steamer, and the steamer brings you to the train. A prominent landmark on the shore road is a tall obelisk erected long ago at the Fall of the White Mares – *Eas nan Làirean Bàna*, I suppose. It surmounts a mausoleum built for himself by a former proprietor who is remembered in the district as 'Long Sammy of the Coach and Pair'. He encumbered the estate with so many debts from his gambling and debauchery that it had to be sold. When his son came back from the army and found what had happened he brought a ladder and a sledge-hammer, went up and took out his rage on the obelisk with a single blow. The top is missing to this day.

But what of the people who live here now? Well, Donald Angus Cameron, the narrator, has been one of the Blarosnich shepherds (succeeding his grandmother) since he left the township school at the age of 14. A sensitive lad, he recalls in *Sons of El Dorado* that the first time he saw the Aurora Borealis he thought 'the Lord was returning, and that everybody at Blarosnich would be carried up bodily into the vast aerial palaces scintillating about us in the sky – everybody that is, except me, for I knew the Lord would leave me behind, since I had a guilty conscience over things normal to boyhood'.

The narrator's mother, Rhona Campbell, died when he was seven. She was a native of Inveraray, daughter of the Duke of Argyll's game-keeper, an outstanding piper. Her husband, also Donald, is the tenant farmer. A quiet man, he too is a piper, and his deep knowledge of Highland plant and bird life is sought in letters from naturalists. His mother, the narrator's grandmother, is a star turn, a true original. A crofter's daughter, she is the last person to have been born in Eilean a'Cathmara, on whose sunken skerries her father was lost.

At the age of 17 she came to the mainland to live in the crofting township. She married the local ferryman, whose name was also Donald Cameron, 'Don the Ferry'. In due course he became skipper of the yacht owned by the Blarosnich sporting tenants. By the time the yacht was sold the couple had saved enough money to rent

Blarosnich from the Government, and to buy enough ewes from the outgoing tenant to stock an adequate herd. (Why the Government owned Blarosnich is not explained; perhaps it had something to do with the Forestry Commission.)

Although choc-a-bloc with core values – horror of debt, respect for the dignity of labour – the grandmother is no caricature. When she moved to Blarosnich 'she was glad to put the mountain of Craig-clamhan between her and the sea and the little sea-battered island'.

Mirren, the maid, comes from the crofting township. She mainly works out of doors with calves and fowl, gathering and washing eggs, and spending fine summer weather in the hay-parks. She and Alec – the other farm shepherd, a man in his fifties who lives at Pitlobar in the summer and in a bothy adjacent to the farmhouse in the winter – are in love, but neither has the courage to express it.

Alec's paternal grandfather was born in Eilean a'Cathmara in 1795, while his mother, Maggie, was from Eriskay. His head is full of Gaelic literature and tradition, and he is a poet. We may be grateful to the author for avoiding the corny word 'bard'.

Another semi-detached member of the family is Teacher. At the start of the book she is living with her husband Niall the Ferry, who has a drink problem. In the middle the narrator attends her school. By the end Niall is dead and Teacher has moved into the farmhouse, where she becomes a sort of unpaid but much-loved housekeeper, sleeping in the big bed with the narrator's grandmother.

The tenants at Sallachie are Sandy and his wife Violet, who reads tea-cups. Their son Black Fergus, a tearaway, is two years older than the narrator; they go everywhere together. In particular, they enjoy visiting Irish navvies ('Paddies') camped at the Forestry Commission plantation.

The sporting tenants in the Big House are two sisters called Florence (nicknamed Florence of Arabia for her generosity) and Philippa (nicknamed the Cannibal because she is rumoured to eat raw meat). The sport is purely for their guests. With them is an aged and incontinent General. Normally in residence during the summer only, when war comes in 1939 they move in permanently. They have a gamekeeper, Duncan, the best piper in the district, whose wife is a Wee Free. Florence, Philippa and Duncan all feature in *Sons of El Dorado*, where we're told:

The hirsels of soft winters in the south or the strength of Lord Lovat's herds did not symbolize riches for me nearly so much as the bony fingers of two eccentric women who were the sporting tenants of the estate. During the summer months they lived at the big house in the manner to suit their position. As a boy I was not fascinated by the ladies' tiny stature and birdlike features, the odd clothes or odder manner of shouting at each other down silver ear-trumpets when they condescended to visit my grandmother. It was their claw-like hands which hypnotized me. The fingers bore rings whose diamonds, according to my grandmother, were worth several farms of land, diamonds which could 'Buy a proprietor out of his father's bed'.

I pondered on this for years. Could the best herd in Dingwall market itself, or whole mountainsides of forest and deer, farmhouses and townships, really be bought for just those few, tiny pieces of sparkling glass? They could, without doubt, as I was told after every visit the two ladies made to Blarosnich.

Though comical, the ladies also seemed formidable to me and I never summoned enough courage to ask them about the stones that gave such distinction to the withered fingers. I never came closer to inspecting the diamonds than a bad mannered stare would allow. But I shared an intimate friendship with the ladies' gamekeeper. He had gone to Canada as a young trapper with the Hudson Bay Company—'The old H.B.C.' as he would mischievously say to provoke my grandmother, 'Here Before Christ',—and had frequented the Whisky Flats of Whitehorse in their heyday.

I pestered him so repeatedly with questions about the desperate sourdoughs defying the Arctic and Indian arrows as they struggled over mountain passes to reach Klondike that it all seemed more vivid than our own perpetual struggle to keep the sheep's long fleeces from balling in the snow.

The most notable of the many guests who pass through the Big House is Eddie, who would nowadays be called a 'champagne socialist'. In *Sons of El Dorado*, however, we learn of another, unnamed, with whom the narrator falls in love.

The profound thoughts and words 'fitly spoken' in those night watches from the rising and falling pulpit of a ship's bows were not always Solomon's or Keats's *Bright Star* which I had committed to memory during repetition classes in the township school. Those words addressed to the ocean night concerned a pair of 'star-crossed lovers'.

I was one of the pair and rising seventeen when it happened. I fell in love with somebody who came to stay at the Big House. But nothing could be done about it, or at least not much, for the rigidly guarded kirk truth of 'The rich man in his castle, the poor man at his gate' put a barrier between us.

To begin with I tried to sit as near as possible to the Big House pew on Sunday. But the fires that raged in my adolescent heart got out of control and even sent convention up in flames so that I dared to breach the unbreachable Big House at its weakest point—through the post.

The names of Big House guests could easily be discovered from the servants in the township as well as their likes and dislikes. But how was I to brave the impersonal coldness of ink, the unresponsive hardness of nib and the obstinate blankness of paper when addressing, anonymously, the loved person whose precious voice I had heard in utterance over nothing more (or less) than Sunday's paraphrases? I spent hours trying to spear on my pen the words expressive of my feelings. In desperation I even resorted to my grandmother's compendium of life and death, the Bible, but found nothing to my purpose. In the end I sent a couplet:

> *Had I read the stars above you*
> *Would I still have dared to love you?*

At the time these words summed up the tidal-wave of adolescent emotions that were partly responsible for me wanting to leave the security of home for a wanderer's life at sea . . .

The house of my birth ceased to be home when Herself, that rugged, marvellous old woman who was my grandmother and the indomitable spirit in a hill gathering, at last went, as she would have said, to meet her Maker. The place in my life once occupied by the Big House visitor, whom I had loved desperately, was successively taken by others. I fancied each was the great purpose to life. Yet, when physical passions had been assuaged, the warmth of human understanding that promised to be an oasis in my seaman's life proved to be a mirage. I was alone but not lonely.

There is poetry in prose all over *The Field of Sighing*. We are told on one page that 'all day long the pewter-plated sea ran in and out of the rocky coast with thunderings and sinister suctions like a giant sucking a rotten tooth', and on the next that 'standing like silent, brown robed monks, the deer waited in the lower braes for the ring of the axes to end'. The narrator cuts sentimental verses from newspapers and writes poems of his own in moments of emotion, as when he spends a winter's morning watching the roe in the Earl's

Park, or the family hears that the *Royal Oak* has been sunk by a U-boat in Scapa Flow.

There's less poetry, but more *about* poetry, in *Sons of El Dorado*. Its narrator speaks of an English priest in the diamond-fields: 'Padre gave me a "shot" also not of penicillin but of self-confidence. Over the years I had dropped into a habit of jotting down things which came into my head, including occasional scraps of verse.'

He scribbles a poem on the fly-leaf of a Spanish grammar. Padre suggests he send it to *The Tablet*. He does so, it's published, and he receives a cheque. 'Consequent upon Padre's visit, from that thatched hut high above the Venamo River, with the good Padre smoking his pipe, no doubt to drown the smell of smoked tapir, drying fish and insect repellent, I made my debut in print.'

What he tries to capture in his verse, he says, is 'a world like all markets that spins on an axis of want'. Next published – he doesn't say where – is a poem about Petare Market. And he contributes a prose piece about an old man called Luis and his two dogs ('Night in the Forest') to the magazine of the People's Dispensary for Sick Animals. 'In these small ways, each as exciting to me as finding diamonds, a horizon opened beyond the days at sea and the mosquito-wearying nights of a prospector's camp.'

It will be clear from all this that Donald Cameron is a creative artist. How accurate then is his portrait of the Field of Sighing?

Well, there's no such place. Our map was specially created for the present edition in the spirit of *Treasure Island*. Blarosnich is nowhere – and everywhere. In fact, the author takes pains to connect it with every single Highland county. It's on the west coast, yet suffers chronically from drifting snow. The *Royal Oak* sinks 'just along the coast', which suggests Caithness or Sutherland. The market is in Dingwall, which suggests Ross-shire. The narrator's father has a cousin who farms in the Black Isle, which is close to Dingwall, yet can't find time to go and see him. Perhaps it's no wonder, given that 'Don the Ferry' went to the games at Fort William, which is a lot further south. The presence of Catholicism and the mention of Lovat's herds suggest Inverness-shire. The sporting tenants' musical nephew, John, who seldom comes north from London, makes the Big House sound like Dunvegan. Eilean a'Cathmara is said to have 'swarmed with gannet colonies' which provided the natives with much of their diet; this is inspired by St Kilda – as, I suspect, is the remark that 'neither Florence of Arabia nor her sister went to any of the three islands whose sporting rights they held in addition to those of Blarosnich and Sallachie', for St Kilda consists basically of three islands, owned for centuries by the MacLeods of Dunvegan.

So it goes on. Though there's no place called Blarosnich, there are two called Achosnich (*Ach' a' Chosnaich*, 'the Day-Labourer's Field'), one near Golspie in Easter Sutherland, the other on the outermost tip of Ardnamurchan, where Donald Cameron is in fact a very common name. The passengers of Don the Ferry's yacht are described as 'the select of the land—gentry like Cameron of Lochiel, the Dunstaffnage, the Rudds of Ardnamurchan and Winston Churchill'. Dunstaffnage, like Ardnamurchan, is in Argyll. So is Oban, where women go to buy dresses. So is Inveraray, where the narrator's mother was born. So is Glenorchy, the *real* patrimony of Sir Duncan Campbell, whose descendants' Breadalbane estate came to extend all the way from the island of Seil south of Oban on the west coast to their principal seat at Taymouth in central Perthshire. And the Pictish place-name 'Pitlobar' suggests a location in Perthshire – or elsewhere along the eastern fringe of the Highlands.

Even allowing that the picture is composite, there remain some strange features. Venison breakfasts are eaten at lambing time, and grey seals on Eilean a'Cathmara climb 'right up the cliffs', so many having fatal accidents that Alec doesn't need to bring his gun. 'His friends among the seals died naturally in sufficient numbers to yield all the oil he needed.'

Some of the English is not quite what we might expect. Sheep's udders are often called 'breasts'. The countryside is criss-crossed with 'lanes'. The narrator refers to 'poets of the Gaelic' rather than 'Gaelic poets' and, as we have seen, to 'the Dunstaffnage' rather than 'the Captain of Dunstaffnage' or 'Dunstaffnage'. We hear of 'a scalp of bees' – is this Gaelic *sgeap* 'a hive'?

In universal Scottish usage, when a lake happens to be in Scotland it is called a loch, yet the author refers to 'the lake which fed Labharag burn'. Conversely, he picks up the word 'kirk', seldom used in Highland English, and runs with it as a substitute for 'church' – 'in kirk', 'kirk-supper', and (of a shirt) 'dirtier than if I had worn it a dozen Sundays to kirk'.

The narrator refers to his grandmother as 'Herself', introducing her as 'Herself, as my grandmother was called'. This must be the latest occurrence in Scottish literature of Sir Walter Scott's curious habit of making Highlanders speak in the third person. One wonders how young Donald addressed her. Had he shown due respect he would have called her *Seanmhair*, still used by many grandchildren (even non-Gaelic-speaking ones like the narrator) to this day.

But then, she's no ordinary Gaelic-speaking grandmother. She speaks a great deal of Scots – 'puir lads', 'och the puir wee man', 'never let your gear owergang ye', 'keeping your neb at the grunstane', even 'there's nowt sae queer as folks' – what language is that? A bit of it trickles down, so that the narrator talks of 'Postie' and 'a puckle of hoggs'. There's a tradition of this in Scottish literature, for three reasons. One is that down to the nineteenth century in areas like Perthshire, Aberdeenshire and Easter Ross there were genuine Gaelic–Scots bilinguals. Another is that until primary education was made universal by the Education (Scotland) Act 1872, many Gaelic speakers, girls especially, picked up English not from books or schoolmasters but from anybody who fell in their way – at harvests in the Lothians or in east-coast herring ports, for example. The narrator's grandmother would have been born about 1860, and he tells us that she 'never received a formal education'. The third reason is that some novelists have substituted Scots for Gaelic as a signal to their readers that what is being spoken at a particular point is not English. Simon Taylor does this openly in *Mortimer's Deep*, but earlier writers such as Neil Munro were less explicit, leading alien imitators such as Amy Murray to misunderstand their purpose, with very quaint results.

Astonishingly, although the grandmother is a Presbyterian of 'stern Christian principles', instead of preparing for the Sabbath she presides every Saturday evening over a domestic ceilidh, with music and dancing, to which the neighbours are invited. And her tastes in music are curiously Kennedy-Fraserish. She plays the harp and sings songs such as the 'Eriskay Love Lilt', the 'Eriskay Lullaby' and 'Caristone' (a mistake for Kennedy-Fraser's 'Caristiona'). This goes with the narrator's fondness for the term 'cromag' for a walking-stick – did he get it from Kenneth Macleod's 'as step I wi' my cromag to the Isles'? Even the dances performed are posh – 'the Eightsome,

Miss Hebburn Belches, Hamilton House, the Duke of Perth or the Dashing White Sergeant'.

There's some good Gaelic. The *caoidh-chòmhradh* or 'mournful expressions' of the wind form a neatly poetic phrase, as does the *Mìn Choiseachd*. I can well imagine that the narrator's grandmother would be called 'Yonder Cailleach' in the township, as he tells us, if we may assume that it's for *a' chailleach ud thall* or the like. But he praises an Englishwoman for calling things 'him' and 'her' without mentioning that this is normal in Gaelic, which has no neuter. And he ought to have known that, as a Pictish place-name, Pitlobar (which he translates plausibly as 'Croft of the Leper's Portion') could hardly have been named after Alec's mother Maggie, social outcast though she may have been. But then, maybe he's joking . . .

Some strangenesses are little things, such as a bit of nonsense about a she-holly in Eriskay. Others have to do with the grandmother's personal habits. Eccentric though she is, it's unlikely that an island-born snob would relish crab-meat, for in her time shellfish was the food of poverty and famine.

Odd little verses are scattered around the book, such as a 'Skye prayer' in English rhyme. Those which can be classed as charms or incantations are whimsical adaptations of material collected by Alexander Carmichael. 'Music of the lyre' in his 'Prayer of the Teats' (*Carmina Gadelica*, vol. 4, p. 65) becomes 'music of the byre' at p. 155 below. This is no typographical error, for Cameron would like us to think that he is citing Blarosnich variants of oral traditions. 'Lord Lovat's herds' at p. 97 are from his own imagination – the quatrain as it stands in *Carmina* (vol. 4, p. 117) is:

> *Better the reward of it under my arm*
> *Than a crowd of calving kine;*
> *Better the reward of its virtues*
> *Than a herd of white cattle.*

In general terms his view of Gaelic literature is a little off-key, but then, even Neil Munro was weak in that area. Nothing is quite as bizarre, however, as his Presbyterian grandmother's taste in verse. Her favourite poets are those who represent medieval Catholicism in its decadent last phase – Giolla Críost the Tailor, Blind Arthur, the

Bard Macintyre, Isabel of Argyll, Red Finlay 'and, of course, Duncan son of Colin, the Good Knight'. She cites them constantly, and the Book of the Dean of Lismore in which they are preserved 'was a second Bible at Blarosnich'.

I have said that she is a snob. It goes deeper than that. *The Field of Sighing* appears to describe a caste system which, in its time, had little place in reality outside India. The narrator attended the township school, yet has almost nothing to tell us about the township people and cannot speak their language. His grandmother has never set foot in the township – not even to attend church – since the day she drove her cow up to the farm. The township people are believed never to wash their hands. Big House and Farm meet at predetermined social points, but 'not a soul from the Big House gate-lodge would be allowed past our front or back door' because they are Catholics. Within the farmhouse there is an astonishing list of who is allowed to go where (p. 106). It, too, involves a kind of sectarianism which is alien to the Highlands.

Who, then, was Donald Cameron? Clearly he knew a lot about the Highland farming and landowning classes, and about shepherding, but nothing about crofters. The religious attitudes he describes may perhaps be found in Ulster, and there are one or two pointers in that direction – the name Mirren (*Muireann*) is more Irish than Scottish, and the Irish spelling *lochán* appears at p. 36. On the other hand 'punkah' (p. 48) suggests an Anglo-Indian connection, while the narrator of *Sons of El Dorado* says 'shall' and 'shan't' (confirming him as a speaker of R.P.) and remarks that in his grandmother's theology 'a kind of Hindu fantasy surrounded the Second Coming of Christ, an incredible affair involving trumps and other unlikely paraphernalia'. He certainly has a colonial attitude.

> It was pleasant to sit and absorb the life of downtown Caracas. Thoughts of the immediate future occupied me. Should I go back to sea for a couple of trips and try to recover my lost weight? But I could summon no enthusiasm for the cold and dreary north when the sun was here and the fantastic throb of life, sanguine, impulsive, fearless—the life that in overflowing spilled out such things as the boys in jeans flexing their buttocks, and further up the slope, their darker sisters luring the dreamer away into the bamboo thickets, luring with the magic of full, velvet breasts, half-bared in temptation.

Donald Cameron comes across to me as a person with Indian connections whose father had been a naturalist, and who enjoyed summer holidays as a child on farms in various parts of the Highlands. I see him sitting in the sunshine of the West Indies turning his memories into connected prose with the help of his father's nature notes and the only two Gaelic books which he happens to possess – Watson's *Scottish Verse from the Book of the Dean of Lismore* (1937) and volume 4 of Carmichael's *Carmina Gadelica* (1941). Where he found his translation of 'Ceathrar do bhí ar uaigh an fhir' (p. 60) I don't know, but it was a much-anthologised poem in its day. When he goes on to write *Sons of El Dorado* he makes just one mistake – in *The Field of Sighing* the son of his father's Black Isle cousin is drowned with the *Royal Oak*, now he reappears as an officer of the Black Watch in British Guiana!

But then, nowhere is *The Field of Sighing* described as autobiography. It carries no introduction, preface or acknowledgement, but was written 'for WILMUS / remembering big seas'. Wilmus sounds like a Dutchman and was clearly a sailor. Had the book been strictly factual, one would have expected a dedication to Fergus – a suspiciously similar name? – who inspired the narrator to join the Merchant Navy, or perhaps to his father or to the memory of his mother or grandmother. Again, he is at pains to tell us how, before he went to sea, he burned or otherwise disposed of a chestful of personal memorabilia accumulated during the first seventeen years of his life, for fear of its becoming a source of amusement or offence to members of his family. No one who has done this goes on to furnish his family, in book form, with an infinitely richer and more detailed source of precisely such amusement and offence. No, *The Field of Sighing*, it seems to me, is an account of an English boyhood transplanted into a Highland setting in order to disguise the author's identity and satisfy some inner longing. It's his autobiography in an aspirational rather than a literal sense. 'How lucky I thought we were in the Western Highlands,' he declares, 'to have three of the four gem-laden hawker dragonflies.'

A few years ago I published an anthology of poems by 100 twentieth-century Gaelic poets. As the biographies of these men and women came in I became fascinated by the thought that they added up to an ethnographic record of the Highland experience of the twentieth century. They offered infinite variety in matters of detail, but conformed to a small number of general patterns. One of the commonest of these patterns can be recognised in the biography on the dust-jacket of my 1966 copy of *The Field of Sighing*:

> Born forty years ago in the Western Highlands of Scotland, Donald Cameron attended the local township school, and at fourteen became a shepherd on the mountain farm rented by his father. At the age of seventeen he joined the Merchant Navy in which he has been ever since, except for a spell as a lumberjack in British Columbia and a year on a Venezuelan plantation. He is, he says, 'happily unmarried and still lives for the pleasure of the moment'. Among his main interests are eating and drinking, bird-watching and skin-diving. He has no particular ambitions 'except perhaps to go exploring in South America in whose ports I feel most at ease'.

There's no doubt who wrote those words. Cameron has a distinctive style. It involves judicious use of conjunctions and subordinate clauses, the sparing deployment of punctuation, and a tendency for semantic shifts to occur in mid-sentence, for example at p. 130:

> There were red and black currant bushes, gooseberries and raspberry canes whose fruit went in almost equal proportions, one half to us and the other to the birds in spite of scarecrows and Mirren's efforts at placing rattling pieces of tin to keep the pirates away. Responsibility for part of this daylight robbery could be laid at the door of our own domestic hens who concentrated their raids on the strawberry beds which my father specially cared for.

This use of subordinate clauses can well be seen in 'the Merchant Navy in which he has been ever since' and 'South America in whose ports I feel most at ease'. One can well imagine however that his friends and shipmates will have had difficulty in identifying the narrator of *The Field of Sighing* as the Donald Cameron they knew. Hence this passage in *Sons of El Dorado*: 'For some reason I never had a noticeable Highland accent and my grandmother thought it wonderful that I spoke "Big House English". Though this anomaly pleased her, it galled me. I would much rather have had her own Gaelic.'

A few words, finally, about who our Donald Cameron is *not*. He is not Donald Cameron, Fort William (1905–96), author of *While the*

Wild Geese Fly: Tales of a Highland Farmer and Auctioneer (1985). Nor is he Alasdair Maclean (1926–94), author of *Night Falls in Ardnamurchan*. I stress the latter point because for most of the past twenty years I was convinced that Donald Cameron *was* Alasdair Maclean, and I once said so in print (*West Highland Free Press*, 8 March 2002).

My judgement was based on what I now see as a series of remarkable coincidences. Maclean's family were Gaelic-speaking crofters from Sanna, the neighbouring township to Achosnich in Ardnamurchan. He was not himself a Gaelic speaker, having grown up mainly in Glasgow. He spent his summer holidays in Sanna, and just one full year at school there. He served in the Merchant Marine and the British and Indian armies, then worked as a laboratory technician in London and Canada. I'm not aware that he ever visited Venezuela, but he begins the epilogue to *Night Falls in Ardnamurchan*: 'For the first two more-or-less adult decades of my life I was a wild rover. I rambled and tumbled so convincingly that I became an honorary dishonourable citizen of three or four countries in two or three continents.'

In the late 1960s Maclean became a student of English Literature at Edinburgh University, then worked after graduation as a librarian in Kirkcaldy. A very private man, he never married. One of his first poems was published in *The London Magazine*. 'Why not write about the old life at Pension Santa Cruz,' someone says to Cameron in *Sons of El Dorado*, 'and send it to the *London Magazine*?'

Claiming credibly to have been writing poetry since he was 20, Maclean burst onto the Scottish poetry scene in 1969 – the year after *El Dorado* was published and Donald Cameron disappeared from view – with twenty-one frighteningly good poems in *Lines Review 30*. He followed them in 1972 with another thirteen in Faber's *Poetry: Introduction 2*, then two full collections, *From the Wilderness* (1973) and *Waking the Dead* (1976).

Night Falls in Ardnamurchan, his only full-length prose work, was published by Gollancz in 1984 and reprinted by Birlinn in 2001. It leans, as does *The Field of Sighing* to a greater or lesser extent, on a journal kept by the author's father. What's more, as Maclean points out, 'Ardnamurchan had its own Lord Lever in the shape of a Victorian magnate called Rudd, a former partner of Cecil Rhodes and a very wealthy man in his own right.'

It will be recalled that Rudd (who bought Glenborrodale Castle) was one of Don the Ferry's passengers, and the feeling that the 'Field of Sighing' is more Ardnamurchan than anywhere else is confirmed by *Sons of El Dorado*.

On our wind-struck hill farm we knew only too well that our feet trod on no fortunes other than those we wrung with our bare hands from the hills where the sheep grazed. Yet even those mercies, vouchsafed to us as my grandmother believed by the Lord, had in fact come to us in a roundabout way by the big finds of diamonds in South Africa. No less a family than the Rudds of Johannesburg brought their yacht and their famous guests into our quiet West Highland waters. Much of my grandparents' rise from one-cow crofters to tenants of 8,000 mountain acres derived largely from the Rudds' generosity during the years of their association with the Highlands. But by the time of my own boyhood on that sheep-farm, the Rudds' yacht had gone from those summer-placid inlets.

There the similarities end. Cameron's mother dies young, Maclean's lives to old age. Cameron is snobbishly patrician, Maclean is a proletarian intellectual. Cameron goes out of his way to convey an essential goodness – his grandmother's parsimony turns out to be because she gives it all away, her loathing for Eddie the socialist turns to sympathy when his pacifist views land him in jail – but Maclean is acerbic. If *The Field of Sighing* is a feel-good book, *Night Falls in Ardnamurchan* is a feel-bad book. They may not be by the same author, but they make a neatly contrasting pair, and could be claimed, together, to portray the life and death of a Highland community in the twentieth century.

For help in compiling this introduction, the publisher (Hugh Andrew) and I would like to thank Ian Abernethy, John Bannerman, Ann Cameron, Ewen Cameron, Stewart Conn, Pamela Maclean, Marion Nicolson, Iain Thornber, Andrew Wiseman and my wife Máire. I am solely to blame for any errors. But if the author of *The Field of Sighing*, or his next of kin, is still out there, whether in Canada, the West Indies, or even in El Dorado, we would love to hear from him. He wrote a wonderful book.

Ronald Black
Edinburgh
June 2003

BLAROSNICH

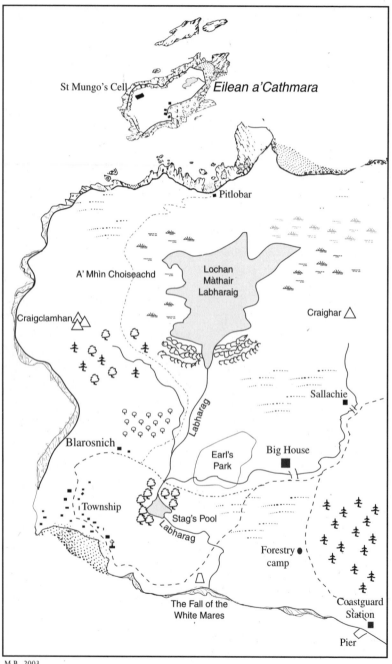

St Mungo's Cell

Eilean a'Cathmara

Pitlobar

A' Mhìn Choiseachd

Lochan Màthair Labharaig

Craigclamhan

Craighar

Labharag

Sallachie

Blarosnich

Earl's Park

Big House

Township

Stag's Pool

Labharag

Forestry camp

The Fall of the White Mares

Coastguard Station

Pier

M.B. 2003

1

Twelve-winded sky

Not a glen or lochan in all the Western Highlands was so aptly named as our hill-farm—Blarosnich—The Field of Sighing. I know of no other stout stone house so buffeted as ours was by the wild winter gales. The winds seemed to lift up the house, foundations and all, and then drop it again. And so it was for the first seventeen years of my life. But long before that, winds had caught the last remaining leaves in autumn and whipped them furiously against the window-panes. I grew up with the desperate tearing which sounded as though the twigs wanted to climb through the window to escape the winds' threat of winter.

By this time of our year the plovers had gone, leaving Blarosnich lonelier without their sharp, rippling trill. The autumn winds tore the last leaves off as though from a calendar. One by one the shrivelled leaves flew away into the air, tokens of each summer day now spent. In summer, when the wind was not so wild, it merely sighed day-long through the bourtree windbreaks, threatening nothing worse than to drown the corncrakes reigning in the meadows.

Bouts of north-east weather came even in spring at Blarosnich. Snow stayed until May on Craigclamhan so that we had a late lambing. The bourtrees were untruthful of the first warm days and only put on their dust of green with caution. So many winds drove these trees this way and that through the years that they could no longer trust the spring. They guarded Blarosnich against the winds which swept down from the black mountains beyond the farm and those which came inland from the Atlantic. Spring at Blarosnich was not a sudden succulence. It was a slow weaning away from winter. I watched the peregrine falcon many times blown about the sky like a bit of paper, so that his nuptial acrobatics had to start all over again when the hurricane relented.

The sighs of Blarosnich, Field of Sighing, were not always sighs. Titanic shouts came from the south-westerly gales. Playful breezes would sometimes come from the rocky kyle, heavy with the tang of salt-water and seaweed. Other winds, seeming to come from all quarters at once, would dry out a mown meadow in a fraction of the time taken by a wary sun.

A thousand scents came with the winds, heady scents of sea and heather, and mountain scents from Craigclamhan, scents with hints of bees, airs sweetly redolent of the whole uplands. By sniffing the air the people of Blarosnich, as well as their beasts, could sense the day's weather. We could tell how far away the spring was when Craigclamhan gleamed white through lowering March clouds. We could tell at once when the summer's gentle breezes became rougher and changed their sweetness for a sharper tang. The strongest wedder sheltering on the hill, the most reluctant heifer emerging from the winter byre, depended on the airs that blew about Blarosnich.

One of the most ravaged-looking victims of the unpredictable West Highland weather on our farm was the clump of sentinel trees on the high ground of the long, rutted lane leading up to the house. Through more than a hundred years storms had scoured and twisted the hawthorns' trunks. Lashing gales had mutilated the branches and their thorny armour. Deformed limbs reached out towards the house like scraggy cattle standing, all turned one way to face the winter onslaught. A Scots pine reared up in the vanguard of the crippled clump. This tree also bore scars and had limbs maimed by the south-western flagellation so that it seemed to have lost all resemblance to the pine family. The hard, tough wood of the hawthorn was made so by the airs which hardened and toughened every human body born to the Field of Sighing.

For as long as I can remember, I depended on the mood of the winds, and kept my ears open to interpret *caoidh-chòmhradh*— 'the mournful expressions'. My grandmother called the winds' noises by this name, growing angry when the winds blew down the chimney, scattering black sooty flakes on her griddle of golden-meal farls.

Caoidh-chòmhradh, 'the mournful expressions', were blowing about the hills of Blarosnich on the late April day in 1925 when I was born within the farmhouse's tough walls. The day's mournful expressions were certainly of the kind that came from the south-westerlies, for the record in the journal of Blarosnich said so.

The journal lived in the kitchen above the meal-ark, and hung by its string from a bacon hook. My father kept it, not because he wanted to write, but because the book was essential in the life of Blarosnich. Our own large, thin diary resembled those in other farms. Everybody consulted the close-written pages because they contained notes of important information and events, and were as necessary to Blarosnich's future as they were fascinating about its past.

The journal contained plain and factual entries as a working book should. We could open it if we forgot when cows had been taken to the bull, or if we wanted to know when the tups had been let out on the ewe-hills, or on which days lamb sales were to be held, or when coal-boats sailed, and, later in the year, the days when the horses would be wanted by the gamekeeper to cart stags home for the sporting tenants.

The journal entry made on the day I was born resembled thousands which had been written before and the thousands written afterward. Only the last part differed. 'Hard south wind slackening before dinner,' it ran, 'then veering round Craigclamhan and freshened to promise of a night-gale. Ordered tar and paraffin. Paid Duncan for dog-fox shot on the burn side of Craighar. Three pairs of sandpipers on lochan and starwart by the Earl's Park. Two fine cock crabs from Postie. Wee boy came before second milking, eight days overdue. R is in fine feckle.'

I was recorded along with the winds and birds and the dog-fox and the two cock crabs from Postie. R was my mother, Rhona, who had no need of any clock other than the changing time of nature. I came into the world 'before second milking' and that was near enough so far as the journal was concerned. Clocks were of no consequence in our lives, we who had no buses or ferries to catch. Morning and evening milking, the coming of the sandpipers, the departing greenshanks, hatching time in the black-backed gulleries, the calving of the grey seal-cows, the deer rutting, the gathering of the hirsel, the marking, clipping, dipping and then the lamb sales—these marked the days and seasons of Blarosnich.

An entry went into the journal every day and it always included the wind's direction and force. As treasurer of the local anti-vermin society my father paid out for all the foxes, hooded crows and weasel tails brought to the steading by gamekeepers, township men, and lads employed by the Forestry Commission, and such payments went into the book. The coming of the waders to our freshwater lochans and the first appearance of wild flowers on the hills were always written in with the same brevity and accuracy. Postie would bring lythe or great oily mackerel on days when he failed to have crabs. Friday was never fish day for us because my grandmother wanted to show her contempt of Catholic superstitions. But the lodge folk at the Big House, who were 'of the other side', only ever wanted Postie's catch on that day.

The journal's reference to me as 'wee boy' indicated the one disagreement between Rhona, my mother, and Herself, as my grandmother was called. I had no name until the minister came up to borrow the mare for working his glebe lands several days later. He stepped up into The Room and demanded to know the name given this new member of his flock.

My mother wanted me to be named Angus after her father who had been gamekeeper to the late Duke of Argyll and a renowned pibroch player. On the other hand, Herself wished me to be Donald after her husband. A compromise solved the problem. I became Donald Angus. Our family called me Donnie because my father was Donald also, the township and neighbours referring to him as Young Don, for they remembered *his* father Old Don.

Old Don was much respected although Herself made sure of it. Not a soul in the township's twenty houses would dare to call the old man by the familiar bodach in my grandmother's presence. She would have driven them down the lane with her great wooden beetle as quickly as she drove begging tinkers from the door. Her late husband could not be mentioned as anything but The Captain.

The Captain had been long dead before I came into the world

and made my first appearance on the journal's pages in company with the sandpipers on the lochan. But his presence was nevertheless a powerful influence in my boyhood—a presence as strong as grandmother's own. The old lady did not speak of her man as The Captain from any common pride. She honoured his memory not merely because he had been a devoted husband but also because by a just combination of luck and self-help he had 'got on in life'. In Herself's eyes getting-on was an activity nicely mixed of both practical and moral values—'keeping your neb at the grunstane' she called it. None of *her* folk were going to be like the township louts whose only work appeared to be cycling off to collect the dole.

She remembered the day when Don-the-Ferry had kirked her, carrying her away down to one of the twenty township dwellings after the simple ceremony. But down there on the seashore she had dreamed dreams beyond the but-and-ben. Those were dreams of a bright silver which none could tarnish until Don-the-Ferry became The Captain. And in these dreams it was no clatty coal-boat that The Captain was to steer up the coast from Glasgow. No McBrayne steamer full of tourists for Iona was Don-the-Ferry to captain.

In those far-off days of dreams for her man, the sporting tenants of Blarosnich were rich. They owned a yacht on which the famous of society spent summer days cruising the islands. The yacht's passengers were the select of the land—gentry like Cameron of Lochiel, the Dunstaffnage, the Rudds of Ardnamurchan and Winston Churchill. Herself had every reason not to forget 'Lord Randolph's son' for was it not he, born to be a leader of leaders, who called Don-the-Ferry *The Captain?* Just as she had dreamed, so it had happened. Her man became captain on board the best of all the boats on Highland waters.

Grandmother's success made no difference to the way she lived. Instead of putting on airs because of her husband's position, as many in her place would have done, she merely prepared for the next stage in the realization of her dreams. It would have been so easy with The Captain's new money coming in to go off to Oban or Edinburgh for big dresses, or to mods to display herself and her fine voice. This was not my grandmother's way. She put the precious sovereigns into the family pinner-pig, dreaming now of the future. With the gentry yachting, like stalking or fishing, was a pastime which any fickle whim could bring to an end. The Captain himself caught his wife's ambition. Together they held expectancies for their adolescent son, who in the course of time was to be my father.

Grandmother never allowed her success and her ambition to over-ride her sense of what was proper in the social order which she accepted as God-ordained. A ferryman could certainly be made into a captain, but not a proprietor in the West Highland sense. Don the Captain was of one-cow crofter stock and, as she put it, 'the young pig must always grunt like the old sow'. The Captain's grand uniform with its gold buttons was not worn by a man who came from the laird order of society. The desire for higher social status never entered Herself's head. Indeed, she held titled and landed people in contempt unless they were good Highland-bred folk who lived and worked on their ancestral acres. Too many such people had denied their trust and gone off to the gutters of London and Paris squandering the large portion the Lord above had given them.

In spite of such moralizings, Herself was glad to use the previous sporting tenants as an aid to her own plans. By the time they sold their yacht The Captain had saved sufficient money to rent Blarosnich from the government. He bought enough ewes from the out-going tenant to start a hirsel. The day came when Herself drove the croft cow up to the Field of Sighing—the eight thousand acres of mountain and moor surrounded on three sides by the sea. She was happier on that day than even on her wedding day.

The Field of Sighing's six-roomed farmhouse came above the manse on the social ladder the top rung of which was the Big House of the sporting tenants. Yet Herself remained as unaffected by this further rise in the world as she had been in her role as yacht master's wife.

During the fifty years my grandmother lived after driving the cow up to Blarosnich she never once returned to the township where she first went as a bride. Not a social in the schoolroom or a silver-potted tea at the Big House would make her stir. She was sought after at the biggest mods and most important Highland gatherings, but the shepherd on the hill and the cattle in the byre were the only ones outside the house who heard her beautiful contralto voice and the sweet sound of her harp. Neither heaven nor hell would have induced her to leave the marches of Blarosnich. Death alone did that and then Herself, waxen and still, had no choice but to go.

Living in the narrow strath between the sister peaks of Craigclamhan and Craighar was the fulfilling of yet another dream for Herself. She had been born, the only child of a crofter, on Eilean a'Cathmara, the largest of three small islands on the other side of Craigclamhan mountain. The grazing ground there was so poor that when she was a girl she had often spent two hours collecting enough young nettles for a midday boiling with a bit of rabbit or, more likely, a roast gannet. Though the little island lacked many things, it swarmed with gannet colonies. The cliffs above the sea on the island's north side were honeycombed with nesting puffins. By harvest time the young gannets would be waddling in fat, and they too were gathered and salted with the puffins against the long hard winter when nobody could cross the kyle to poach red deer on the mainland.

One man only was left on Eilean a'Cathmara, and grandmother, his daughter, was the last person to be born there. Before the famine of 1847-49 the island had supported a big township. Grandmother's father was drowned while fishing in the treacherous surf of the sunken skerries, so she and her mother ferried their few sheep across to the mainland. Nobody had lived on the island since. Occasionally, during the herring season, fishermen went ashore to use the old black-houses which we kept in repair for our shepherd who went there from time to time to attend ewes and lambs.

For the first years of her life Herself looked across the water at the fat pastures on the flanks of Craigclamhan. At thirty-five she was mistress of it all and Eilean a'Cathmara besides. Though she advised her friends and neighbours to keep 'yer neb at the grunstane' nobody ever worked harder than she did. She built Blarosnich up until its wedders were the pride of the Dingwall market and until breeders came from far away places like New Zealand after her son's cattle.

Her black-lined hands were as leathery as a horse's breeching. Burns from branding irons in the sheep fank had deformed them. They were gnarled from many winters out on the hill rescuing ewes whose long fleeces had balled with snow. I knew her hands in that state when they were full of character like the old worn hawthorns on the lane. Once they had been the shapely hands of the young girl at the oars of her father's long boat nosing its way through the sunken skerries of Eilean a'Cathmara.

Contrary to appearance my grandmother's hands could be gentle. I loved them and used to ask her if mine would be like that when I became a man. She smiled in answer and I knew she was thinking of The Captain of whom five years shepherding at Blarosnich took their toll. Afterwards Herself's hands ruled over the eight thousand acres. The farm became her only love. She never forgot that The Captain had brought her to it.

All my life The Captain had been clear to me. Herself always spoke as though he were not already dead but as if he were only out on the hill rounding up a puckle of ewes and might be expected home at any moment. He was more clear to me than Aunt Jessie, the only relation I ever stayed with outside Blarosnich. The Captain's yachting cap and jacket still hung in the farmhouse hall. They gave out faint odours of mustiness and dankness when I passed them with my candle at night going to bed. His skene-dhu lived on the mantelpiece of The Room. Only my father was allowed to use it when he went off to the lamb sales in his best kilt.

Sacred though these things were the large photograph of The Captain in the kitchen formed our family altar. When there was nobody else in the house Herself would talk Gaelic. She also spoke Gaelic to the photograph, and every day she said good night and good morning to it. I used to wonder if Herself had scared The Captain as much as the camera appeared to, for the faded portrait showed the terrified eyes of a cornered animal. Despite the

8

vignette effects, a full and generous mouth peered through the photographic mist and mildew spots, though the nose was spoilt by being too 'quhaup-nebbit'. This long, sharp, curlew nose was the only family resemblance I could trace in my father and myself. But I hated my nose as a boy at school because the other boys laughed and called it a beak. But my nose was nothing. For years I held a grudge against The Captain because of jeering in the playground.

Once the evening milking was done, the calves fed, the oil lamp lit on the kitchen table and the last grace for supper said, everyone took out his night work. My father wrote up the day's events in the journal, a job which came before anything else. Only after the journal entry was complete would he turn to mending our boots or to cleaning his gun or making bar frames for the beehives.

Rhona, my mother, made jams or pickles now that the fire was clear for that day of animal food and cooking pots. Herself sat in The Captain's chair knitting until sleep stole over her. Snores would replace the click of her needles for a while. Then she would wake with a start, look around at us accusingly, as if somehow we had complicity in her doze, and announce that it was high time for Christian souls to make their peace with their Maker. She set her knitting aside and slowly went upstairs to bed.

Before my father got the Good Book down from its shelf for the day's reading I would have finished my homework and sat thinking out ways and means by which Herself's knitting could be destroyed—that is, if what I saw on the thick bone needles was intended to be worn by me.

From my earliest years I knew it was wrong to say anything against The Captain. I also knew it was wrong to repeat tales told about him by other boys at school. And nothing could ever be said and no question must ever be asked about The Captain's and Herself's early years down in the township. It would have been catastrophic for me to tell my grandmother that I hated the jerseys and stockings she incessantly knitted for me, year in year out. For being a good boy and having learnt to strip the cows of their last porringer of milk I would be rewarded by Herself going to the wardrobe where she kept The Captain's starched dickies and

9

butterfly collars, her secret supply of boiled sweets and the family birth, marriage and death certificates.

She would choose a pair of old stockings from what seemed an inexhaustible supply and rip out what was left of the tops by moths. The heels were always full of holes. I suspected that she had so many pairs because she preferred to knit a whole new stocking than darn the heels and toes. Herself had the same plain pattern for my stockings and jerseys as she used on the knee-length bloomers for her own use and the baby-wear for the township children.

My grandmother did not sense that her own appreciation of these things went unshared. In no way did I feel flattered when I was told that the stockings she was ripping out for me had first been made for The Captain going off to the Games at Fort William twenty years before, or that the shepherd's cape she was saving for me when I became a man had been homespun by The Captain's mother. I dreaded the day when I would have to wear the cape, though I felt thankful that at least the evil day was postponed—the cape was not going to be cut up into jackets and coats for me to wear now. My clothes seemed bad enough to me as it was. They looked so obviously homespun and homemade. During the summer the crofters' children at school wore bright cotton shirts and dresses bought from the travelling grocer or the pedlars. Yet I sat at my desk or sweated in the playground in thick jerseys of shades varying from grey to gingerbread brown.

The economic running of Blarosnich depended upon the sale of the lambs and the wool-clip. Herself could not be moved from the belief that wool was the only respectable material to wear, and moreover that it must be worn every single day of the year, come sun or snow. The fact that other boys or girls at school only had cheapjack goods from Manchester to wear confirmed my grandmother in her belief that the township women were nothing but tea-bibbers who did not even know how to hold a pair of knitting needles. 'Not a decent stitch to their backs', she would repeat firmly, 'Not since the day I knit their first nipper suit with my own hands.'

Quaint and old-fashioned though Herself seemed to me even

when I was very young, I relied on her a great deal after my mother died when I was only seven years old.

'Our Rhona' was the proud proprietary brand name given her by my grandmother. She talked every day about my mother so that together with The Captain, whom I had never known, my mother grew larger rather than smaller in my mind as I got older. 'Our Rhona' was, however, as much an expression of praise from the old lady as it was an expression of contempt for the township wives.

Rhona was everything they were not. They preferred bought bread to baking their own, and said grace in English rather than Gaelic, both things being regarded by Herself as treason to the Highland way of life. These same township women, abrogating the rights and duties of the hearth, were guilty also of trying to brighten their dull lives by the bringing of city gadgets into their homes, and worse, by the use of cosmetics.

'Our Rhona' had fallen for none of these temptations, as Herself regarded them. Yet she and my mother were opposites in many ways, and that may have been why they lived so harmoniously under the one roof for over eight years. After my parents' marriage Herself wanted to move up the strath into a disused cottage. But Rhona insisted that her mother-in-law must remain mistress of Blarosnich. So the cottage was never warmed. Only once in those eight years did the two women disagree.

Rhona's enthusiasm for making jams and jellies led on to cider brewing. She knew of Herself's horror of drink but tried to balance this with the old lady's equal love of economy. Rhona was also aware of my father's embarrassment at sheep-clipping time when the neighbours and shepherds came over to help and were given orange squash in place of beer or cider which they dispensed at their own clippings and which my father much enjoyed.

Even in The Captain's time the orchard at Blarosnich had been extensive. With so much wind the ground beneath the trees was always thickly dotted by fallen fruit which could never be stored. Rhona used these windfalls for her cider—pointing out to my grandmother the saving this effected. The cider made it unnecessary, she said, to order the crate of cordial for the sheep-clipping, a crate which usually arrived with several bottles broken as a result of their long journey in steamer and ferry.

I was twelve before I heard the sequel to my mother's cider enterprise. Herself rather frightened the township children. The girls only saw her when they brought cows up to our bull, for decorum naturally ruled that my grandmother watched the courtship when females were in attendance. From their earliest years children knew the importance of getting their cows mated once they saw them becoming amorous up on the crofters' grazing common. Most families had only one beast. To let it run dry for longer than necessary would be a great loss. So, though they hated doing so, the village women and girls struggled between them to bring their cows up our lane.

The children feared our bull more than they feared my grandmother. He was a heavy Shorthorn and inclined to break out after Herself had set a limit to his performance. The bull always wanted to pursue his lovers down to the township and occasionally, amid cries and much running about, he succeeded in doing so. The girls and their mothers thought Herself had something of a witch about her because of the bravery she showed in going after the bull and driving him off with resounding wallops of her cromag. At such times the girls handed her the fee with sweaty, trembling hands and were gone as quickly as possible from the bellowing bull as he gored the closed gate with his thick horns.

Blarosnich affairs provided an endless source of gossip for the township and, in turn, their shortcomings occupied Herself's mind. For many years we had Mirren. She did the churning and made the special Highland cream cheese called crowdie, she fed the calves and looked after the fowl. Mirren came up from the township every morning brimming with all sorts of exaggerated tales of her neighbours' face paintings and powderings and coffee drinking which was then the rage.

At school I had no defence but my fists against the sarcasm of the other boys. But these hardy implements could not be used against the girls who were by far the worst teasers.

'Hullo Donnie,' one would begin, 'I know you folk at Blarosnich are so grand and respectable but you can't still be mourning for old Queen Vickie with all your grey jerseys. Is that a new one?'

When I pretended not to hear such remarks it would only cause saucier ones. 'What a pity the cailleach can't make you a nice jersey out of those blue drawers she's always tripping over.'

Out in the playground one day I heard about my mother. The girls had tired of playing needle's eye, going to and fro beneath outstretched arms. They went to their other favourite game of mimicking either the minister, the deaf chatelaine at the Big House or my grandmother.

One girl was giving a lively version of the old lady, who was stiffening with rheumatism in spite of numerous activities, and who now leaned on a short cromag. The impersonating girl had Herself's snatchy voice perfectly. I could not count the times I had heard Herself say, in exactly that voice, 'I've been maimed for life by the sins of my own kith and kin.'

I asked my father once what had happened to his mother's leg. He mumbled something about an accident. I thought of the thresher and mowing machine or even Herself's own scythe which she still wielded in her battle against the bracken on the hills.

'Maimed for life by the sins of my own kith and kin,' the playground girl went on in a squeaky, petulant voice, 'and that only because a bottle of cider exploded against her old varicose veins.'

I ran the whole way home from school that day and asked Mirren if what I had heard was true. Mirren looked both pleased at receiving my confidence and cross at being cornered. As always when divulging township scandal or family secrets she abjured me to 'swear by your Maker not to breathe a word of it to the Mistress.' And Mirren told me the story of the exploding cider bottle and how the flying glass cut my grandmother's leg and how she resigned herself to lameness as a just reward for allowing alcohol into a Christian home. Afterwards, the windfalls rotted where they fell and made no more cider than their own decay produced.

Rhona, by all accounts, was a 'topping' baker—high praise indeed because in our district the best that could be said of either a good beast or a beautiful girl was that they were a 'topper'. Nobody ever tired of what the late Cameron of Lochiel's ferryman said when the chieftain asked his opinion of the Lady Hermione when she arrived as a young bride, 'Och, she's a topper.'

Rhona must really have been a topping baker, for whenever we ate the bread which Mirren baked Herself would remark to me 'Your poor mother would turn in her grave to see you fill your belly with *that*.'

Mirren, however, was only allowed to bake when Herself was too busy out of doors. Coming from the township where nobody was supposed ever to wash their hands, Mirren's idea of hygiene was regarded with some suspicion, and my grandmother preferred to preside personally over the griddle and oven. Rhona made her absence felt in this because Herself disliked working in the house.

Whereas my mother had been an ideal wife and housekeeper, Herself felt her rightful place was out on the hill or in the sheep fank with the shepherds. She could do a man's work quite as well as any man around Blarosnich. Her deerstalker hat and long clothes, high Edwardian boots, the eye-glass slung over her shoulder like a rifle, were known for miles around. She could easily have been mistaken for an odd mixture of Victorian sportsman and an Old Testament prophet stalking God on the mountain.

I cannot recall the taste of my mother's renowned bread and cakes, but I can clearly see her rotund form bent over the mealark as she measured out the flour—flour which seemed to get into her soft brown hair. When I first began to go to school, my mother came down the lane to fetch me at the end of the afternoon. This was probably because she wanted an hour or two alone with me before we returned to the busy kitchen where she could spare me little special attention.

On those afternoons we would sit beside the burn while she heard my lessons or told me of her own childhood and the grand castle-folk whose guns and rifles had been looked after by her father.

The news that I was to have a brother or sister came to me not from my mother on one of those afternoons together, but from children in the school playground. They despised me for not already knowing such a thing and laughed when I denied it. Rhona confirmed the children's remarks and after a while came for shorter and shorter distances to meet me from school. The girls in the playground jeered and said my mother was so big and so heavy that there would surely be twins and, they said cruelly, that would mean Rhona would stop loving me for she would be too busy. I worried about this, though without really believing that Rhona could ever stop loving me. She did stop, however, for her new son was stillborn and she herself died giving birth.

Of the death itself hardly anything comes to me out of the past except the following day when the doctor came. I was hiding in the barn, my place of escape when anything unpleasant was happening in the house. Nobody could ever find me among the rows of fleeces and sacks hung up to dry.

On that awful afternoon, Mirren flung the back door open and fled across the yard and up the steps of the bothie where Alec the shepherd slept.

'They've cut her throat,' she cried over and over in a demented way, a gruesome chorus which the township children were pleased to take up afterwards.

I bolted from the barn into the house, expecting to see some mad man rushing about, brandishing my father's cut-throat razor. All that had happened was the doctor, in accordance with my mother's wishes, had severed her jugular vein. She had a fear of being buried while still alive, a fear not uncommon in our part of the world.

Rhona's coffin was put on the Forestry Commission's lorry and smothered with flowers from the local gardens. I had never seen so many men before in my life. Long files of them came from mountain farms around to follow the slow-moving lorry with its bright, sad load of flowers. I could not really believe that my mother lay underneath them.

We made the oystercatchers angry by stopping on the shore to build a funeral cairn. Neither the thousands of flowers nor the red peony petals which my father told me to drop into the yawning hole impressed me so much as Alec's masterpiece. In his role as the Blarosnich shepherd, he had dug the grave. The top sods were neatly rolled round a pole in one long unbroken carpet. After the service, while others hurried away to take the traditional whisky and cheese by the gate, Alec unrolled this grass carpet so that the ugly scar was healed immediately. I loitered behind to watch him. My mother would have approved of this neat work- manship. And somehow this made her burial more acceptable.

Herself and Mirren had not attended the funeral because that was the men's responsibility. But all too soon they heard of the whisky though not before we had heard of events up at Blaros- nich. While we men were away, going about our part of the funeral, my grandmother and Mirren had set about theirs. The last rites included the burning of the clothes in which my mother died and also her mattress.

We arrived home to find one side of the steading turned into an inferno. Flames shot up taller than the rowans by the house. The crackling and roaring of the fire drowned the cries of escap- ing fowls and animals. Smoke belched from every opening, accom- panied by long yellow streamers of sparks. For a moment, when I first saw this spectacle, inaction seized me. Then released, I began to follow Herself, but curiously wanting to laugh and enjoy the great blaze. My grandmother was already in her seventies, yet she ran to and fro, foaming at the mouth, directing operations like a demon. When I saw the old lady with skirts tucked up inside her long drawers, her face lacquered jet with ash and burning, I thought she was the big black Devil whom she had described so frequently and adequately over the years.

None of us could imagine how the fire was prevented from spreading to the dwelling house—except Herself who claimed it as a miraculous intervention on the part of her Maker. Mirren had taken the mattress out and poured paraffin over it. According to Herself, Mirren had been too lazy to take the big mattress down to our usual place by the ford for burning things. But according to Mirren this was too far, even for her strength, to carry the mattress. So unthinkingly she dumped it just beyond the steading, on the hay-shed side. Unthinking also about that day's particular Blarosnich wind, she set a match to the pyre. Luckily the new season's hay had not yet been brought in and so only a few tons remained from the previous winter to feed the fire.

The double event of my mother's funeral and the hay-shed fire became the hegira of our local calendar. The black tide-marks of smoke stained the barn walls permanently. Births and marriages, bad winters and good harvests were dated by that day, which afterwards was always called the Big Burning. I can remember the heat of the steading cobbles, the comic apparition of Herself as chief fire-fighter, and the wonderful colours of the flames suddenly erupting to singe the windbreaks' green leaves.

Yet these things are not so clear still as the funeral. I see those oystercatchers rising from the shore as we stopped to build the cairn. I feel the dank, silky texture of the peony petals I scattered into the hole. I see Alec on his knees in his best trousers unrolling the neat green blanket over the mound. The tears were in his eyes and I had not seen a man weep before. Men only cried when they were drunk, Herself had told me. But she was wrong, for Alec, I knew, was not drunk.

2

Herself and the tailor

By his twelfth birthday Black Fergus had already distinguished himself by being the talk of the countryside. Township parents gave Teacher strict instructions that Black Fergus must not, under any circumstances, sit in the same desk as their daughters. They regarded Fergus of Sallachie as a serious threat to the quiet tenor of township life. Like the rest of us, he pulled the girls' dresses up but he did so more often and to more girls than we did. Fergus showed greater inventiveness in enlivening our games of mothers-and-fathers.

I could never be sure whether Black Fergus made a speciality of shocking the grown-ups or whether he merely failed to see why they were shocked. He certainly did not understand why Teacher brought in the minister after one of the smaller boys had paid my friend a penny for the privilege of seeing Fergus's extraordinary claims to manhood. But when he reached fourteen, Black Fergus's reputation had spread beyond the schoolyard wall. The maids from the Big House dreaded meeting him at night along our lonely shore road and seldom went about after dark without escorts.

Fergus of Sallachie was two years older than me. By my second book in school he had become my best friend. Everybody had a 'best' friend and Fergus was mine. Perhaps the closeness of our two families encouraged this. He and I were the only farmers' children in the school, and our families were involved together in many farm affairs. Few tenant-farmers like us, who only had the minimum of hired labour, could exist without the help of neighbours.

Sheep handlings called for a common effort. Because the nearest town was a day's journeying away we had to rely on neighbours for spare parts when machinery broke down. Our common enemy the fox brought us together. We could not fight him alone. Efforts by the old gamekeeper to hold the fox at bay did little to protect our scattered hirsels. The Forestry Commission was planting more and more of the rocky slopes. And as the young firs shot up tall and green, the foxes multiplied. The slaughter and plunder in the flocks grew worse.

At Blarosnich we prided ourselves on the prices our lambs fetched. We talked with satisfaction of the acres my father was bringing to new life with the tractor. But the folk at Sallachie were better at killing the fox. Black Fergus became as expert with a gun as he was with a girl.

Fergus was always up at Blarosnich. The road winding round the foot of the mountain gave the easiest way. But it twisted and turned so much that Black Fergus usually came over the hill and up our lane to school. He often called at the house with urgent messages about fox dens. Sometimes he brought the supply of lamb, because his family and mine took it in turn to kill for our own needs as well as the Big House's.

When my mother died Black Fergus took her place as a companion on the way home from school. In the mornings too he waited for me at the bottom of the tups' hill. Entering the playground together caused as great an uproar as two foxes going into a hen house.

I would wait to see him running through the bracken of the tups' hill before collecting my lunch and meeting him by the burn. As long as I had known him he had always been called Black Fergus. His hair was thick and blue-black like a raven's plumage. His skin was swarthy too, as though he lived wild up in the mountains and was coloured by the wind and sun.

Fergus wore long trousers soon after his twelfth birthday to cover the black hairs which spread over his legs and which in no time at all appeared on his upper body too. The transformation of boy into man was followed with interest in all the wonderful accompanying details. The girls, alarmed and astonished by his hairiness, called him King Farouk.

Despite the long corduroy trousers, the girls had many opportunities to see Fergus's hairy chest. Few people around Blarosnich or Sallachie ever went swimming, even in the hottest weather. But between May and September Black Fergus was seldom out of the water. The shore was normally the preserve of crofters' hens which picked fastidiously among the seaweed littered at the water's edge.

Nobody in my family had ever been swimming, not even Herself who had lived on a small island until her seventeenth year. My grandmother feared the sea. Her home had been Eilean a'Cathmara—Island of the Sea-Fight. Her father had been lost on its sunken skerries and the sea had never been the same for Herself afterwards. In its peaceful, sleepy summer moods when low swells moved towards to the cliffs, the sea seemed to her to be waiting and watching. And when breakers thundered and broke as big as houses against the bastion rocks of the cliffs during gales, she feared the sea would scale the perpendicular cliffs and devour the last traces of scurvy-grass and sea-pinks. Herself never regretted leaving the Island of the Sea-fight. For her the sea was vicious and wild. And when she moved to Blarosnich she was glad to put the mountain of Craigclamhan between her and the sea and the little sea-battered island.

My grandmother could not understand that anyone should want to swim in the sea. I was forbidden to go bathing off the cliffs. If I must cool off like the cattle then I could sit in the top part of the peat-brown burn. The top but never the bottom part, which was deep and flowed into the dangerous Stag's Pool.

And just because the treacherous coast and Stag's Pool were forbidden their fascination grew, helped not a little by Black Fergus's own enjoyment of them. Because I was hot and sticky and wanted to peel off my thick grey jersey, I willingly followed Black Fergus after school. But it had to be done with guile for gossip in the township always reached Blarosnich. And so I persuaded Fergus to go by way of the woods on my secret visits to Stag's Pool.

Our burn was called Labharag—the Little Loud One. In its lower reaches two other burns joined it and together made a good sized river, so that the Little Loud One was no longer a descriptive name. The river was still loud but not little as it pounded over boulders and waterfalls. One of the waterfalls tumbled like a tress of hair into a churning basin—the Stag's Pool.

For a long time no persuasion would induce me to jump into that particular part of the burn. Too many warnings had made me timid and too many stories from Herself's childhood filled me with caution. The pool's depth was unknown. My father and Alec the shepherd had once dismantled an old deer fence. There was nowhere to throw the barbed wire except into Stag's Pool. Although the water was clear, those thousands of yards of rusty wire had sunk invisibly into untold depths. The place was sinister.

The disappearance of the barbed wire did not impress Mirren. She told me of the stags, demented by biting clegs and flies, which had plunged into the pool and were unable to get out again. She swore the place was bottomless and that the stags' death had put a curse on the water.

I first dived into Stag's Pool the summer after Black Fergus had taught me to swim. Once the initial dive was done the place lost some of its terrors and also some of its glamour as a forbidden thing.

The roe-deer leaping at our approach through the woods seemed to inspire Black Fergus with the same lightning movement. His clothes came off, tugged over his tousled, jet hair and were flung carelessly on the ground or a nearby bush. Then Fergus ran and dived, curving beautifully through the air in a swarthy flash. The pool became a threshing floor. Black Fergus, laughing and shrieking, flailed the water with his ripening muscles, winnowing fine drops out of the choppy waves.

I dared not hesitate on the bank or else Fergus would clamber out, lithe as a young seal, lift me in his arms and jump in again carrying me with him into the boiling vortex at the waterfall's foot. After a time, I forgot about the barbed wire waiting like a water-sprite to entangle me.

Perhaps no two boys were ever as happy as Black Fergus and I, wrestling and writhing on the forest floor, plunging over and over again into the pool to cool off, and contorting our young bodies with exercises we hoped would miraculously give the Charles Atlas torso we admired in magazines.

In the early spring, before the grass was shooting or the burn seemed warm enough for our quicksilver splashings, Black Fergus and I went off for whole Saturdays, ferreting on the hills, hunting wild cat and roe, fishing with homemade rods and plain hooks, combing the far caves for pigeons, writing messages on the sands, sharing an old pipe and whatever tobacco we had stolen from his father and our shepherd, leaving our mark in a thousand ways and in a thousand places over the country, and being ourselves marked by its sights and sounds and smells.

Whatever the fascination of the rock-pools or the islands, and no matter how exciting it may have been to watch the rough play of the young seal bulls down on the skerries, Black Fergus and I were always home in time for Saturday ceilidh, the highlight of the week.

While cleaning my best boots ready for the Sabbath, I watched my father shave Duncan the gamekeeper. Herself kept a smart weather-eye on the piece of newspaper where the cut-throat razor deposited little mounds of whisker-speckled lather. She did not trust my father's aim with the lather. We all believed that years before some of the barbering mess went flying into one of Herself's kitchen pots.

'I wouldn't be wanting his white whiskers thickening the broth again,' she would mumble, moving the two stock-pots out of danger.

Herself was not happy on a Saturday night until Duncan's red face, shining like an apple, was finally cleared of lather and the newspaper screwed up and thrown into the fire. The stock-pots were too precious to be spoilt because they stayed simmering on the stove every day of the year.

With Duncan done, Alec would come in from the bothie, dressed in his kirk clothes. Then we would all wait for the ring of hooves on the steading cobbles announcing the arrival of the Sallachie folk.

I always went out to help Black Fergus unharness and stable their big chestnut mare, while he enquired what was for supper and what latest development had come about in the courting of Alec and Mirren. The existence of the courtship was hotly denied by them both, though we all knew they had been 'going strong' for years. Before leaving the stable Black Fergus would ask me if we could make Alec an apple-pie bed again, so that the shepherd would think it was Mirren's doing and perhaps be encouraged to make further advances in her direction. Black Fergus was most anxious to help this courtship along and he regarded the affair as if it were his own.

By the time we came out of the bothie, leaving as neat an apple-pie bed as we would manage. Fergus's parents had gone into the house. Violet and Sandy were both small and round, their faces lined with laughter. Everybody loved them, with certain reservations on the part of the gamekeeper's wife who was a very religious Wee Free and therefore had bitter things to say of Violet's fortune-telling from tea leaves. Her views of her husband's pipe-playing, on the other hand, had never been heard. Presumably she approved, for nobody within twenty miles of Blarosnich could play the pipes as well as Duncan.

Before the gamekeeper got his pipes out, we all went up to The Room to eat. My father said grace, and Black Fergus said 'Amen', a louder amen than anybody else's and an amen with a surprising degree of cheekiness in it. In fact, it was Black Fergus's decidedly irreverent amen which put the edge on the long love-hate relationship between Fergus and Herself. She knew all about Black Fergus's skill on the shinty field and in the sea and his exploits among the girls. Herself was prepared to overlook these because Fergus could kill foxes, which were the bane of our life. She could not, however, forgive Black Fergus for his Saturday night 'Amen'. It filled her with horror, and once she got as far as to ask me whether Black Fergus believed 'in his Maker'.

The supper itself featured as a great ceremony and I looked forward to it with renewed excitement every week. Herself took immense trouble and pains over the meal because this was the best one of the week. Vegetables never appeared with the hot dish and nobody made a pretence by calling the meal dinner, which the Big House ate at that hour. Our dinner gong consisted of a whistle strenuously blown by Mirren before the cuckoo clock in the hall announced midday.

The Saturday supper may have lacked vegetables, but more than made up by the variety of different breads to eat with the savoury dish that sizzled in the oven until the grace was said and Mirren scurried along the passageway, her hands covered in cloths like boxing-gloves, carrying the still-bubbling first course of 'these Thy gifts' which my father so emphasized in his paean of thanksgiving to the Father above. The blessings themselves, usually old-fashioned fare, could be delicious things such as barnyard pie, baked crab or hare patties.

Even the homely haggis, which inevitably appeared when we killed a sheep, surprised us by its flavour. With heart and liver, lights and oatmeal in the stomach bag, Herself was like a mediaeval alchemist in the way she blended herbs and onions. The game-keeper had a particular partiality for haggis and we renewed our delight every time he addressed the hot dish in Burns's words,

Fair fa' your honest, sonsy face,
Great chieftain o' the puddin' race

Piles of sweet things overloaded the Saturday night table. Everybody thought it a duty to sample from the seven or eight platefuls as a tribute to Herself's baking. For Black Fergus and me duty did not enter into it. Seldom would as much as a manse biscuit be left over for the rest of the week. Fergus and I claimed far more than our fair share of Balmoral bonnets, raspberry fingers, Queenie's nut slices, wholemeal shorties, petticoat tails, sweet oatmeal biscuits, sponge gingerbread, Braemar fruit cake, curly murly, and hogmanay bun.

I would not have said so, but I could not believe that my mother's baking had been better than Herself's. Even as an old woman of eighty she never ceased to astonish us with the variety of her Saturday spread. In later years if her memory failed she might inquire of me whether we had cinnamon biscuits at the previous ceilidh, because she could not think of offering similar things two weeks running. And Saturday supper was all the more enhanced by having to make do during the rest of the week with dropped scones or golden-meal farls spread with jam.

Despite a huge meal, everyone took on a new youthfulness.

We cleared the kitchen for dancing. Even old Duncan, whose hand shook so much that he was afraid to shave himself, played the reels and jigs, his fingers moving firmly as the rest of us weaved through the Eightsome, Miss Hebburn Belches, Hamilton House, the Duke of Perth or the Dashing White Sergeant. Duncan's newly-shaven cheeks looked more apple-like than ever as he blew into the bagpipes, one foot thrust forward tapping in time to the music. Many of the sets consisted of four pairs. Violet invariably partnered Sandy, and although both were as round and plump as dumplings, they moved with agility through the most complicated reels. Alec paired Herself. He was far too shy to ask Mirren as this would have been an open and public admission of his interest in her. Mirren clung to my father's arm. But her eyes looked only at Alec.

Matched and paired as they all were, there was nobody left for me except Black Fergus. We danced, though dancing was hardly the word for our rough play. We were like two of the young seal bulls we watched down on the skerries. No matter what the tune or the manner of the dance, Fergus hooked his arm in mine, or we crossed hands, and then we swung until sparks flew from our boots as they struck the flagstones and sweat darkened our shirts. By the last bar we were like whirling devil-dancers. Fergus declared that 'the Paddies' up at the Forestry nurseries danced like that in the township socials. And if the big Irishmen did so then we must follow suit.

Violet made a concession at every Saturday ceilidh of partnering her black-haired son just once. But Fergus did not change his tactics. He swung his mother round until she laughed so much that they had to stop.

'Take Mistress Cameron for the schottische, Fergus,' she would eventually get out between fresh attacks of laughing. But Herself would brush the offer aside. Not only was Black Fergus too strong and wild for my grandmother but she was not sufficiently recovered from Fergus's suspect 'Amen' before and after supper.

If Mirren saw Black Fergus go towards her for a set she would run to the door. Because I was Fergus's partner in the rough swinging, I too was avoided by the women, though they knew that Herself had taught me the steps almost from the day I could walk. So Black Fergus and I were left to work off our excess energy together. My father was inclined to lift Mirren off her feet but he never attempted our speed. The others did not mind the wild swinging and were rather disappointed if Fergus and I did not put our best into it. Old Duncan especially loved to watch and would round off the evening with a very fast Strip the Willow to encourage us.

Black Fergus and I were tireless but the older people liked to pause. While they sat breathing heavily and fanning their faces, Herself took the harp from its corner. I succumbed to her spell each time she played. How could those knobbly hands, I wondered, produce such sweet sounds, sweeter than the stirring skirl of Duncan's pipes? Even when very old, Herself's fingers lost none of their dexterity nor her voice its alto richness.

Hearing the sad words of the Caristone lament in the kitchen, now quiet so suddenly after the noise, I could imagine Herself as the Lady of Clan Ranald in the song, sitting on the shore watching the two ships, one sailing to the west with a happy bride, the other returning with the bride dead.

I knew most of my grandmother's songs by heart because she sang them in the byre. She strongly recommended singing to the cattle while milking. The cradle and boating songs helped the cows to relax and release their milk, or so Herself assured me. She helped our ceilidh guests to relax also. But she was a good performer and understood that to make the best effect she must neither sing too many sad things nor go on too long. We all knew that when she put her harp away she would get Mirren to make more tea.

We knew also that Alec's song would have to come before this. Shyly, every Saturday, as though he had never asked before, the shepherd requested Herself to sing the 'Eriskay Love Lilt' or the 'Eriskay Lullaby'. That far island was his mother's birthplace and he never tired of hearing either song. Nobody would have wanted to deny Alec his simple pleasure, for though he was the most silent of men, he was confidant and friend in need to us all, including Herself.

No matter what storms or gales blew, even in the worst winter nights, our Saturday ceilidhs took place. We admitted defeat only if the winds of Blarosnich had piled the drifts too deep for the Sallachie folk to get their trap on the road. But the heaviest wind-driven deluge would not keep them at home. And no matter how cruelly the rain or hail beat down upon them as they got into the big tub-trap at the end of the ceilidh there were always shrieks of laughter louder than the shrieking winds.

Duncan and Mirren climbed into the trap and rode as far as the township. I could hear Violet jokingly rebuke her son as she settled herself on the leather-cushioned seats. 'Fergus, leave Mirren alone or I'll hammer the life out of . . .' and the rest would be drowned in squeals of delight as Black Fergus pushed his mother into Duncan's lap.

I cannot remember any such evening at the Sallachie house, although my father and I often went there to supper after handlings. The Saturday ceilidhs always took place at Blarosnich. Everyone knew Herself would never go beyond her own marches and there would be no proper music without the sound of her harp.

Rheumatism began to plague my grandmother, so that eventually the furthest she could move from the house and steading was the Earl's Park on the far side of the burn. Herself went there on Sunday morning after we had all been sent off to the kirk which she could see from the top of the hill. Dressed in her pale lavender-grey, Sabbath dress and black tippet shawl like a barnacle goose, she walked up the old drove-road and picked her way carefully over the stepping stones of Labharag. Then slowly, already tired by her efforts, she wandered across to the hill where our land and the crofters' common pasture joined the Earl's Park. Long stone dykes enclosed all three properties and these stones de-claimed the history of Blarosnich as they did a big part of the county, and much of the Western Highlands besides.

When the lairds had been denied their heritable jurisdiction by law in 1747 the Highland's proud tradition of clanmanship was broken. The chieftains ceased to be petty kings and became big land-owners instead. With long years of battle over, they had more opportunity to think of their way of life. They acquired the tastes of the age for fine living and imported silver and clothes from France, wines from Madeira, fruits and spices from the East.

Unfortunately, the high living could not for long be paid out of the smallholders' rents which were still often made in kind, such as a pair of cocks or a portion of barley. So the old lairds rented and sold their ancestral lands to the people of the south who wanted wide open spaces for breeding black-faced sheep.

The Clearances began then. Crofters' lands and birch woods were stripped to make room for the flocks moving up from the Cheviots and Pennines far south of the Highlands. Evicted tenants struggled to the cities and colonies or simply fell by the wayside. Whole glens were taken over, townships disappeared under the creeping sea of bracken. At Blarosnich we knew enough about bracken. We understood that the rape of the land which happened so long ago was not yet over. The people of our part of the Highlands were as reluctant in those far away days to go abroad as we were. They were herded down from the hills to the present township on the shore.

Up the drove-road came the men of Eilean a'Cathmara, gaunt-faced with hunger, wondering at the stubbornness of God in withholding manna so long in this stony wilderness. But when they reached the shore they found God had cast their bread upon the waters. Manna, in a strange form, was provided for decades to come. Each tide had left an unusually large amount of tangle behind, seaweed which only needed to be burnt in a kiln to produce valuable alkaline for making soap and glass. By the end of the eighteenth century the new shoremen could earn £20 for a ton. This fortune shrivelled when the landlords took part of it as rents for the miserable black-houses and shore lands. Yet the people managed to live. In fifty years more the price of the manna dropped to only £3 a ton. Most families were so poor that they were obliged to do corvée work to pay off their dues to the big land-owners. They laboured at building stone dykes to fence in the new thousands of black-faced sheep.

Many miles of such dykes were built at Blarosnich. They filled me with horror as they also did my grandmother. She remembered how her family had stumbled over crag and corrie, carrying wooden litters full of enormous stones. I could hardly lift some of these rocks myself when I grew older and helped my father to repair the dykes, yet they were carried, often for miles, by people of both my parents' families.

Herself sat on a stone stile up by the Earl's Park on Sunday mornings. My grandmother kept her eye on the tups because she did not want them to escape to the ewe-hills and bring lambs into the cruel world of March. The township folk said that she was only up there on the Sabbath inspecting the dykes to see if any gaps were left by their own township cows being pushed through to make a free visit to the bull. But although Herself might very well have looked for such tell-tale marks, she certainly never went up there Sunday after Sunday to view what the township women were wearing to the kirk on the other side, even though she carried her spy-glass over her shoulder.

The old lady climbed the hill for other reasons. Because she could not go to kirk and lose sight of her beloved Blarosnich, she went to the stone stile because she could watch both farm and kirk and still have communion with her Maker. She sang her paraphrases and hymns, happy to have only the accompaniment of croaking woodcock and the music of the Little Loud One.

The prayers Herself intoned to the Almighty were, however, unorthodox. 'Watch and pray' was her motto. And it was engraved in poker work on a picture by The Captain which hung over her bed. And while she kept the Sunday morning watch over stance and hill Herself prayed. As she put the glass to her eye and moved it slowly round to scan the world before her, seeing what mood the chimney at home was in, counting the bullocks, watching the buzzards rabbiting, following the course of the hinds stampeding across the moors to the soft waters of the lochan, she recited a strange litany.

She prayed to God in the words of Giolla Críost The Tailor, and not those of John Knox who came a century after. The destruction of the hirsels by foxes obsessed Herself. The lambings seemed to become progressively worse. Night and day my grandmother's thoughts were on the hill with the ewes whose breasts had been bitten off, and with the lambs whose stomachs had been ripped open by mothering vixens. But once upon a time, wolves had been a greater menace. Giolla Críost The Tailor wrote his fiery verses urging the Almighty to bring about their downfall.

And so every time a fox was mentioned at Blarosnich, Herself quoted The Tailor. During her Sabbath morning watch over the mountain acres she poured out her flood of Gaelic praise in passion. I often thought she should have been a minister because her rhetoric was matched only by her singing.

In later years Herself liked me to return from kirk by way of the hill so that I could help her on the walk back to the house. A long way off, as I came up through the green bracken I would hear the jumble of verses repeated as the spirit took her and not as The Tailor had written them.

> It was by Thee that Adam's seed was made with red-raspberry cheeks.
> Thou who hast blessed the land of Thy people, do Thou curse all sinful folk who are against Thee.
> There are accursed broods of whelps who work evil against the king's children; Let us hear of the slaughter of these hurtful heads for every leafy glen is full of them.
> These who declare war on Adam's children do Thou O King of Sun restrain them.
> We have many a wild dog's skin as cover for harp and lyre, but no fewer are the skulls, cold and empty that we have of that wild and evil brood.
> Father of Christ let snow fall from Lochaber to Renfrew and let there be ashes in Connel from their bony bodies.
> Murrain and plague, cancer and poison on all those that slay the herds. May the Son of God, with renewed purpose, cut off that mis-shapen brood.

Herself never received a formal education yet poets were her companions. Old poets especially lived with her, though words by that youngster, Robbie Burns, were painted on the bread-plates. She much admired his idea of social justice as expressed on the plates by 'A man's a man for a' that'.

Possibly my grandmother regarded Burns's queer mixture of English and a Scots dialect with suspicion, particularly since Burns praised drink. Having the Gaelic, Herself made no secret of the fact that she thought it the only Christian tongue. *The Book of the Dean of Lismore* was a second Bible at Blarosnich. The anthology had been compiled in the early sixteenth century and contained works of all Herself's favourite authors from those earlier turbulent centuries of eloquence, Blind Arthur, the Bard Macintyre, Isabel of Argyll, Red Finlay and, of course, Duncan son of Colin, the Good Knight.

These men and women, with their music of the Gaelic tongue, were my grandmother's daily friends. But none was closer to her than Donnchadh MacCailein, for not only was his verse often on her lips but he was once connected with Blarosnich. Before riding out to his death at Flodden, Sir Duncan had owned Blarosnich. He was seventy when he died on the Field of Flodden, an old man who could look back on many years among the same burns and corries which we knew. Sir Duncan had been laird of Blarosnich, the Field of Sighing. But of all his lands only a tiny parcel called the Earl's Park still remained in his family, and only so they might retain their ancient titles.

The Earl's Park was unlike the grass parks of our farm. We used these for pasturing the home cattle. But behind the thick stone dykes of the Earl's Park life ran riot, and had run riot for so long that an almost impenetrable forest had sprung up. I loved to clamber over the walls and lose myself in exploration of its dark, soughing tunnels. In bad weather our ewes often broke into this part of Blarosnich, making themselves snug dens under the hanging canopies of earth which clung to the roots of storm-felled trees. Majestic rowans stood in the Park, overburdened in September by bright scarlet berries to the delight of blackbird and thrush.

Birch overran the Park, growing so dense that when one tree died from suffocation it remained upright, imprisoned in the tangle of branches. This forest floor provided an ideal lek where blackcock displayed its bubbling chorus. And here too, among the unchecked wilderness of briars and bracken I found a boy's paradise. The present earl's factor and woodmen had never been known to visit the Park and it had become a sanctuary for birds.

In good weather and bad, in summer and winter, the wren burst himself with strident and jubilant trills. By the end of April, when a bright carpet of wood-anemones littered the forest floor, the willow warbler had returned from Africa. His sweet descending cadence continued all day. Also arrived from the warm south was the redstart, most gorgeous among the score or more of species which bred in and around the Park. With songsters like these we had no need of nightingales.

Herself taught me the flowers of the hill. Never a day passed when she did not come back to the house with something stuck in her shaggy old deerstalker hatband, which already bore a decoration of chestnut neck feathers from pochard drake and white ptarmigan tail-coverts. Even on the bleakest day of February, when our land seemed lost under an eternal crust of ice and snow, she would find dog's mercury in the warm twilight of the Earl's Park. And in November she often came home bearing primroses and violets in her hat.

Herself's memory was remarkable not only for poets of the Gaelic but also for flowers. Although she occasionally forgot the rota of cakes baked for Saturday ceilidhs, she remembered where flowers had been found in previous years, even on the island of her childhood days. When we went over to Eilean a'Cathmara, we would be closely questioned by my grandmother on our return. What state were the trees and flowers and bushes in, she would ask, and had the accursed bracken claimed the chickweed pastures which once fed man and beast. And if our trip across to the island happened in summer, we had to be sure and bring home a bunch of screeby to liven up the salads.

Many of the wild flowers and bulbs which came into the house at Blarosnich were used for age-old herbal cures whose recipes Herself had brought from the island. My grandmother had terrifying pills the size of tennis balls for giving the foals a tonic. But the young horses raised as much objection to having them thrust down their throats as I did to other concoctions made for dealing with my worms. And when the worms left there were cresses and meadowsweet to cleanse the blood.

The old lady could hardly wonder I did not show enthusiasm

for her nightcap cup of tea infused from fried elder blossom, speedwell and wild rose. But in spite of medicines which could be produced from wild flowers, I was an ardent collector. I pressed them between the pages of an old *Encyclopaedia Britannica* my father had bought at the sale of the last outgoing sporting tenants. The present occupier of the Big House was Florence of Arabia, who irritated my grandmother by choosing every visit to Blarosnich at a busy time of the farm's day and demanding that her house guests hear the harp there and then. Nevertheless, Herself displayed an unusual willingness to be long-suffering over these unreasonable requests, for Miss Florence was everything the previous tenant had not been.

Florence of Arabia personally made sure that all her stalkers and fishing friends closed gates and did not litter the moors with picnic tins and bottles, and she had no sympathy for the hunter who broke the ancient code of honour and returned to the Big House leaving a wounded deer out on the hill.

Miss Florence earned her nickname through her generosity. She gave each member of her staff a present on their birthday, and every bride from far and near received a wedding gift. The one drawback with this otherwise much appreciated institution was that all the gifts consisted of leather goods from Egypt. The housemaids and gillies found themselves accumulating at an alarming rate a collection of perfectly useless book-covers and travelling sets, souvenir boxes and pouffes, handbags and wallets, all with views of pyramids and passing camels tooled with varying degrees of skill on the soft leather. Besides the outsize pouffes, which took up an inordinate amount of room in the small Highland houses, there were the even more conspicuous stools shaped like camel saddles complete with brass knobs. In our own house The Room displayed several small tapestries depicting, in the style of Victorian oleographs, love scenes between fat sheiks and veiled women.

Florence of Arabia only spent six months of the year in our neighbourhood. During her stay she never went anywhere except in the company of her sister Miss Philippa, who was known as The Cannibal. Though, naturally enough, none of us had ever been to dinner at the Big House, we had it on the best of authority that Miss Philippa ate raw meat. Mirren's cousin was parlour-maid up at the Big House and assured us that the meat was not just under-done, but that huge raw and perfectly bloody steaks were served to and devoured by the younger mistress.

I could never believe that Mirren's cousin told the whole truth because both ladies were tiny and thin and merely nibbled at the smallest pieces of shortbread when they took tea at Blaros-nich. But I agreed with Mirren that both Florence and Philippa had long, horse teeth, noticeably darker in shade than the old false ones which Alec kept in his waistcoat pocket for social emergencies.

Besides being deaf, Florence of Arabia alone of the two sisters could drive their large open motor car. Miss Philippa sat beside her, pumping the rubber horn as though she were in an ambulance on its way to an accident. The whole countryside consequently knew when and where they were going. The horn, however, had its uses. Its sound, blown by a wind across country, would give Herself warning of an impending visit. She could then run and put on a clean apron ready to receive the weird sisters and their often weirder guests.

As a young boy I used to be as spellbound by the two sisters as they appeared to be by my grandmother's music. Miss Florence would sit almost on top of the harp, pushing her silver ear-trumpet in front of Herself so that not one word might be missed, though neither she nor her meat-eating sister understood anything of the Gaelic. Miss Philippa also leant well forward, mouth open, horse teeth bared as though to bite the music.

I would pass my gaze from the beaky, bird-like faces to examine Miss Philippa's claw-like hands, for Herself had told me that the rings on the bony fingers were worth several farms of land. Could those few pieces of sparkling glass, I wondered, really buy scores of ewes, whole mountainsides of forest and deer, farmhouses and townships? They could indeed, I was told after every visit the ladies made to Blarosnich.

Miss Philippa's diamonds, however, were easier to understand than the doddery old man they sometimes brought with them.

How could anybody expect me to believe that he had once been a general in command of thousands of men at the front line? He drooled and slobbered over himself and several times during the short visit had to be conducted up the garden to the lavatory, because his 'waterworks were worn out', as Alec explained to me. It was the shepherd who did the conducting and kept his grey dentures in readiness for such occasions.

Herself was consulted about cures for the General's malady, but my grandmother did not meet with the same success as she had over Miss Florence and her 'queer turns'. Herself liked to hear nothing more than how much better Florence of Arabia felt on the herbs of Blarosnich than on all the prescriptions of Harley Street. None of us, neither Miss Florence nor Herself nor the Harley Street men, understood that my grandmother's homemade mixture of *meuran nan caillich mharbha*—dead women's thimbles, was only a stronger dose of the digitalin drugs of Harley Street which were also made from foxgloves.

When Herself finished her music, the sisters waited while the General went down the garden again to the 'wee house' and gathering their shawls and gloves and bags departed as they had come with a fanfare of horn blowing. The horn had no effect on the township hens. They often became victims of the ladies' car as it shot along the shore road. With the General on board, posted royally among the tartan rugs on the back seat, there was no doubt a justifiable excuse for speed.

3

Shepherd's delight

The lake which fed Labharag burn was naturally called the *mathair*—Mother of the Little Loud One. Long, reedy arms of the lochan stretched across half of the moor between Craigclamhan and Craighar. During a summer day the hunter on the hill would pause with his gun, absorbing the beauty of the place, watching the ducks as they dived after freshwater shrimps. Yellow flags were reflected in the still, glassy water.

The hirsel moved among the lush grasses and sedges like woolly summer clouds. And more blue than the June sky or the distant cobalt sea was the cerulean flash of blue-aeshna dragonfly. His vast blue eyes had a thousand sensitive cameras focussed on every bright spear of lakeside plant for unwary blue butterflies. Snail-hunting wheatears flitted restlessly across the moor, waving their white rumps and ignoring the screaming peregrines. The place became such a paradise on summer days that the gamekeeper felt reluctant to use his gun against the red-breasted merganser. But use it he must if any trout were to be left to nibble Miss Philippa's hare's-ear fly.

This *lochán mathair*, Mother of the Little Loud One, was the scene Florence of Arabia tried regularly every year to put on canvas with her paint brush. The arras of colours, however, was too subtle for her palette. As a result, the annual summer painting never varied, for she seemed to see nothing except bell heather and the startling vermilion of distant rocks, blood-soaked by the sunset. These landscapes were often framed and given as Christmas presents when the supply of Egyptian leather goods ran out.

Here also, by the cool lochan shores, the picnic things from the Big House were set among the grasses. The heavy silver and the finest of rarities from Harrods were unloaded from the wicker baskets on the bank between the otter tracks. The ladies and their genteel guests never saw the otters. Only the working shepherd on his pre-dawn round watched the young cubs playing by their breeding holt or the bitch teaching them to swim.

To me, the lochan was neither an artist's canvas nor a picnicker's playground, though during my life I walked its length and breadth on thousands of days, and often before sunrise. For me, in those chill early hours, the Mother of the Little Loud One was all grey. Rocks and heather were uniformly charcoal, awaiting their colour from the sun's first touch. Before dawn, the boulders looked grey and round like the ewes heavy with carrying. At first light the ewes would paw the ground and prepare a couch for lambing.

But although I loved the lonely lochan before daybreak, it was only because Herself was up and about and came to knock on my door soon after five o'clock that I ever saw it. The flannelette sheets and the woollen blankets made a chrysalis I was reluctant to leave, though the hot water bottle had gone cold hours before. Confused between fleeing dreams and the flicker of the candle Herself brought and set in my room, I struggled into my clothes and boots. Below, in the kitchen, I ate breakfast in silence, still half asleep.

In those days Blarosnich carried a stock of nearly a hundred score of ewes and yearling ewes, or hoggets. They had a natural, geographical setting of three hirsels—the far shore of Pitlobar, the Craigclamhan flanks, and the lochan moor. For the four weeks of lambing and much of the summer and autumn, Alec returned to live at his old home on the shore beyond the moors. He was meant to live there all the time. But following his mother's death and his own illness he divided his time between our bothie and the bleak little house on the Pitlobar shore.

My father was thankful enough for this arrangement. Few men would face the privation of the shepherd's house across the mountain. By comparison, at Blarosnich we were sophisticated cosmopolitans, for within a mile we had the life of the township and its sixty or so inhabitants. But Alec's home lay over two hours walking and climbing from even the nearest steading, which was our own, and even that journey was impossible during part of the winter months.

The far shore had never been as difficult a hirsel to shepherd as Craigclamhan. The mountain face there was bare and treacherous and few of the winds took kindly to it. My father herded it naturally enough and left me the lochan moor now that Herself could go shepherding no more. When age and rheumatism forced her to give up I was fourteen years old, a man ready to take his place on the hill.

A print of the Good Shepherd hung on the half-landing at Blarosnich. Many Highland homes possessed this picture which showed the Saviour rescuing a lamb fallen down a cliff. But by my twelfth birthday I already knew that the hymn about ninety-and-nine being safely within the fold was seldom, if ever, true of a hill-farm. All of the sheep were out on 'the mountain wild and bare'. We considered ourselves lucky if only a quarter of the lambs died. Only too often the losses were greater than that, especially among the Craigclamhan hirsel.

The lambs seemed to be deliberately perverse in getting themselves lodged immoveably on the most unlikely of mountain ledges, or drowned in burns racing with melting snows. And their dams, who ought to have learnt from experience, were no better. They seemed adept at choosing the bleakest summit or most exposed stretch of moor for labouring.

Florence of Arabia went to the lochan to paint a pretty picture. I went in those dark, early mornings not knowing what I would find. In the kitchen I put on my oilskins wondering what troubles awaited me by the lochan shore. Herself gave me a 'piece' and bade me make haste, for most of the ewes seemed to prefer an early hour for lambing and I had a long journey in front of me. My grandmother called the moor *A' Mhin-choiseachd*—The Easy Walking. The lochan shores were indeed the flattest part of the whole peninsula and before the Clearances supported a large township. But the climb up through the grey-scree braes to the immense rockface buttressing the moor was not easy walking.

Once I got outside the house, the wind and lashing rain washed the last sleep from my puffed-up eyes. From his chain in the yard

I would free Smoky, a shaggy little collie who was much more interested in putting up woodcock and chasing rabbits than working the hirsel. While Smoky had half an ear cocked for my whistling, and half an ear for exciting sounds blown on the winds, I looked into the hen house to see if wild cats or foxes had made any disturbance during the night. Then the dog and I would set off in earnest along the fank wall. Beyond the grass parks lay an hour's climbing through braes, where, in April, a lacework of little burns tumbled down releasing the floodwaters of Craigclamhan. Amongst the strange sculpture of giant boulders I would hear the bleat of lambs who had already lost their dams. And by the time I reached the moor sweat had made my clothes as wet inside as the rain made my oilskins. The wool was glued to my skin in an uncomfortable hot, clammy wetness.

Yet, indescribably, I felt a sense of power. Peering through the still-grey gloom of mist or driving rain, trying to discern the blank faces and grey bodies of the flock, I knew the lambs' safety depended on me. Old stone dykes, running for miles across the hills, could no longer be relied on. The sheep broke through them where the stone had collapsed, often under the large herds of stampeding deer. If stone walls alone had confined our flocks, the sheep would have been able to wander far beyond them, scrambling through the gaps, going in their innocence as far as Sallachie and the Forestry lands beyond that. But they seldom did.

No animal was ever more tied by instinct and tradition to the place of its birth than the black-faced ewe. Born on a particular part of the moor or mountain, the female lamb, growing to a two-year-old gimmer, would give birth to her own firstborn in the same part. Only the ram lambs were sold at the autumn sales with the four-year-old ewes whose place in the flock would be taken by ewe lambs. In this way four female generations were always on the same ground. Multiplied through many generations this tradition produced an inbred sense of home. And just as the knots from high Arctic waste lands returned every winter to our mudflats, so on going up from handlings the ewes left the densely packed flock of their own accord when they reached a barely discernable grass-track leading to their own home territory.

The hirsel was unerring in its knowledge of the hill and of the best places for shelter in bad weather. The stone dykes were much more useful as windbreaks for the sheep than confining them to the home marches. Indeed, throughout the long winter when deep snow blanketed the hills it was shelter afforded by the dry side of the walls which saved many from death.

But we could never leave the sheep alone even though the shepherd disturbed them or his dog sent them running just at the moment when they were pawing the ground and preparing a lambing bed. There was the constant danger of prowling foxes, and sometimes the township dogs which could be as destructive. There were dangers from hooded crows and gulls, and other dangers of a hundred kinds attending the birth of a lamb.

Knots flew south to us every year by instinct and there was instinct in me also. By my fourteenth birthday I could clamber about the moor and find the difficult births without ever really knowing why. Gradually, after my climb with Smoky, light would begin to filter through the mist. The ewe would settle in her chosen bed, watched over by last year's female lamb which had now become a hogget. The hogget could do nothing to relieve the mother's kicking limbs and hour of agony.

If there were no complications the ewe would lick her lamb clean and the tiny creature would be on its feet within minutes. But the strangeness and pain of motherhood often seemed to blind the ewe. Running back and forth, wildly answering her bleating lamb, the dam was unable either to see the lamb or be capable of following the sound of crying.

Hoggets which appeared so interested in their mothers' last lambing sometimes could cause the shepherd most trouble when they became gimmers the following year and gave birth themselves. They often got up from the bed and trotted away, leaving the new-born, slimy bundle unlicked. And then, if the lamb was not to die, the shepherd must be on hand to bring them together. Sometimes the gimmer would not allow the lamb near her sore breast and both had to be taken all the way down to the fank and left in a pen.

These would be the straightforward births, occurrences we took for granted. Sometimes there were half-born lambs crying in desperation as their dams ran around in mad agony unable to free themselves of the birth. In spite of being in such a terrible condition the ewe would run from the shepherd, racing him over steep-banked burns and crags before he could complete the delivery by force. The difficulty usually occurred because one of the lamb's legs was bent backwards.

Sometimes ewes became overheavy with lambs and got onto their backs. These died within a few hours if the shepherd did not arrive in time to turn them over. Hooded crows and black-backed gulls often swooped down on these unfortunate animals and ripped the bellies open with their beaks. Twins also posed a problem because their dams, being on a mountain covered with snow for much of the winter, seldom had enough milk for two mouths. A foster mother would then need to be found or else the lamb had to be carried back to our kitchen and fed from a bottle. One of the first things I can remember about Rhona, my mother, was her feeding a weak lamb on the kitchen floor. She warmed the drops of milk in her mouth and then, almost mouth to mouth, she passed the milk into the quivering little animal.

Because still-births were not unusual, and there were ewes whose udders were painful for want of milking, it was sometimes possible to get an orphan lamb or twin fed by them. But we knew that a ewe's sense of smell was strong and that she could not necessarily be relied upon to accept an adoption. Even though I might have made the changeling a coat from the dead lamb's skin, the ewe would not always be deceived by the smell of her own body on the coat.

For four hours I would tramp the lochan moor, often wet through with feet and fingers numbed by the freezing winds. I was a sorry-looking, bedraggled figure in my oilskins, a different sort of person from the young men of the Big House. They tramped the lochan moor too, but only in the best summer weather when they could wear gay summer blazers.

Still, I never experienced envy. If anything, I despised them, especially when they stopped me and asked who I was, as though I was trespassing on their private estate. My 'piece', eaten in what shelter I could find from wind and rain, seemed to me more real and satisfying than fancy things out of picnic baskets. My bread and dripping was a man's food. *Pâté de foie gras* was for dandies. In spite of all the hardship and danger they involved me in, I loved the hill and hirsel. And wind and rain did eventually give way to warming sun. I could always look forward to the sandpipers returning to the lochan even though I despised the Big House visitors who came there. They made me feel inferior when I met them out stalking. These younger guests of the two sisters looked at me suspiciously as though my shepherding would give the deer wind of their presence.

Suddenly, on the bleakest of mornings, I might find myself warm with happiness because I had saved a particularly fine ram lamb, or because all the ewes during my round had lambed down quietly and I would be able to rush home to a black pudding and venison steak breakfast. At no time in these years did I ever question my place on the hill. I never shared my schoolfriends' ambitions for engine-driving or Highland soldiering or being a speed-cop in Glasgow. I only longed for the summer holidays when I could leave school altogether.

After proper breakfast, wet or dry, wind or sunshine, came school. And the worst that happened on the hill was better than the best that happened in the classroom. Listening to Teacher helping Postie's tiny daughter with her alphabet was not of interest to me. School's only saving grace was the presence of Black Fergus. When he was there anything could happen to liven up the dull hours. But when he left his cheekiness and laughter and defiance of law and order went with him. School had nothing for me and I had nothing for it.

Teacher's love for us was at once her strength and her undoing. She probably loved Black Fergus more than all the rest of us put together. He knew this and took advantage of it though he would have laid his life down for her if the need had arisen. She knew I missed Black Fergus and sympathized with me. Her own attainments were limited in an academic sense. If the answer books were stolen, as they were frequently during Fergus's reign of terror, it was an embarrassment to Teacher. She could never set me any algebra or arithmetic until another set of answers arrived a week later from Glasgow.

She only enjoyed teaching Scripture and singing and was never happy when her pupils got past the age of ten. After this, the senior girls had to specialize in needlework, while the big boys did gardening or helped Niall the Ferry with his boat. Niall was Teacher's husband.

Before my last book at school Teacher lost her Niall. We were not at all sad that he was dead. Afterwards Teacher came up to Blarosnich to sleep with Herself. Despite her great size and strength, Teacher was nervous and felt afraid to spend lonely nights in the school residence which was beside the kyle, some distance from the other houses. Whatever criticism the township people may have had about Herself, whenever troubles came they always turned to Blarosnich, knowing my grandmother practised as well as preached her stern Christian principles.

The new arrangement worked well because Herself was fond of the big, bouncing Teacher and felt sorry for her coming to such a pass after so many years with the ferryman. Of all the township men, Niall was the chief target for sharp tongues. He was often to be seen, in broad Christian daylight, drunk. Because there was no public house in the neighbourhood, Herself concluded that Niall was only a ferryman in order to obtain liquor from the steamers. My grandmother had a dread about any of us using the ferry; it was, she said, the height of folly to put one's life into the hands of a notorious wine-bibber. Now Niall was dead. He would give Teacher no more black eyes and she would not need to wear sunglasses in class to cover the bruises.

Niall's death was received nowhere better than up at the Big House. At one time Florence of Arabia had considered giving up the sporting tenancy because she so hated the ferryman. The two sisters and their frequent guests used Niall's boat more than anybody. But they could hardly have complained of Niall's drinking, for Mirren's cousin insisted that after one dinner party alone over twenty empty wine bottles had been carried from the Big House. The ladies' objection to the ferryman concerned more serious things than alcohol.

In those days, the most important member of the Big House was Susie, an ageing dachshund. To call Susie a 'German sausage' was a strategic mistake for those whose strategy involved being friendly with Miss Florence and Miss Philippa. Both sisters were anti-German to an astonishing degree. They made a particular point of referring to Susie's breed as 'dash hound', though it was difficult for us to think of her either dashing or being a hound. Susie lived exclusively, as far as we could tell, on one or other of the two ladies' laps, which made it difficult for us to accept her need of a bright red modesty belt as protection against possible overtures from township mongrels. The mongrels did not fail for lack of trying. At times it seemed as if the whole canine population was congregated on the Big House doorstep with the express purpose of embarrassing the two sisters. These would-be boarders had to be repelled by the gardener and his watering hose.

Herself had no time or patience with such nonsense. A dog's place was in the yard on a chain, when it was not working on the hill or catching rats. An orphan lamb might be most appealing with its close-curled fleece dazzling white in contrast with black hooves and face. But if it did not respond sufficiently well on the bottle, it was served up for dinner without waste of words and sentiment. We took such things as part of our life. We thought Florence of Arabia silly over her dog. She may have thought us hard-hearted about ours. We were not hard-hearted but hardy.

Much to my grandmother's annoyance, the Big House ladies brought Susie on their visits to us. Susie loved to hear the harp, they said. Poor Susie's agonized whines could not possibly be interpreted as enjoyment, despite Miss Philippa's protestations to that effect. If Susie loved the music then her appetite for the shortbread was a consuming passion. This also annoyed Herself. She baked the shortbread especially for the two sisters. But they only nibbled, Herself suspected, so that Susie could gobble the rest. It was awful to watch the crisp, rich shortbread being swallowed whole by that fat dog, knowing that we ourselves only had it as a treat on Saturday.

'*What* a good girl,' Miss Philippa would say to Susie, 'to finish the last cake.' Then she would turn to a seething hostess, 'You know, Susie *loves* the good fare at Blarosnich. She will go home now and turn up her nose at the lovely supper cook has prepared for her.'

'May the Lord on His throne above keep me poor and sane,' my grandmother would say to nobody in particular as the Big House car went down the lane and Susie barked her appreciation of Miss Philippa's performance on the rubber horn.

In spite of such indignities and insanities suffered at the hands of the sporting tenants, Herself remained staunchly diplomatic in all her dealings with the Big House. It was advantageous for us to be on good terms with the two sisters. They paid us top London prices for the mutton and garden produce, milk and cheese we supplied, and in addition they allowed us quite a free hand with game and deer on the hill.

But not even the good fare of Blarosnich could prolong Susie's days and at last the fat little dog was buried in great style on top of the hill facing the sorrowing ladies' bedrooms. When the first snow fell, covering the top of Craigclamhan like a nun's wimple, the dust-sheets were brought out to cover the Big House furniture. The sisters went south to their estate in Sussex before going on to Egypt for sunshine and more leather presents.

In the year following Susie's funeral, when the ladies returned in the late spring they had added three creamy Pomeranians to their family. The new dogs were named Knight, Frank and Rutley. The sisters soon discovered that none of the trio had a musical ear and consequently they were only brought once to see us at Blarosnich. But Susie was not forgotten.

Miss Florence went into the school residence one day with a basket of game she wanted put on the steamer. She got no reply to her repeated knockings on the open front door. Thinking her deafness had denied her the call to enter, she went inside to put the basket on the table. The bedroom door was ajar and through the narrow slot Miss Florence saw something which shocked her beyond any shock she had ever had. Florence of Arabia had travelled the world a great deal, especially in her younger days. She had been swept along by hysterical crowds in Indian race riots. She had been robbed by bandits in the Chinese mountains.

But none of these or similar misadventures were as bad as the one now confronting her in the bedroom of the school residence.

On the unmade bed lay a tartan rug—a very familiar and special tartan rug: Susie's. It was the very one in which Susie had been lowered into her little grave the previous autumn. Miss Florence realized at once that a dreadful deed had been done.

When Niall the Ferry came into the house, Florence of Arabia leapt at him as if demented. Though small and bird-like and past her allotted threescore years and ten, Florence flew at the grave robber, feeling the strength of God and St. Francis within her. Using her silver ear-trumpet as the best cudgel to hand, she advanced, flailing the air with her weapon and screaming suitable abuse. For many months afterwards she triumphantly showed visitors the dents in her ear-trumpet, nobly incurred in her primitive attack on the evil Niall.

The Big House ladies wasted no words in giving their opinion of Niall the Ferry. But Teacher had loved him, in spite of their frequent quarrels and the black eyes which she brought with her to nurse at Blarosnich until the drink had taken its toll of Niall. It seemed odd to think that Niall was dead now. I could not get used to the idea of Teacher sleeping permanently with my grandmother in The Captain's room with 'Watch and Pray' over the big feathered bed. For weeks after Teacher came I would lie in my bed in the next door room trying to sleep. But her sobs were too heart-rending to ignore. The beatings she had suffered from Niall were terrible. But Teacher had been happier with Niall breathing whisky fumes over her in the night than with Herself, whose boiled sweets of comfort always tasted of camphor balls.

Quite often Teacher had not returned to the schoolhouse by the time I came down from the lambing on the hill.

'You look tired, Donnie. Get away to your bed. Don't trouble to come down my way,' Teacher excused me from squeezing my long legs under the low classroom desks. And for the last three months of my compulsory education I seldom appeared in the one-room school. The only work Teacher could devise for me was reading. But I found it impossible to concentrate because all around me infants intoned Scripture or poetry.

Being the oldest and biggest in the room I felt embarrassed and out of place. I was now unusually tall for a boy of my age. A downy moustache appeared on my upper lip. I did not change, but my body did, suddenly confronting me with intoxicating sensual pleasures, filling my dreams at night, making me absent-minded during the day.

I did not altogether like the disturbance in my life, yet there was no denying that it had its good side. I could understand now why city people liked to lie on beaches and why the young sporting men from the Big House stripped on the moors and let the sun play with their nakedness.

All that May and June a delirium possessed me, a fever of yearning for things I could not identify. The burgeoning spring flowers and their heady smell seemed to be more sensuous than I remembered from previous springs. My body made demands on me. It had to be dealt with like an unruly dog. I wanted to roll on the carpet of yellow tormentil covering the hill. And when the sun beat down on my back it made me yearn for strange excitements.

To calm myself I swam in the burn. But as I emerged, quivering with sensation, the sun began again. The breezes seemed to be laden with desires. The Blarosnich winds touched my newly sensitized body. I stretched my arms above my head and opened myself to the sun. The breeze towelled me and dried off the clear, crystal drops of water that clung like dew to the mysterious tufts of wiry hair which was so different from the silky hair of my head.

Going on with my work after such a swim was distasteful. I could think only of abandoning myself to the sun and dreaming in the sun. Herself disliked Skye folk whom she regarded as lazy and untrustworthy. But I recalled, and now understood, their old Prayer and said it to myself many times over,

> *O that the peats could cut themselves,*
> *And the fish swim into the shore,*
> *And that I could lie on my back in the sun*
> *And sleep for ever more.*

47

When summer came and the rains returned I was still subject to violent moods and seizures of longing. Mists clung to the hills just as the haymakers' clothes clung to their bodies during their long battle of winning the meadows. But in spite of the mists and the rains, the enclosed strath was like a tropical jungle, so great was the humidity. My father and Herself passed up and down the parks, turning row upon row of soaked grass with a mechanical precision. Their thick clothes did not bother them, nor did they seem to attract the clouds of midges and clegs which came to suck the tingling new life under my sweaty vest.

The days in the hay parks were long to me, longer and more tedious than ever before. I kept looking towards the lane, praying for a township cow to come bulling so that I could have an excuse for leaving the meadow for a time. I strained my ears, hoping to hear one of the beehives swarming, or to catch the sound of the Big House car's horn that would draw the others away, leaving me free to dash like a panting stag to the burn. The clegs and gadflies might follow me but I would lie on the bank, fanning them away with bracken, marvelling again at this new body of mine, filled with an exquisite wonder as each sensuous stroke of the green punkah passed electrically over my skin.

I discovered that physical contacts of many different kinds aroused the new sensations. The fronds of bracken on the burn bank was not the only one. The cold iron legs of the desk at school pressing against my own legs stirred me in a peculiar way. So did the innocent enamel bucket I held between my knees when milking in the byre. And when my body was actively occupied in this way, my mind was. Images and imaginings passed before my inner eye in a cavalcade of sensation which my body craved.

Smooth, hard things sought out the bones under the muscles, and hardness responded to hardness. Soft things, like my milking beret and my shirts and my canvas shoes had a special quality too. They became part of my body, an extra skin put off and on night and morning. I found that their own smell excited me because they were bitter-sweet with my own sweat. All the animals around me were roused by smells. And now I enjoyed my own much better than the dead carbolic odour of my family or the sickly perfumes that lingered in The Room long after Miss Florence and her sister had left the house.

For a long time I thought the change in me and my own efforts to indulge and encourage it were known to none but me. But my restlessness did not escape Herself's sharp eye. I took the strictest precautions when going into her bedroom to look at my marvellous man's body naked and full length in the wardrobe mirror. But in spite of her lameness, my grandmother shared her Maker's power of omnipresence. Her spy-glass missed little of life and movement that stirred between the summit ridges on either side of the strath.

I had already sensed her crossness one day when I obeyed the summons on the farm whistle to join my father in the next park for the afternoon *strubag*. Herself poured out my pint of tea. As she handed it to me I saw an unusual, hurt expression on her face. I did not know what it was all about until I went to bed that night. My family rarely, if ever, talked about matters of a sexual nature. I remember when I first saw my father in the fank covered with blood. He was castrating the ram lambs with his knife and teeth. I asked him why they had to be cut but he was embarrassed and could not answer.

On the evening following Herself's day-long, hurt expression I went to my room and found my Bible opened. A sheet of blank writing paper was placed on top of the page. A tiny window had been cut in the paper to draw my attention to a particular verse in Genesis:—'And the eyes of them both were opened, and they knew that they were naked; and they sewed fig leaves together and made themselves aprons.'

Surprisingly I knew for the first time in my life that I was prepared to displease Herself and my father and that I did not care if they were hurt. It was easy for them to thumb their Bibles. They were old and did not understand. Certainly, I was not going to stop swimming because a dried-up old woman might catch sight of me through her eye-glass a quarter of a mile away.

Herself, however, was disturbed. She prevailed upon Alec to take me aside and discuss the matter after Black Fergus and I had

49

spent a happy Sunday afternoon at Stag's Pool with the Irish woodmen.

'Six grown men you were, down in the water with not a stitch between the lot of you, and it the Sabbath too,' Alec said. But his attempt to deliver a sermon was not convincing. His eyes twinkled and in the end he merely told me to be more careful on future occasions.

'You know what Herself is,' he concluded.

I did indeed know, and I disapproved. I envied Black Fergus for his parents. Sandy and Violet laughed until their eyes watered when I told them about the Bible and the sheet of writing paper. Violet expressed all our feelings.

'It's not as though Mistress Cameron,' she said, 'hasn't seen a bit of courting tackle in her own day.'

We laughed again. But Violet was kind-hearted. She would not have spoken to Herself in that way. The tub-trap drew up on Saturday night and she came into our kitchen a model of propriety, her generous bosom well hidden by a modesty vest as she danced under my grandmother's eagle eye.

And I certainly would never have repeated Violet's remark to my father. We had a curious relationship. I would have liked a thick mat of hair on my chest like the one Black Fergus now sported. I envied the Irish woodmen their adventures with the Big House maids. But it was my father upon whom I wished to model my life.

He was tall and thin like me. He smiled uncertainly when the Big House stalkers asked if I were his young brother. He was not given to talking, and shared with our shepherd the reticence of men who have spent years of solitude on the hill. My father left school at thirteen, though he soon learnt the complexities of our Highland life. Professional naturalists asked his opinion about bird-life and red deer, or they listened closely as he told them about the distribution of otters. Men from the Ministry of Agriculture frequently came up our lane to marvel at my father's experiments.

His first love had been the hirsel. But his ambitions went beyond wedders and ewes. He never forgot the rape of the Western Highlands during the Clearances, though for reasons different from Herself's. When my father climbed to work among the bare screes of Craigclamhan, he remembered that our ancient forebears had come that way through dense oak forests and clinging gardens of birch and pine. The sheep barons from the south cleared the last of the woods and drove the crofters down to shore communities or to Canada. It did not take long for the sighing winds of Blarosnich to strip the forest soil from the unprotected hill, and leave nothing but bare, inhospitable rock. Any saplings which sprang up in defiance were soon nibbled by the sheep in winter.

Before the black-faced sheep were brought, the Highlands had been cattle country. But their grazing grounds soon disappeared under bracken. Beautiful to look at, bracken was a menace to us. It spread like a green leprosy and Herself regarded it as an evil equalled only by the fox. The sheep were not heavy enough to trample it down and too fastidious in their choice of food to eat it, so that the bracken rioted unchecked for decades. The breed of small, hardy black cattle that roamed our hills before the sheep came had died out long ago. Nevertheless, my father still dreamed of a great shaggy Highland herd that would out-winter and require little attention.

With this object in mind he spent every free hour clearing the land beyond the old grass parks. The endurance of those families forced to build the stone dykes in the last century must have been like my father's efforts to clear these lands of boulders. The sour rush acres were cut open with his plough. On many nights, as I went reluctantly to bed, the spluttering of the tractor came in through my open window.

A stranger visiting Blarosnich might well have concluded that my father was a weak man dominated by his old mother. To think this, however, would have been to misunderstand the workings of our hill-farm. My father was only a young boy when The Captain died. Herself had to decide either to carry on the running of Blarosnich or to go back to the crofter-fisher community in the township. Her son never forgot that it was her iron will which saved the Field of Sighing intact for him.

From long experience he knew that farming like ours was not

learnt at agricultural colleges or from textbooks. What did lecturers and authors understand of Herself's skill in changing lambs from one ewe to another? How could a scientist appreciate the herbal lore by which she cured sick cattle after the vet had despaired of them? Where the weather was concerned, my father always consulted Herself. She had an uncanny instinct, like a red deer. She could sense the coming of a gale or snow-storm hours before it reached Blarosnich.

When he came of age and married Rhona, he was wise enough not to push Herself into the background. When Rhona's golden bread no longer graced our table he was glad Herself was still there and able to run house and steading. My father and grandmother were very much alike except that he had also inherited The Captain's patience. He was a man of mountains and moors just as The Captain had been a master of tides and rivers. My father ploughed large tracts once full of boulders. Nothing could stop him from taking on such impossible odds. In him, both parents met. The silent wisdom of ebb and flow mingled with the shepherd's stubbornness. He would go away to lamb sales entrusting the whole of Blarosnich to Herself even when she was an old woman. He left me to Alec's care, certain that the little shepherd had more to offer me than Teacher in her one-room school. Sometimes when Herself made loud complaint because we brought half the hill into the house on our boots, my father would give me a sympathetic wink. But he would not rebuke Herself. He knew the pain it caused her straight back to get down and scrub the stone flags I was so careless about.

My father seldom failed to notice the outward marks made by any carelessness of mine and saw at once if I had left a badly-dressed hay-cock or grew impatient with the sheep. Yet he seemed totally unaware of my inner conflicts which were, often as not, the cause of any shoddy work I did about the farm. He could identify each note of the waders' clamour at sundown, but remained deaf to the voice asking to be heard amid the crashes of my adolescent blunderings. I could not imagine that he had ever been young. It did not seem possible that he would have stood when he was a boy in front of the long mirror in his mother's room to admire the lines and budding muscles of his body and to put out his tongue and feel the coldness of the glass.

He would have regarded my fascination with the reflection of this naked body which belonged to me as unquestionably sinful. On the other hand I could not think it wrong. The otters and deer, I felt sure, gazed at themselves in the lochan's moonlit waters, just as our old cows stood in the shallows of the burn to look at their summer heaviness.

Speculation as to whether my father would have indulged in mirror worship did not help me because the wardrobe had not been in Herself's room during his boyhood. My mother bought it on coming to Blarosnich as a bride. We had got most of our grander pieces of furniture from auctions although they were seldom used afterwards. The mahogany commode from the castle itself, festooned by carving, did nothing but collect dust over the years while it waited for an illness of sufficient gravity to justify such luxury.

Herself had always wanted a sewing machine. When the aged post-mistress died we bought her foot-pedal Singer, together with a willow-pattern tea service. I had never bid at a sale before and I could not resist the sight of so much blue china. Its attractiveness was not dimmed for me by the many thin brown cracks which veined the set: these tell-tale signs alone now told of goodness knows how many years when the old post-mistress and her two sisters laid a Sunday table for beaux who never came. As a boy on my way home from Sunday School I used to stare at the three old women sitting with the door open, the table spread and a beckoning smile on their wrinkled faces. But I would never venture near them because Mirren had assured me they were waiting to pounce on the first unsuspecting male.

My grandmother was as delighted with the Singer as I was with the blue china. But she never once used the machine though one of my cups frequently appeared on Saturday's supper table because it had a special little draining ledge for a moustache just right for the gamekeeper.

Likewise, nobody ever sat at our large writing-desk, which came from the next parish manse, to compose the important letters and documents which the broad top and bundle of quill pens demanded. We used the desk's long drawers for storing apples. And the wine glasses in The Room press had certainly seen no ruby shades of port since the day the auctioneer sold them as part of the contents left by the last tenants of the Big House.

Alone among these things was the wardrobe, very much in use for the best clothes as well as The Captain's butterfly collars and old stockings. I knew that nobody but myself enjoyed the full-length mirror in its door. The patches and blotches wrought by time on the silvering in no way married my secret pleasure. Like our writing-desk, the wardrobe originally belonged to the next manse. Had the minister, I sometimes wondered, turned a vain eye upon his rotund body swathed in frock coat, or even upon the hairy suit of his Maker's likeness? Had his wife, who had mothered so many children that the family was obliged to leave for their education in the city, ever looked with wonder at her pregnant body in the mirror?

Bodies! What odd things they were. Looking at the half-boy half-man in the ex-manse mirror I was also confused. In my home emphasis was put upon the fact that Man occupied the most superior place in Creation, because he was God's special project and had been given a body modelled after the divine likeness. Yet for all this privilege the poor body also appeared to have been an error by the Almighty. Although in part divine, the body must be concealed as much as possible, buried in woollen combinations, dark grey Oxford shirts and hideous stockings. Women seemed particularly offended by the divine handiwork and carried their bosoms around like crosses, unwanted flesh that must be well covered at all times.

But the sight and the smell of my body intrigued me besides its own involuntary reactions to touch. I would have loved to have had the mirror in my own room so that I could reassure myself more often about the works of creation. I well understood that my thoughts, not only in this but in so many matters, differed entirely from Herself's and my father's, Alec's and even Black Fergus's.

Similar discrepancies between preaching and practice worried me in other directions, such as the Jews. The kirk and Sabbath School constantly referred to the Jews as God's Chosen People. We had two little wooden boxes in the house into which I reluctantly put part of my pocket money, one for African lepers and the other for a mission to the Jews. It was also much stressed that Jesus was of Jesse's rod—a confusing term in itself and one which in early years I associated with an aunt of that name living in London. An elaborate plan of the old Temple at Jerusalem surrounded by incomprehensible details of the Twelve Tribes was the largest picture in our house.

All this respect for the Chosen People went only so far. Perhaps respect stopped short because the holy, inspired Word of God was contaminated by the unspeakable word 'circumcision' which appeared so frequently in connection with the Jews. At any rate after the Bible was closed at night or the kirk emptied on a Sunday, our awe of the Jews naturally reverted to derision. Even Herself, so careful of her tongue, had been heard to use the term 'dirty yid'. Despite such conviction we had no actual contact with Jews except in the form of a travelling haberdasher. Everybody liked him and bought birthday presents or combs and hairpins from his bulging suitcases; we were amazed by the variety of goods, and wondered if the open cases would ever be got to close again upon the mountains of aprons and handkerchiefs, bottles of iodine and frilly pink garters. I used to look closely at the Jewish pedlar. To me he was half a kind of holy man because he belonged to the Chosen and half a great debauchee because people's uncomplimentary remarks about his race often included references to blood, such as Black Fergus's 'blood-sucking Jew'.

Muddled ideas about the Chosen People persisted for years and continued into the period when my adolescent body preoccupied me. I certainly enjoyed sucking my own blood from cuts and scratches and I liked to bite the muscles developing so firmly on my long arms. The advent of Hitler hardly resolved my Jewish muddle. At the time of Mr Chamberlain's flight to Munich I had at least got as far as understanding that Jews in the Old Testament were acceptable whereas modern ones were not. Yet when Hitler began to treat the Jews exactly as I had heard everybody for years saying they *should* be treated, Highlanders in quiet western glens became extremely indignant. They were quite unaware of any contradiction in their attitude and the war mood gradually built up.

Meanwhile Mr Chamberlain still hoped to preserve peace and I still stole into Herself's room to view myself from behind and front. I admired the pattern made by the sun in a brown version of a modesty vest on my chest, tanned where an open-necked shirt exposed it to my Maker's fresh air. Narcissus-like I watched the pink extended tongue in the mirror advancing to meet my own on the cold glass. I was not nearly so afraid of being discovered at this pastime by Herself as by my father. His sense of propriety forbade him even to wash in the kitchen.

For an overworked and worried farmer like my father the presence of a restless and moody son like me must have caused constant embarrassment and annoyance. I knew that he hated to hear of my idling in the sun on the hill. Yet he never nagged or bullied. Rather he tried to ignore my gauche youthfulness and to regard me as a man. And on those terms we went on many happy outings together.

Awkwardness forgotten we would take evening strolls together to the head of the strath after ptarmigan and grouse, or, at Herself's bidding, we would go into the garden and gather gooseberries, chatting amiably as if no difference had ever arisen between us. We were like brothers as we laughed and shovelled coal side by side from the bowels of the old coaster on its yearly visit to the township. And we soon became rivals in our shepherding of the hills. I used to wonder what he would say to me at the end of the day when the ear-snippets from my lambs were counted and the fruits of my stewardship made known. Would I be worthy of his trust in me?

It seemed to me that so many ewes had died on their backs during my first full time lambing-season of the lochan hirsel. Too many lambs had ben savaged by ravens and crows or washed away by burns in spate, or had simply perished from the grass sickness. In the four weeks of lambing I had covered endless miles back and forth across the lochan moor, keeping a morning and evening vigil against the hirsel foes—the fox and the hoodie, the snow-storm and south-west gale. There were hidden enemies which I could not fight, like the woolly kidney disease which had nothing to do with the other balls of wool that developed inside the lambs from sucking the ewes' matted breasts.

But when my father and Alec set out with their four dogs to help me gather the flock, the whole hill soon teemed with sturdy lambs. From across the moors the dogs drove the ewes from every corner of the overhanging burn banks, down the corries and round the crags. The big wedders were routed from the high summits, and the unshorn yearling hoggets appeared lost and confused now that their dams were occupied with the new lambs.

Alec and my father could not be seen but I heard their whistling above the cry of curlew. Other victims fell to the peat moor's predators. I sometimes saw a desolate plover seeking her nestlings devoured by a hooded crow. With pitiful crying she would search the moors for days, unable to accept the terrible loss. The forlorn plover affected me more than the plaintive double note of curlew. But all around the monotonous, unison bleating of sheep filled the air and I had little time for birds as the dogs gathered stray ewes into little puckles that soon met others, swelling gradually into a sea of rippling fleeces bright in the June sunshine.

Neither of the dogs I used was properly conditioned to shepherding but they had that inbred sense for driving sheep that sent them into a frenzy of unbounded energy. On each side of me they sped mile upon mile to bring the little bevies into the main galaxy. The dogs' shaggy coats were entangled with twigs, their pads swollen with thorns or cuts from the grey scree. But nothing could stop them as they flashed like thunderbolts through the heather and over the stone dykes. The fastest burn or a toss from the horns of an obstinate ewe did nothing to slow them down.

A last, the various groups met and merged as one in front of the panting dogs. Slowly, like a cumulus cloud, we moved over the cliff escarpment and through the heather braes. Seeing them all together I was deeply impressed by the number of dazzling white fleeces on such well-fed lambs. The others said nothing. Theirs was a silent acknowledgement of another year's miracle. I knew Herself would be up at the attic window, glass at the ready, viewing the magic of spring swarming through the lower braes.

By eight o'clock Black Fergus and his father joined us in the fank, the stone walled enclosure containing the handling pens ranged around the shedder. The shedder was a long, narrow passage where the ewes were divided from their lambs amid agonizing cries and baaing. My job was to catch the ewe lambs around the middle and present them to Alec who snipped their ears and docked their tails. Black Fergus livened up the proceedings as he and his father castrated the tup lambs.

Fortunately the days of knife and teeth for this particular operation had finished the previous year and people had no longer to work covered in blood. We now used a special, pincer-like castrator which severed the testicle cord without it being necessary to open the bag. Only the dogs and the township women resented this bloodless revolution. Previously they had shared the delicacy of lambs' fry. Nobody would dare have appeared at the fank now because Black Fergus brandished the stainless steel pincers in a bawdy fashion at any intruder—unless the gaunt figure of Herself was seen hovering over the fank wall.

My grandmother would not be far away because she was impatient for Alec and my father to empty their pockets of ear snippets. The dogs were impatient also, since they had the lambs' tails thrown to them. But at last the two men seated themselves on the shearing stools. Like a pair of Chinamen scoring mah-jongg they counted the blood-stained pile of snippets from ewe-lambs and new wedders. Nobody spoke until they had cross-checked each other's heap.

Then Herself would be told the total number and she began to translate it into scores, the unit in which her Maker had numbered the days of Man. She traced the figures in the thick dust of the fank with her short cromag. Could there really be such a heavy crop, I wondered, over eighty per cent of ewes that bred? Herself fixed me with her ancient eye. Was I really the heathen who consorted with Irish Catholics to break the Sabbath in Stag's

Pool? But even if I had been roaming the hills 'Eden clad' the Lord seemed to have prospered the work of my hand.

Herself never made rash statements and was obliged to go through again the arithmetic in the dust.

'A sight of lambs,' she said to herself, 'a sight of lambs.'

Then she turned to me. No words were hers to express her surprise and joy at the lambing. From under the sack apron and long brown skirt she drew a paper bag from her underskirt pocket. From the creased bag she offered me a piece of her favourite rhubarb rock. And only somebody who, like me, had been raised amid the sighing winds of Blarosnich would understand that this was high praise indeed for having brought home so rich a harvest.

4

Greek fret

Prince among the poets, at least for Herself, was Duncan the Good Knight. He was also a hero like so many other lairds killed at Flodden. The Good Knight's father, Sir Colin of Rome, had visited the Eternal City three times and won his spurs in Rhodes in battle against the Sultan of the Ottomans. Included in my grandmother's Gaelic repertoire was a mediaeval poem whose loveliness appealed to me especially. It peopled my mind with heroes from an age even more remote than that of our own Highland heroes.

> *Four men stood over a brave soldier's grave*
> *The tomb of proud Alexander—*
> *They spoke without exaggerations*
> *About the king from lovely Greece.*

Herself inflamed my imagination with stories about 'lovely Greece' and its marvellous heroes like Alexander the Great. I cared more about Greece than anywhere else in the world at that time of my life. Iceland was the exception because so many of our birds came from there. But given the opportunity I should have left Blarosnich at once to go and see the islands of Greece. The poem *Ceathrar do bhi air uaigh an fhir* lit a spark in me which my discovery in an old copy of the *Encyclopaedia Britannica* fanned to a flame.

I was sitting by the fire one night. Herself's knitting needles made the only sound. To pass the time I was pressing wild flowers between the *Encyclopaedia's* pages. Suddenly my heart began to pound and I thought Herself would hear it above the clack of her knitting needles. I glanced at her to see if the commotion inside me had broken her fireside trance. It had not. With trembling fingers I laid aside my flowers and turned the pages. Across the top in large letters stood the word GREECE.

I could hardly believe what the book showed. Instead of the heavily armoured and absurdly helmeted warriors I had imagined from Herself's Gaelic poem, I saw figures moving through a landscape of endless sunshine and fragrant gardens. They were noble men and graceful women—exactly the sort of men and women I day-dreamed about.

At first I was almost shocked to find my own dreams in the *Encyclopaedia*, and I was amazed that what I thought wonderful had also been thought so by others. I could hardly manage the Greek heroes' curious names. But how like Black Fergus coming out of Stag's Pool was Doryphoros. My friend, when he came shining with water from the pool, flexed his muscles which now stood in mounds like a Greek statue's on his fast-developing body. His heavy body resembled the solid manly figures of the Greeks. He used an ash rod while doing his Charles Atlas exercises like Doryphoros after Polyclitus. Black Fergus had the same litheness and strength, the same rhythm of muscle, perfection of symmetry. Fergus, intent though he was on becoming like Charles Atlas, would have thought me daft for avidly devouring pictures of statues.

Certainly the real Alexander in the *Encyclopaedia* was far more of a handsome hero than the old and hoary 'proud Alexander' I had imagined from Herself's poem. When I came to Europa on her bull, again it was different from anything I could imagine happening with our cattle. Poor myopic Mirren would rather have died than ride our Shorthorn down to the township. In spite of all my dreaming none of the women I knew could possibly possess the ripe, graceful body of the Aphrodite of Cyrene. Her breasts were full and firm yet the right size for the body, quite unlike the tired and drooping bosoms of our women who seemed to accept their shape as a divine curse to be covered up with shifts and ridiculous pieces of chiffon.

The *Encyclopaedia's* pictures burned into me like a brand. I had discovered something in that article about Greece which was going to influence the emotion of my newly-gained adolescence. If those strong, good-looking men and those richly curved, serene women had really existed in 'lovely Greece' and were good enough to be put in the *Encyclopaedia's* pages, then there could not be very much for me to feel guilty about. It must be my family's attitude to these things which was wrong, not my own.

By her attitude to the Jews, I perceived Herself's belief that what went on in olden days was one thing but what went on today was another. Old Testament Jews could do no wrong, modern ones could do no right. And although I knew that Herself disapproved of my antics spotted through her eye-glass, she would no doubt have admired the *Encyclopaedia's* picture of Praxiteles's Hermes. The child in Hermes's arms seemed the most natural and beautiful representation of life I had ever seen. The baby belonged to the gracious lines and firm body of the man. So how, I asked myself, could this be 'ungodly'?

Immensely encouraged by my fireside discovery of Greece, I wanted more. To my further excitement I found that among the books we had got from the last sporting tenant's sale was a whole set dealing with Classical things. These books had been fortunate in escaping the fate of many. Volumes thrown into auction lots at sales around Blarosnich were often carted away by their new owners to fill the ignominious role of providing spills for pipes and lamps. Before I realized what books meant I had torn strips from old volumes for Alec's pipe. Herself would have been outraged if a match had been wasted on such a thing. Although mildewed from their exile in our barn, the Classical books had miraculously escaped the flames to live again for me. I began to read, not understanding everything, but feeding the fire within myself nevertheless.

I learnt about the gods. I absorbed the myths. I stared at the photographs of mountains and streams where the beautiful gods lived, and longed to see the whiteness of the columned temples built for them so long ago. Why had not our nineteenth-century lairds put such wonderful buildings on the top of Craigclamhan as Pericles put on the Acropolis at Athens? Why did we have to have endless miles of dull stone dykes instead of a marvellous Parthenon?

In my Bible I had a brown postcard of Inverary, the only written communication I ever had from my mother. It showed the castle in whose grounds my grandfather had been gamekeeper. But in the light of my recent discovery, the building looked like a squat hen-house compared with the marble temples of Greece. I dimly understood that there had been a spirit about those athletes and the verses written in their honour and the buildings and sculpture set among olive groves to celebrate their victories. I loved Greece. Its spirit was mine. I could have worshipped Apollo in his high mountain place at Delphi. It would have been so much easier than trying to worship our old, white-bearded, forbidding God in the dull, tiny kirk down the road, which stank of varnish and wet raincoats.

Bible language had been used at Blarosnich all my life. No other book could be read on Sundays, the Sabbath of the Lord when the blinds remained drawn all day. This custom was a precaution against the non-religious members of the township, and was quite pointless since none of them were likely to come up to Blarosnich on a Sunday and intrude upon its piety except in the rare case of a cow being brought to our bull. But in such an event the fee payment would have to be put off until the Monday.

In spite of familiarity with the Scriptures they remained obscure to me. The paraphrases we droned Sunday after Sunday had none of the beauty I found in the Greek verses I devoured. The Bible had always seemed dry and remote. What did they expect me to make of 'Thy righteousness is like the great mountains?' But nobody needed to show me the beauty in Aeschylus's description of a high mountain—'mighty summit, neighbour to the stars'.

Although the Big House constituted the manor of Blarosnich, its dour Victorian turrets did not convey the subtleties of the Field of Sighing. Yet surely Andronicus Cyrrhestes the astronomer had known the eight winds of Blarosnich before he built the delicately beautiful Tower of the Winds at Athens.

Even the stones of Greece had the spirit of the winds about them. The trees and flowers were part of their existence. The oaks sprang to life at the birth of the nymphs and the last twig fell as their souls left the light of the sun. The shepherd boys had an understanding with their flocks. The sheep were not like ours, representative of just so many heads at the Dingwall market or the size of the woolclip cheque.

From the old books and from some instinct newly-sensed within myself I saw that human nature was part of all nature. A sweet harmony flowed between those splendid Greek bodies and the trees and the birds, the smell of trampled hyacinths, the grasshopper 'drunk with dew', the feel of golden pomegranates.

I returned to my own flock on the lochan shore filled with admiration for the Arcadian gods who were the essence of *Fhinnghréicc*. They were lovable and by being partly human understood the human. They were another creature altogether from our night-shirted or funeral-shrouded old man riding in the clouds whose forefinger was perpetually raised against everything beautiful.

Louder music than the chiffchaff's familiar song haunted the Earl's Park for me. Pan and his pipes set the roe dancing and drew the most gorgeous of red admirals to his rocky haunt. The silent birch park was, above all;

the forest home of revelling Dionysus,
Without sun, without wind, without storm,
Where the god roams
With the nymphs that nursed him.

Pan became my imaginary companion as Black Fergus was my real one, only slightly distinguishable from Pan where hairiness of legs was concerned.

But Fergus and I were both grown up now. Gone were the carefree Saturdays when we roamed the hills bolting rabbits out of their warrens with our ferrets. We had more urgent things to do than to suck the sweet juice out of crowberries to quench an idle summer thirst, or snuggle close together for warmth round a winter fire of heather shaws until the black billycan began singing. Now we were boys no longer but working shepherds. We crossed the same sheep tracks amongst the heather only with the gamekeeper's cairns to bolt foxes out of their dens. We carried guns as Alec and my father did and stood by the holes waiting for the vermin to appear.

If neither of the fox parents lurked in the den we spread out through the rocks and surrounding braes to lie in wait, certain that it would return before morning. I came to know much of our hills and waters intimately from lying with loaded gun watching for foxes. As these adventures often lasted several hours my eyes would wander from the paw-beaten track to where the sunset had calmed the turbulent kyle into a millpond of shining ormolu-varnish. The red flushing of a spring sun which seemed reluctant to leave the afternoon sky bathed everything in sumptuous colours, from the violet shores to the rose snows still lingering on the peaks. Then the bird babble down on the wrinkled saltings would suddenly become a chaos of screaming and yelping as a gunshot brought our watch to a violent close. We stuffed the dead fox with poison and left it as a lethal gift for hooded crow and raven.

Black Fergus's nose possessed uncanny skill in picking up foxes' scent in the forest, a musky, bitter smell like the faint, unpleasant tang of wood-anemones. He would follow the vixen's spoors across the snow as if they were signposted. Yet, besides having such keenly developed natural senses, Black Fergus loved mechanical things. When he had reached what seemed to me the advanced age of sixteen, he fell in love with my father's tractor, which was the first in the district. I had no interest in machinery at all. It did not exist in the Greek landscape of my mind. The winged feet of Hermes did not rely on clutches and gears.

Fergus's almost nightly appearances to give a hand with the tractor work helped my father to forget his disappointment over my own indifference. Afterwards, Black Fergus went home to Sallachie and read himself to sleep with trade magazines and text-books on internal combustion engines. He wrote off for a corres-pondence course.

Black Fergus's new, and to me disruptive, interests did not completely interfere with our old way of life. When he could tear himself away from the tractor we still went up to the Forestry camp to join the Paddies. I used to go on the pretext of digging out the foxes' breeding dens in the stronghold of the dense woods. And sometimes we did justify this aim. But usually Fergus and I just loitered about the woodmen's huts listening to the accordion whose only music, like the men's songs, came from Ireland.

Although the woodmen lived rough, the amber light of the forest seemed to have given them strong faces and a special glow of happiness. They seldom cared to cycle down past the township and its closed doors, but stayed instead around their huts writing letters or fishing or completing their long ritual of washing themselves and their clothes.

Black Fergus and I liked the Paddies because of their stories, true or not. Like a caravan settling round a story-teller in the desert, we sat for hours listening to the woodmen's tales of the terrible Black and Tans or of their cousins in the Boston police or of their past Herculean labours in the Bog of Allan. A star among the Paddies was Festie who played on a hand-saw with a violin bow and who could shoot cherry stones out of his mouth further than any of us. And there was quiet little Ned who had two fingers missing and a sad story of watching his eldest brother being shot by the Black and Tans.

Kevin told the best stories. He was a tinker lad and much too independent to work for anyone, least of all a government department. Kevin was his own master, walking a fine pony stallion to service through a score of townships. When he came to our district, Kevin shared a shakedown with his fellow Irishmen and never failed to weave a web of magic round us with his exploits.

We drank thick black tea as our friends regaled us with adventures that happened in Glasgow where they were roadmenders or when they were working on London building sites. We sat tense, the tea bitter on our tongues as Kevin told us of his stallion's misdemeanours or of ghosts which haunted every barony in Ireland. I wanted to live up there in the huts with the woodmen.

But every evening came to an end. I had visions of Herself standing like another ghost at the top of the staircase in her long nightdress, awaiting my late arrival with great plaits of hair round her shoulders and the wrath of her Maker inscribed on her candle-lit face. Herself firmly believed that night had been created for sleeping. Except for the earliest winter evenings and the Saturday night ceilidh she went to bed 'with the lamb and rose with the laverock.'

66

Shortly after my first lambing season, and no doubt partly owing to its success, I was allowed to fulfil a dream of mine. This sent me into a delirium of excitement which excluded everything else. My father and Herself had agreed, surprisingly without demur, that I could visit my mother's sister Jessie in London. My aunt wrote saying she would like to see me again, especially as eight years had passed since we had last met during her stay at Blarosnich when my mother was alive. I only had the vaguest recollections of Aunt Jessie. Herself did not care overmuch for the city woman whom she called the Darling Duchess. But because Aunt Jessie was my closest relative on my mother's side still alive, Herself, fair as always, said it was only reasonable that I should go south of the border as soon as the clipping was over.

The prospect robbed me of sleep. I confessed to nobody at home, however, the real cause of my excitement. I was going to see for myself something of the Paddies' big world. I would be able to visit Kevin's brother Joe in a much-talked-of place called Camden Town. And further, I would actually be able to see in reality many of the Greek statues familiar to me from the *Encyclopaedia Britannica* and the previous sporting tenant's books.

When there was good heart in the herbage floor and a spell of hot weather, the old fleece on the sheep started to rise on a new growth. It was essential to have this soft under-rise before we could gather the hirsels and start clipping. We clipped in the big root-house where the last mountain of mangels had long since been fed to the cattle. Three long stools stood to one side of the shed. Alec, Duncan and my father sat on them against the wall, while the sheep struggled helpessly on their backs between the three men's knees. To prevent any kicking, especially from the heavy tups, the legs were tied.

Black Fergus and his father also came to the clipping. But they spurned the use of stools and clipped the sheep on the ground, opposite the others. In the course of time, I preferred to clip in this way, and although my father made no comment, he disapproved of the method. On another matter he was openly cross, and that was when I went on all fours in the fields, going along the furrows thinning roots with my hands as the Paddies did when they came to earn a few extra shillings with us after work. My father used a hoe and considered that I should also.

Two years lay ahead of me yet, before I should be considered good enough to take my place in the shed with the clippers. Shearing required skill. I gained experience by clipping the strays which had missed the general gathering. My job, nonetheless important and often much more tiring, was 'crogging', in which I had to manhandle the ewes and wedders from an enclosure to the shed. I usually walked them between my legs.

The sight of blood seldom affected me. I had grown up in a way of life where the butchering of lambs, the cutting up of stags and the castration of rams were part of a day's work. But I felt queasy if a ewe's horn came off in my hand whilst I was crogging. The hole in the skull gaped in a grisly way, although I thought nothing of dabbing the same beast with tar if the pointed shears accidently cut it.

Clipping days, strangely enough, were festive in spirit, and memorable for a well-spread table. And with my crogging I could cause a lot of merriment. All the men took great pride in their work. They disliked using the archangel tar tin too often on nicks from their tools. Beginning at the back of the sheep's head, the hand-clippers would work their way round and bare the chest and right foreleg and so down to the tail. If the wool had a really good rise to it, the men might work their way through as many as ten ewes or more in an hour. Keeping five pairs of shears supplied with sheep meant that I crogged one beast almost every minute as well as passing the tin of tar to and fro.

The speed of the operation largely depended on whether Herself had come out to roll up the fleeces as they fell, the creamy insides so revealed looking like the softest tissue ever made or grown. Many of the fleeces were fouled or wet and could not be folded. They had to be hung in the barn where they often stayed for months waiting to be packed.

I failed to understand the gamekeeper's skill with the shears. As long as I could remember Duncan had come to Blarosnich on Saturday nights to be shaved because his own hand was unsteady. Yet on the shearing stool he was the undisputed master. He took full-length sweeps with the clippers and rarely asked for the tar tin. His old, trembling hands seemed to know the anatomy of every ewe and ram. I would crog him a big three-year-old wedder with a double coat because it lived in the high summits and had missed the previous year's gathering. Wedder sheep like these had fighting spirit and I made sure Duncan had them to deal with just to please Black Fergus who was often on bad terms with the gamekeeper through too much poaching. But not even the huge horns of a troublesome ram or the lack of rise on a delicate gimmer could disturb the gamekeeper's assured and expert manner of rolling back the unbroken fleeces.

We stored the rolled fleeces in the loft above the stable. When the clipping ended we brought out the long 100 lb wool-bags. They hung down through the trapdoor to be filled by Black Fergus and me. Fifty or more fleeces went into each bag if they were well packed. We took it by turns to get down inside the bag and trample the wool which the other passed down. This was a dirty, oily job but because Fergus was involved it never failed to be hilarious.

Fergus would look up at me from the long, dark sack and make it swing like a ship from side to side, singing a bawdy song he had picked up from the Paddies at the Forestry Commission. And then there would be Mirren's screams of delight and frustration when she carried out a *strubag* of tea and piping hot scones from the kitchen. Hearing Black Fergus's strong language she would pierce the wool-bag with one of the enormous sacking needles used for sewing up the filled bags. Mirren's formal objection to Fergus's bad language was that Herself would hear it.

'The Mistress will skin you alive,' she cried to the entombed Black Fergus.

But Mirren's true concern lay in prodding the sack with a needle to make the sweating Fergus emerge with an unsuppressed desire to catch hold of her. His unshaven face appeared, full of mischief.

'Do you want a rub of the old relic?' he asked referring to his week-old growth of beard.

Before Mirren could think of further back-chat, Black Fergus would swing himself out of the wool-bag with surprising alacrity, and have her rolling on the mountain of wool until not a hairpin remained in the pilgrim bun at the back of her head. If Alec heard the commotion he would run to the barn and give Fergus encouragement. Alec loved to find Mirren in such compromising situations and urged Black Fergus on to further horse-play. I think the shepherd would have given anything to break his reserve and be as bold as Fergus. But he could not, and though we knew Alec and Mirren were in love seriously, they could never bring themselves to do what Black Fergus did.

Fergus understood this and his horse-play was intended to tease the pair, even perhaps to tease them into an open declaration. We all read the signs of love between them, but they did not satisfy our own idea of a love-match. In early spring Alec always came over on a special trip from Pitlobar to set the croft potatoes for Mirren's widowed mother. The shepherd also cleaned their chimney once a year and did other such like jobs for the two women. Reports had it that Alec had been known to leave our bothie and slip down to the township late at night to talk with Mirren through her letter-box. Black Fergus made no secret of the fact that he thought all this a feeble way to carry out a courtship. He lost no opportunity of catching hold of Mirren if Alec was nearby and of being rough with her in a way that would never have entered his head otherwise.

Of all the clippings I had seen in my life and of all the fun there had been, no day had meant so much to me as that particular morning when the wool-bags were ferried out to the steamer, for that morning I started on my journey south to London.

The previous night I hardly slept and was up and out an hour before my usual time. But one thing occurred which I had failed to reckon with. Before even I reached the top of the steamer's gangway my enthusiasm for the fortnight's holiday fizzled like a wet log. Looking back at the group of friends and relations on the stone jetty a pang of loneliness clutched me. I had never even been as far as the Dingwall market alone before. I clung to the pile of woolsacks on deck as the last remaining piece of Blarosnich accompanying me.

Misery must have shown in my face, for a pleasant American voice enquired, 'Are you sea-sick?'

I looked at the brightly dressed woman and her husband. They had been touring the islands.

'Sea-sick?' I replied. 'Me sea-sick? No, of course not.' I tried to make it sound as if I had been travelling on that steamer with woolsacks every day of my life.

'I've never been sea-sick,' I said quite truthfully. To prove it, I jumped off the woolsacks and strutted down the deck. The Americans walked beside me and complimented me on my kilt and asked what family it represented. Before docking we had become sufficiently friendly for the woman to ask if I wore anything underneath. Curiously, in spite of keeping Black Fergus and the Paddies company in their bawdy talk and singing, I was shocked. It seemed out of place for this woman to pry into my personal habits.

Nevertheless, I concluded that they both meant to be kind and I was pleased that they took notice of me. I was conscious of cutting a fine figure in my Highland clothes. Not another person had a pair of shoes as splendid as my new ones. My father had made them, and fitted them with fringed overlapping tongues. And I wore the white shirt I had bought from the Jewish pedlar specially for my holiday.

By the time I reached Edinburgh I felt as though we had crossed the whole of Europe. I had met many people during the long day and Colin was the only one who impressed me.

Colin was a Highland soldier returning to his regiment after home leave on the Isle of Mull. I arrived early for the train south from Edinburgh and sat in a corner already tired and dreading the night's journey to London. I was half wishing I had never left Blarosnich, where, like as not, Black Fergus would be out with the new ferryman fishing. Then the compartment door had been slid open with a bang.

'Move over, mate,' Colin said, though nobody was there but me.

He slung his kitbag onto the rack, and aimed his cap at the opposite corner.

'Booked,' he winked at me, 'that seat's booked if any bastard wants it.'

'Who for?' I asked in innocence.

'Nobody,' Colin said with another, broader wink, 'at least, not yet.'

Colin was so large and so noisy and so friendly and obviously so experienced and familiar with the world where the train was taking us, that I warmed to him at once.

'Are you going all the way to London?' I asked wanting to be reassured.

He looked at me with mock contempt. 'I would hardly be on this bloddy train if I wasn't, now would I?'

He began to pull the blinds down.

'London,' he said, 'you can stuff it.'

But I knew he was only pretending. I imagined him making the best of all the wickedness there was to be had in London.

Colin surveyed his handiwork with the blinds which were now all pulled down and fastened. He threw himself onto the seat and stretched his legs out. 'It's the only way to keep the bastards out,' he said, looking again at the drawn blinds.

I could not ignore the strong smell of strong drink that surrounded Colin. Herself would have had something to say about that. She would not have approved either of the way he opened bottles of beer with his teeth, spitting the metal caps onto the floor. Who, I wondered, did he want to keep out of our compartment? Was he on the run?

I did not care, as long as I did not spend the night journey alone; Colin could be guilty of any crime at all, and I still would not have minded.

My new soldier friend switched the lights off. When I asked him why he did so he said that we would each have a whole side of the compartment to sleep on. People on night trains never came into darkened compartments when the blinds were drawn, he assured me in his easy worldly-wise manner.

Colin took a long time in deciding to unbuckle his white webbing belt as a preliminary to settling down for the hours ahead. I had to hear, not unwillingly, about his exploits round the world.

For fear that I should disbelieve some of the more incredible of these he jumped up at intervals and put on the lights again to show me appropriate tattoos collected, as far as I could gather, from almost every exotic port between Hong Kong and British Guiana. These stories, backed up by lurid details, told me that Colin loved soldiering. The only thing wrong with it, he said, was the letters. Not enough letters from home. 'Write to me,' he said pleadingly. 'Every day if you have the time,' he added, to emphasize the importance of mail from home. I promised I would write and printed my address in his little notebook so that he could answer. With stubby fingers he wrote his long army number and his name on the inside of a cigarette packet and handed it to me.

'You will, won't you?' he insisted before we settled down full length on the seats.

I lay with my eyes open. It seemed as if another boy had left Blarosnich so long ago. I felt as though my whole life had been spent travelling. In the gloom of the compartment, London and Aunt Jessie seemed as unreal as Blarosnich and Herself. I was desperately tired but could not sleep. Light darted in swift arrows through slits in the sides of the blinds as we thundered past other trains or cannonaded through stations. Colin could not sleep either. Every time we slowed down or stopped he got up to see where we were and how far we had come from Edinburgh.

The bottles of beer he had drunk rolled about the carriage floor and the beer began to take effect on him. At last he had to unbarricade the door and go to the lavatory. He was so long away that I became concerned and thought he must be ill, or, worse, had disobeyed the notices in the train and had leaned out of the window to meet with a dreadful accident. But I heard him singing after a time, and when he did come back he was not alone.

'This is Ruby,' he announced.

Ruby giggled and kissed him. She was at least twice Colin's age. Her arms were full of bracelets, like the African giraffe-necked women I had seen in pictures from the leper mission magazine we received in return for filling the L-shaped collecting box with coins. Ruby was a good size and had certainly never figured in a missionary magazine. She sat on Colin's knee and put one of the braceleted arms round his neck for support. I became very hot and bothered when she laid her other, fat hand on my knee and, leaning across, gave me a sickly-sweet kiss. They both laughed as I dashed out to the lavatory.

I bolted the lavatory door and sat there, lurching from side to side with the train's sway. Realization came that I had not obeyed Herself's last injunction to me. It was not surprising that an old trollop had tried to beseige me. To the clacking roar of the wheels on the rails I recited the familiar lines to my Maker, beseeching Him to prevent big Ruby from coming into the lavatory after me. She roused some childhood fear in me.

Our family had never paid much attention to stories of ghosts or the influence of the Evil Eye, horrors which haunted our shepherd and many township people, especially Mirren and her mother. My worst dread in childhood had been of the aged postmistress and her sisters sitting on Sunday afternoons like three witches greedy for lovers. But my fear of them had not been supernatural. Even as a boy of seven I had interpreted Mirren's warnings about the trio as a sexual affair. None of the old ladies, however, had rushed out after me as I had been afraid they would. But now on the London-bound train, I felt as if Ruby had been sent to visit their revenge on me. I did not dare to budge from the safety of the lavatory seat.

When at last an uncertain grey light showed that dawn had come on the other side of the lavatory's frosted glass window, I unbolted the door. The corridor was empty except for suitcases. I wondered if Ruby and Colin had ransacked my suitcase during the night, possibly interfering with the presents I was taking to my aunt and cousins.

The compartment blinds were still drawn, although the light was getting strong. And the door was wedged. I knocked on the glass and said it was me.

'Keep an eye on the door a while longer,' came Colin's muffled voice, 'then you can have Ruby all to yourself.'

I was humiliated to think that Colin believed I had been keeping watch on the door in case the guard came and demanded the un-wedging of the door. And I was terrified too that the soldier expected me to follow his example with Ruby. Feeling forlorn and unwanted I went back and sat on the lavatory seat again. With something like an outraged sense of propriety I almost wished the guard *would* come and catch them in the act. I was tempted to give a loud official-sounding rap on their door myself. Only the possibility of Ruby's braceleted arms coming out to devour me prevented my plan.

The train had almost reached St Pancras before I returned for my luggage. The door was open and the blinds were up. Ruby had gone. Colin was his bright and breezy self again, looking none the worse for his night of debauch. While breakfasting on the remaining bottles of beer he boasted about how many times he had made love to Ruby. Then he took my hand and held it in his own hot, hard, pad-like hands and made me promise over and over again that I would write to him.

Without knowing really why, I had resented Ruby and the way that Colin had changed from me to her without a moment's thought. But I could not resist the charm of his carefree ways, or remain cold before his warmth. It was more than I dared to ask if Ruby was also going to send him letters. I was dying to ask if her name would be added to the roll of honour tattooed up the proud muscles of his arms.

5

Crise de nerfs

St Pancras railway station, I thought, must surely be the biggest building in London if not in the world. I did not recognize Aunt Jessie among the knot of waiting people. But she saw me and came sailing over and flung her arms round me, in an extravagant gesture unusual to me.

Released with the same abruptness as I had been embraced, I looked at her two sons, Ian and Peter, whom she instructed to carry my luggage. They looked quite ordinary. Aunt Jessie called the boys 'darling' every time she spoke to them. 'Darling' was lavished without sparing on all her family, and also on her two budgerigars, who used the word themselves.

I had to admit that Aunt Jessie was dashing. She did the talking for all of us as she drove their car deftly in and out of the morning traffic, taking a hand off the steering wheel to light one cigarette from another. I could understand why Herself did not like the extravagance of the aunt she slightingly called the Darling Duchess.

Possibly because of my uncomfortable and sleepless night, I was not taking in much as we drove towards Kensington. Everything in London seemed to be overwhelming, not least Aunt Jessie herself. She talked all the way up in the lift to her large flat. Plainly, Aunt Jessie lived grandly. I felt nervous and shy of their sumptuous home.

My aunt gave me the impression of being too large for everything—too large for the chairs she sat on, too large for the clothes she wore, though I could tell they had cost a lot of money, and too large even for the big sitting-room of the flat. It seemed as if it was necessary for her to overflow all the time, in talk, in gesture, and in kindness.

I was to share Peter's room with him during my stay. My suitcase was on the bed.

Aunt Jessie came to the door.

'Darling, don't you think you ought to have a rest and change?'

I already had my best clothes on for the holiday. I was upset that Aunt Jessie should think me in need of a change. And change into what? I looked at my new shirt. It was already much dirtier than if I had worn it a dozen Sundays to kirk. Not surprising, I supposed, for I had never seen anything so grimy before as St Pancras station. Crogging the sheep at Blarosnich in the dust and droppings had not made me half so dirty.

Four days of my holiday went by like a whirlwind. A non-stop round of sight-seeing left me dazed, though Peter, my constant companion, showed no signs of amazement. He jumped on buses, apparently without looking at their numbers or destinations, he dashed down underground escalators and made his way through the warren of tubes, all without the least hesitation. I would have liked more time to absorb it all. But Peter would not have this.

Peter differed completely from the serious, eighteen-year-old Ian. Unlike Peter, he stayed at home all day, head bent over chemistry books. While reading he twisted a strand of hair round and round his finger. Whenever Aunt Jessie saw this she said automatically, 'Darling, please, *please* don't. You'll be as bald as Daddy.'

Daddy was a dentist and his head was a pink dome. To compensate for this, a grotesque walrus moustache concealed Daddy's mouth. He seldom came home for long, and when he did he spent his time talking in an incongruous falsetto voice to the two budgerigars and drinking whisky from a tumbler.

Only a year separated Peter and me in age, though I was taller than he. My cousin asked if he could be photographed in my kilt, but once he got it on, he wanted to keep it on and go around showing it to all his friends. Since I liked Peter best of all the family I did not object and agreed to wear his grey school suit instead. But Aunt Jessie told us not to be ridiculous.

This was not unusual. She seldom approved of anything Peter wanted. He was not docile like Ian, and his school reports did not compare with his studious brother's. It took me some time to discover that Peter was the bane of his mother's life, while Ian was her idol. The situation perplexed me. I could not understand why Aunt Jessie went to such trouble to make herself gay and charming and give herself such a glossy appearance to outsiders, when in fact her life was far from happy. I had never seen such tangled bitterness before. If Herself was angry with me she showed it at once, but before going to bed that same night all would be forgiven and then forgotten. Although Black Fergus irritated her at times beyond endurance, she did not hold it against him, as Aunt Jessie did against Peter, who, after all, was her own son.

'You'll end up like Daddy, darling,' she threw at him a dozen times a day.

I learnt that 'Daddy' and 'darling' meant nothing in terms of affection. They were only phrases with no more meaning than the budgerigars put into them. Peter appeared to ignore his mother. But he might well end like his father because he had already developed a taste for the whisky bottle.

When other people in the huge, brick-box block of flats emerged in the evenings to exercise their dogs in the gardens around Kensington Palace, Aunt Jessie took Ian out for a similar walk. Because she insisted, I went with them on the first evening.

'Nonsense, darling,' she cried when I suggested that perhaps they preferred to be alone.

But I sensed they did not really want me. And when I discovered that she meant nothing she said, and that the more she protested the truth of anything the less it reflected her real feelings, I made an excuse or pored over the chessboard which Peter used as his reason for not going. It annoyed me to see his mother making a pretence at being fair to both sons alike, when, in fact, she was so heavily prejudiced against Peter. Aunt Jessie did not press me any more and was happy to go off into the park, arm-linked to her favourite darling. They often had long, half-whispered conversations, though I could not guess about what.

The hour without them was an hour released of the curiously tense atmosphere Aunt Jessie generated. Peter's father came home while the other two were out. This happened so regularly every day that I wondered if he contrived it deliberately in order to miss his wife. He whistled to the budgerigars as he hung his hat in the hall. This sound made the birds hysterical. When he opened the cage door they flew into the room screeching and wheeling round several times with a frantic whirring of wings, eventually settling on him, digging their tiny claws into his bald pate or combing the walrus moustache with their bills. While this was going on, Daddy talked to them in a secret language and his special baby-talk falsetto. I had never before seen the sad spectacle of a man who had given up hope in life.

As soon as the door closed behind Aunt Jessie and Ian and we heard the slow grinding lift descend, Peter and I jumped up from the chessboard and let out loud yells and leaped about shouting to show our defiance of the conventual silence which lay over the flat for hours on end because Ian was studying. Then Peter's Japanese-looking eyes narrowed further still with laughter. For an hour, or at least until his father came in, the flat and everything in it was ours.

Many things were purposely locked against Peter. But he had equipped himself with keys and could pick the most complicated lock. The dining-room sideboard received his attention first. His father's whisky was kept there and I was alarmed by the amount Peter drank. I thought his father must surely notice how the level of whisky dropped. But Peter laughed at me. Daddy always went to the club before coming home and when he did get back he was certainly in no state to notice a little thing like that.

We sat in Peter's room to drink the whisky. On the first occasion I took a single swig and at once felt sick. Thereafter I merely watched while Peter indulged his precociously acquired taste. Observing my still-full glass Peter suggested that perhaps I would prefer his mother's gin. While he was gone to pick the lock which guarded Aunt Jessie's bottles, I emptied my whisky into the cactus pots on the window-sill. The drink, when he brought it, was mercifully drowned in lemon squash because the aunt would detect anything more than the smallest depredation of her gin.

Our secret drinking went undetected for four nights. I looked forward to the moment when the lift went down and there was an hour to be filled with Peter's pranks. I was rather sorry not being able to take the whisky, but nevertheless I would still have a lot to boast about in front of Kevin and his Irish woodmen friends when I got back home again. The cocktails could be exaggerated to sound like wild night-long carousals, and in any case I already intended to magnify the incident on the train. For the Paddies' benefit I would give a glowing picture of Ruby's charms.

I had no doubts about how the Irish woodmen and Black Fergus, even at my age, would have tackled both the whisky and the Ruby problem. To them neither would have been a problem. For some time now I had realized there were sides to my nature which I could share with nobody. I had erected barriers to my inner self beyond which none of my relatives or friends could pass. And so the Paddies must never know that I had let the opportunity on the train escape me. Black Fergus must never see the photographs of Greek statues, nor discover my passion for birdsong. Herself must remain in ignorance of the invasions I made into her room to use the long mirror in a way that everybody else would have thought sinful. Even the worldly-wise Sallachie folk would have been shocked at my fascination with nudity. Black Fergus, despite his own love of plunging naked into Stag's Pool, would simply have regarded my mirror-worship as madness. Likewise, my father must never know I felt sick when ewes' horns broke off in my hands during crogging, and that I lived in fear of the animals, not only the dogs but rabbits also, getting in front of his mowing machine's merciless teeth. And I certainly lacked the courage to tell Peter that the whisky made me feel as sick as Ruby's cloyingly sweet kiss on the train.

On the fifth morning of my London holiday, while I was in the bathroom, the storm broke. Angry exchanges came from the living-room. Aunt Jessie's voice, strident and hysterical, was the loudest. Then I heard my aunt run to her bedroom, sobbing. I reached Peter's room in time to save him a beating from Ian. When the elder brother left us to console his mother I heard the cause of the eruption. The dry old cactus plants, like myself, had not been able to absorb the whisky and soda, and it had leaked into the saucers the pots stood in. Aunt Jessie saw and smelt the whisky when she came to do the weekly watering.

The row with his mother and brother meant nothing to Peter.

It was only one more in a series of rows. They had caught him before at his father's whisky and would doubtless do so again. So far as he was concerned they could 'take a running jump at themselves'. But what upset Peter was my own deception. He could not believe at first that I had thrown the precious stuff away.

Nevertheless, he bore me no grudge and gave no sign of being interested in my reasons for getting rid of the whisky. We slipped into the hallway. His mother's voice, still neurotic, was heard declaiming to Ian.

'He's a delinquent! I know it. He's a delinquent!'

'Bitch,' Peter remarked laconically as we sidled towards the front door.

But Aunt Jessie heard our movements and burst upon us with renewed fury. Peter's mouth twisted in a contemptuous sneer. I began to tremble with embarrassment. Yes, I confessed, it was I who tipped whisky into the cactus. I didn't like it, I added. But this only incensed Aunt Jessie, for it made Peter's liking for whisky seem much worse, and his forcing of it onto me as a positive crime.

I was amazed at the state Aunt Jessie worked herself into. While she ranted and raved, it occurred to me that she must often give vent to this quite unbalanced passion. Peter's poor father no doubt got it frequently, and if so, that would explain his reluctance to be in the flat. Ian, it seemed, cleverly avoided being a target by always giving in to his mother's exorbitant demands. He probably found life easier by acquiescence. In this, he was already more like his father than Peter would ever be, in spite of whisky drinking. But Peter came up fighting. He gave as good as he got. I felt sure the only reason she did not strike Peter was because she knew perfectly well that he would hit her back.

The aunt eventually stopped and went to her room. Peter made a vulgar sign behind her back and winked at me. Suddenly I was exhausted. Not even after the sleepless night on the train had I felt so utterly weak. I still trembled inside.

Peter was forbidden to go out. We had planned to visit the British Museum that day.

'Very well,' Aunt Jessie said when I reminded her, 'I shall take you myself.' She spoke as if she owned both me and the museum.

By lunch time, Aunt Jessie was back to normal, except that she called nobody darling. Peter's punishment consisted of having to stay in and do school work with Ian in the tense atmosphere of the living-room.

The trembling inside me subsided. But I was astounded at what had happened. I had not known that people could behave like that. What was the point of living a luxurious life, when behind it all lay the constant threat of violent quarrels?

I had seen plenty of people angry in my time. Nothing was more like the wrath of her Maker than Herself's wrath. But somehow it was different. When Herself was angry it was because of some carelessness of mine or because I had got into mischief with Black Fergus. But Aunt Jessie seemed to be full of hate. I was too young and inexperienced in worldly ways then to imagine why, though I sensed that some other cause, entirely unconnected with whisky, lay behind my aunt's outburst against Peter and me.

She drove me from Kensington to Bloomsbury. Though possibly partly ashamed that she had given herself away and made a spectacle in front of a comparative stranger, Aunt Jessie continued her complaints against Peter. Without taking her eyes from the weaving traffic she talked continuously. I hoped that she would run into a bus, anything to interrupt the flow against Peter. I stopped my ears against strings of adjectives . . . lazy . . . selfish . . . unappreciative . . . wilful . . . headstrong . . . criminal.

We came to the forecourt of the British Museum. But somehow, although this was to have been the secret climax of my visit to London and indeed the visit's secret *raison d'être*, I knew the museum tour was going to be a failure. My aunt, especially in her present mood, was hardly the companion and guide I had envisaged for my first sight of the marvellous sculptures of carefree Greek youth. Nevertheless, she tried to put the awful morning out of mind and did her best to make our museum visit a success. She respected my interest in Classical things.

'If only *he* wanted to look at such things,' Aunt Jessie commented with reference to Peter, 'instead of those infernal comics.'

I did not answer. What would she have said about other books

82

which Peter kept hidden, and whose contents and pictures made comics by comparison seem wholly innocent? Peter and I shared his small but effective library of erotica before we went to sleep each night. Suppose, I thought with new fears, that the books were to be discovered as well as the whisky. It was a possibility that would not bear thinking about.

My aunt, on the other hand, was not at all bashful in making a thorough investigation of all the nude figures we gazed at in the museum galleries. She seemed annoyed that schoolgirls should stand smirking and sniggering in front of Hermes. Like many other people who drifted on a slow current of curiosity through the galleries, Aunt Jessie seemed to be interested principally in the sculpture's age.

'Imagine,' she exclaimed as we fingered a column relief from the Temple of Artemis at Ephesus, 'imagine its having survived twenty centuries.'

This attitude had no appeal for me. The temple might well have been one of the Seven Wonders of the Ancient World. But for me, on that stifling July afternoon in London the carved figures had no magic lingering in them from the goddess of nature, the goddess who, I knew from the books, was the embodiment of fertility and the earth's power of reproducing its kind. A clogging dust of death had settled over those fragments of stone in the museum. It all seemed wrong and so unlike the Greece of my imagination.

The group of silly schoolgirls embarrassed me by dividing their attention between my kilt and the genitalia of Hermes which appeared to be eaten away by a kind of stone leprosy. The whole museum was sickening to me. My fireside dreams of white marble gods in lush green countryside were swept away.

The horsemen and centaurs lacked life and looked dirty. They could have no part in my dream landscape. I walked along the rows of frieze sculptures. But not one of the figures condemned to immortality there could be mistaken for Kevin as he led his famous stallion through a Highland glen. Many arms and legs of the statues had not survived the centuries, but neither had the spirit of their youth. To me, the small, wiry Black Fergus was much more the Messenger of the Gods as he leapt from rock to burn-bank, and ran to bring us news of the lamb sales.

Aunt Jessie helped to bring my illusions of Greece to as ruinous a state as the shattered sculptures themselves. The fine and delicately poised feelings I had about the beautiful remains from ancient Greek life turned sour in her company, tense as it was with scarcely-suppressed anger and resentment. But perhaps the British Museum would have been depressing anyway. The hushed voices and emphasis on the immense age of the objects on view made the place a home of dead things. Hermes with the baby Dionysus in his arms was not after all an exciting version of my own discoveries of the past months. Hermes was only a tomb-stone.

When we got home Peter asked me how I liked it. A curious tone inflected his voice. I told him I did not care much for the galleries.

'Not surprising,' he said, 'neither did I. Mother took me there to learn the facts of life.'

Peter laughed and said that he had learnt a few more since then. I was sorry for him, living in the explosive atmosphere of the flat. The facts of life must have seemed tawdry to him. No doubt his mother spoiled them for him as she did everything else. I began to see things about my own life at Blarosnich which I would never have seen without my visit to London. It occurred to me how lucky I was to have discovered my own life facts on the mountainside with the winds of Blarosnich about me. The musty museum with its dusty statues would have dulled the keen edge of excitement and wonder.

From the day of the museum visit with Aunt Jessie, the holiday deteriorated. My bed was put into Ian's room to keep me away from bad influences. Ian was considerate and careful and polite but I could not make a friend of him. Within a few days Aunt Jessie tired of hawking me around London and I was back with Peter again.

But although we still had an amusing time together on tops of buses and in the tube trains, the green leaf of our pleasures was blighted by the thought of having eventually to return to the flat.

We could never divine Aunt Jessie's mood. The overbearing 'darling' session of breakfast might well have become an unbearable *crise de nerfs*. I came to believe that my aunt caused these upsets deliberately so that she could rush in tears to her bedroom. This seemed calculated to bring Ian from his books so that he could comfort her with strange phrases like 'There now little mother'. I was nauseated.

I also disliked eating at the flat. In the earliest and most gushing stages of my stay, Aunt Jessie had promised all sorts of delicacies. 'Porridge and boiled mutton,' she said of Blarosnich, 'must be rather a bore for you.'

She made me feel ashamed. I wanted to retort that porridge and boiled mutton were better than what she cooked. But such a reply would have been a rudeness of which Herself would never have approved. To console myself I rested content with the thought that we did not *always* have porridge and boiled mutton.

My aunt made remarks about Blarosnich whenever the opportunity occurred and it was this more than anything else which turned me against her. Jokes were introduced into almost every conversation about our way of life, our 'sanitary' arrangements, the food, the apparently ridiculously early hour of rising, our clothes, and above all my grandmother's eccentric ways. Aunt Jessie did not see that her cheap sarcasm was teaching me a lesson. I was beginning to understand in a way I never had before what a wonderful home life I had. And as for Herself, that stern old woman whose puritan ways irritated on more than one occasion, I was never to meet such a sterling character. She had not only filled in my own mother's role but had taught me more than Rhona ever could. I hated Aunt Jessie for making fun of Herself's old sack aprons and of her snoring by the fire at night. Herself in the sackcloth had won and ruled eight thousand wild Highland acres when she was a relatively poor widow with only an adolescent son. Aunt Jessie, coarse with pink gin and comparatively well-off, could not control an eight-roomed flat and two adolescent sons.

My aunt could talk a great deal. Most of it signified nothing. She invented fantastic names for her food, but all the dishes tasted similarly of the nasty brown gravy which came out of a bottle. Aunt Jessie took me into expensive restaurants but again, in spite of the grand French names on the menu, we had the same stodgy food with the same gluey gravy. The plain boiled cabbage which had been standing on the stove for hours did not have the rich flavour of our greens which were picked in the garden, cooked and eaten within the hour.

The only kind of London food I liked was chips, which appeared with at least one of every day's four meals. But they lost their novelty appeal. My grandmother never claimed to be a good cook, but she certainly knew how to make our hill-farm produce exciting. We had a vast range of fresh and dried herbs and a big vegetable garden which Herself still tended. No place in London where we went gave things which excelled the old lady of Blarosnich's stuffed snipe, partridge pies, casserole hare, or the rowan or juniper dressing for venison. Deep-red deer sausages were not the same as the pink sawdust ones of London.

Aunt Jessie invented extravagant food, I thought, in order to show up the simplicity and plainness of Blarosnich's table. I resented criticisms and sly remarks about our Highland ways. Yet the Darling Duchess had spent years of her own early life in a Highland gamekeeper's cottage, where no airs and graces of the horrible kind she sported now had existed. She made me feel raw and stupid and I could only bear with it by recalling that the people at home always said how well-mannered I was and spoke the English of the Big House.

I was concentrating on my soup at Kensington one day when Aunt Jessie suddenly demanded, 'Do you always eat with a penny whistle?'

At first I did not understand the remark. But as the sarcasm sank in I realized how strongly I disliked her. There and then I longed to jump up from the table. I would have run all the way to the railway station for the next train back to Blarosnich where we all made noises with our soup—often of necessity to cool it so that we could get out to work again as quickly as possible.

I did not jump up in anger at my aunt, but neither did I reply.

Instead I tried, for the first time in my life, to stifle the noise which I thought soup naturally ought to make. The main reason I stayed on was Joe.

Joe was Kevin's brother. He gave Peter and me an unforgettable meal in his lodgings at Camden Town. He resembled Kevin and had the warm spontaneity of manner which I admired in all the Paddy woodmen at home. I could hardly wait until I saw them again. Joe, like them was generous not only in his hospitality to Peter and myself, but in his giving of himself wholly to a pair of strangers. If we had asked for his last penny he would not have said no.

Peter and I both thought the Camden Town area of London immensely superior to stuffy Kensington. The Camden Town women were no less extravagant than the Kensington ones, though with character rather than money. In Kensington even the old women looked disdainfully at us as though they expected us to rob them of their jewels. But as we made our way to the shabby street where Joe lived, Peter and I got lots of looks from lots of girls whose intentions could not be misunderstood.

Joe had promised to get some gramophone records of Irish songs for me to take back to Kevin when I went home to Blarosnich on Friday. Since he was working as a baker's roundsman, he did not know exactly at what time he would call at Aunt Jessie's flat on Thursday evening to leave the records.

Peter and I hurried back after seeing our favourite film of *Old Mother Reilly* at the cinema. Neither of us wanted to miss Joe. He had Kevin's high spirits and charm and despite our protests had insisted on giving us presents of money at the end of our visit to Camden Town.

When we went into the sitting-room Aunt Jessie was reading. She raised her eyes and by one of her typical pantomimes of facial expression indicated that we were not wanted because Ian's study period must not be disturbed.

Aunt Jessie stage-whispered to me, 'There's a parcel here for you, darling.'

It was the records. I asked why Joe had not waited to see me.

'You don't really think I would invite *that* into my home?'

All the resentment against her, dammed in me for two weeks, burst the banks of silence.

My face flushed with anger. I turned on her. I did not mind Ian's superior strength. Nor did I care if they wrote letters of complaint to Blarosnich. I told my aunt the truth.

'You are an old bitch, and I'm glad to be leaving.' Still burning with rage I went into Peter's room.

Rigid with disgust, hating her for calling Joe *that*, I stood by the window. But the door did not burst open with a revengeful Ian demanding an apology for his 'little mother'. Even Peter did not come to turn my wrath away with his unhappy silence. An hour passed. I did not know what to do. An unusual quiet had settled over the flat. I wondered if the shock of my truth-telling had given Aunt Jessie a heart attack.

Then, outside in the hall, the telephone rang. My uncle had come home by this time from his club and I heard him answer the persistent ringing. He used a voice as surprisingly bass as his budgerigar one was alarmingly soprano. The fact that it was he who answered the telephone only deepened my suspicions, for normally when the telephone rang Aunt Jessie raced into the hall.

Iron grips twisted my stomach when my uncle knocked on the bedroom door. The call was for me. Could it be the police or a mystified Joe, or was it Ian and his mother from the flat next door ringing through to demand my immediate departure? I had never spoken into a telephone before and having to do so frightened me, although Peter had once showed me how it worked and had let me listen to a conversation with one of his friends.

I picked up the receiver and a noise resembling a human voice squeaked into my ear. I called Peter to come and interpret, but he was nowhere about. Seeing my desperation, my uncle took the phone and by dint of shouting, as people did to the deaf or foreigners, he got the person to speak loudly, clearly and slowly. He handed me the receiver again and at last I knew it was Alec, our shepherd, talking to me all the way from Blarosnich.

And this gesture of Alec's was the happiest event of my whole holiday. I did not know the full details until my arrival home. But that last and miserable night in the Kensington flat was transformed with the shepherd's few half-English, half-Gaelic sentences.

Nearly all my friends and relatives had written to me during the fortnight in London. I sent Herself letters full of descriptions about city life, and I posted the rudest possible postcards to the Paddies up at the Forestry. Alec had several notes from me which Mirren had to read to him, but he could not answer them because he did not know how to write. But he knew how to use the telephone.

After the lamb and cattle sales he always telephoned the news of prices through to the lady housekeeper up at the Big House. Black Fergus usually relayed to us the unpredictable prices that Alec and my father had obtained for our stock. No one would dared to have used the telephone in the lady housekeeper's parlour for any less important event in our lives.

In the evenings, when he was at Blarosnich, Alec changed his cloth cap and put his false teeth in, to walk down to the Big House with the milk. If required, he would help with getting the General in and out of the bath, and this and similar small services made Alec a favourite with the lady housekeeper.

On the Thursday night before I left London, Alec went down the shore road with his head full of schemes. Since I was hundreds of miles away in the land of the stranger, all propriety about using the Big House telephone must be set aside. A call must be put through to tell me the equally important news of how much the woolclip had fetched in my absence.

But I knew the real reason for Alec's call. The little shepherd wanted to be assured once more that I would be on the Saturday steamer when he took the ferry out to meet it.

6

The leper's portion

The clammy atmosphere of London's streets reached beyond the last suburb. The train hurtled northwards but the city's damp heat clung to the crowded carriages, for high summer had brought heat and humidity. The sighs of Blarosnich, when at long last I reached home, were themselves steamy vapours imprisoned under a low ceiling of mist clouds. The heavy scent of bog-myrtle seemed unable to rise in the sultriness lying over hill and meadow.

This sort of weather brought dragonflies to life and they beguiled me from my work in the hay parks. Black as a mandarin's pigtail, as orange as sunset, green as young apples, scarlet as pimpernel, powdered with jersey-greys or electric blues, the dragonflies hovered and shot about their business in flashes of brilliantly iridescent colour. I stopped my work to see if these enamelled and jewelled marvels were darters or damsels, giant hawkers or the smaller aeshnas. On transparent wings, sometimes inlaid like leaded church windows, the dragonflies sped over burn and lochan, moor and forest. I found it impossible to turn the swathes of hay and also to follow the huge golden-ringed with his amazing turn of speed while he used his six feet as a snaring net to catch bees and wasps.

How lucky I thought we were in the Western Highlands to have three of the four gem-laden hawker dragonflies. But none was more gaudy than the brilliant-emerald whose wings were brushed with saffron. While cooling off in the amber shallows of the burn I often saw the female come to bore a hole in the bank with her pneumatic drill-like ovipositor to lay her eggs. We had many red damsels which delighted in the quieter waters and lived on a diet of moths and mayflies. Up on the lochan, large swarms of common-blue damsels would suddenly appear, the males holding onto their mates' necks until suitable reeds could be found for maternity wards.

And in this electric tension of high summer the larks filled strath and moorland with exuberant singing. Their trilling flight-notes poured down on peat bogs blazing with golden spikes of asphodel, the high-pitched outpouring rang over the cloak of wild thyme spread with royal purple across the braes. Their long rhapsodies reached the tangle-covered rocks of the shore and mingled with the murmur of the summer sea.

Although the dragonflies' feeding on the wing went on from dawn to dusk, the beautiful creatures did little to reduce the vast population of unwanted flies. From among all those green aisles of bracken and impenetrable bramble thickets a small fly emerged and drove us to despair. Worse than the fox's cunning was the airy visitation of these green-bottles. They were a nightmare menace to the shepherd on a hill-farm where he could not possibly handle his flock with continual attention.

Happy to have the hundreds of miles between myself and Kensington, I arrived home to find my father coming down from the hill with the tell-tale bottle of dip in his hand. A swarm of the wretched blowflies had attacked the dirty tail-end of a power-ful tup. But the animal's strength was no defence against the maggots which had already burrowed into the living flesh, half way on their two-day journey into the vitals.

Early next morning I was up on the lochan shore with little thought of Aunt Jessie and her profusion of 'darlings' at the station and her insincere insistence that I must repeat the uncom-fortable holiday. Her pettiness evaporated from my mind as I looked for flies hovering over our lambs and ewes, and for holes in the fleeces where phalanx upon phalanx of writhing maggots claimed another victim.

Demented sheep which were badly infected could be detected by their shaking tails or by the way they rubbed themselves against the peat banks up on the moors. When the animal's whole system became poisoned by the flies, the sheep would trot round and round in a useless attempt to get at the gnawing maggots.

Eventually, the poor animal's nervous system collapsed and the sheep lay down to die.

We had to be quick indeed in order to save infected animals. Within twenty-four hours of the flies striking, the eggs hatched and the maggots began to exact the toll of total destruction. The hooded crow would be lucky if even the sheep's eyes were left for him by the seething white mass of maggots.

Apart from the flies, other diseases and plagues claimed summer victims among our flocks. The law obliged us to dip the lambs twice before the sales as prevention against the awful scab. But at Blarosnich we gathered the hirsels down from the hills for a further dipping if the season turned out to be bad. My father strongly supported the liquid arsenical bath which was supposed to make the sheep free from fly and other parasites for some weeks. We all knew, however, that there were wedders returning to the hill still dripping from the chemical while fly eggs underneath were on the point of hatching.

Herself did not think much of the big yellow drums filled with paste that came from the city. The sheep passing through the dipper often had cuts and sores which Herself claimed were poisoned by the dip mixture. She had herded sheep on Eileen a'Cathmara where, in her childhood, there had been no such fancy things as drums of paste. Her father had used tar and seal oil with better results than the new-fangled chemicals.

When the ewes came down for handlings, if an odd one had to be shorn around the tail because of scouring, its chances of survival were much greater if Herself dressed the soiled area with her island mix. The wealth of new grass on the hills meant that the sheep often scoured and this attracted the green-bottles in great numbers. Unlike the little Island of the Sea-fight, Blarosnich was too vast and rocky a region to be herded daily for the fly-struck sheep to be driven all the way down to the fank.

Alec shared my grandmother's belief in the old ways of curing flies in sheep or worms in man. He was responsible for getting our supplies of seal oil. I always looked forward to the handlings at Pitlobar, Alec's side of the mountains beyond the lochan moor.

But I was especially happy when we went round the west shore and over to Eilean a'Cathmara after seals.

Pitlobar was a small house and it stood on the green foreshore. The overrun garden became part of the beach because hardened froth from whelk-egg capsules and bladderwort were littered amongst the buried flower-beds. Nobody knew why the place was called Pitlobar—the Croft of the Leper's Portion—though Alec's own life resembled a leper's isolation when he returned to this old home he loved so much. Local people said that more than anything the idea of living away in the loneliness of Pitlobar made Mirren reluctant to marry the shepherd. Mirren liked life and gossip and the township's friendly ways and she could not understand why Alec wanted to put the forbidding mountain between himself and his nearest neighbour.

I never had difficulty in sharing Alec's love of Pitlobar. After his mother died during my early boyhood, he divided his time between our bothie and the far shore. My earliest memories included Alec's comings and goings with his sturdy little horse. This animal was a black garron as sure-footed in the steep mountains as Alec himself. The shepherd also took his old Galloway cow on the journeys between Blarosnich and Pitlobar, for Alec liked to drink milk and to enjoy the fresh butter and crowdie cheese made from the surplus.

Alec's possessions were always packed into two osier panniers which he had made. Four Aylesbury ducks sat on one of them with their feet tied. Alec never travelled without the ducks either for he insisted that their eggs were the only things worthy to be set before a shepherd herding a mountain-face for anything up to sixteen hours a day. I was always surprised to see the ducks come safely back. All around the Pitlobar coast there was loud moaning and cooing from eider drakes dressed up in dashing velvet black and sparkling white plumage, finery to match the pink breast and pale green nape which glowed with a kind of inner fluorescence.

There were days at Pitlobar too when the kyle echoed with the quivering laughter of great northern divers pausing at our waters on their northward journey. Although Alec's overfat

Aylesbury ducks ignored the great divers' call, I would willingly have sprouted wings and followed them to Iceland. The migration of birds, especially waders, acted as a siren calling me northwards.

I spent a few nights with Alec when his hirsel was gathered into the shore fank. The meadow pipits seemed most indignant that their dainty walk should be put to flight before the invasion of sheep. Sending their rapidly repeated alarm cry *peep peep peep* they mixed with the rock pipits down on the silverweed carpet where Alec once had his lazy-beds of potatoes. But silverweed had grown there long before the planting of potatoes came in. For centuries people had boiled its roots and ground them into a meal for bread-making, though Alec did no more than pick an occasional bunch to dry and mix in his tobacco tin.

The shepherd was immensely house-proud of Pitlobar's three small rooms. The candlesticks were polished like suns and the salt patterns left by sea spray carefully erased from the tiny windows. The royalty souvenir cups, starting with Queen Victoria's Jubilee and going through to George VI's recent coronation, stood monumentally upon the dresser, and this collection may well have been the inspiration for my own interest in china which began when I was still a boy. Alec set dropped scones before his visitors and I felt sure that Rhona would have been proud of them. The damp, sea-musty smell of the house soon vanished as clouds of the herbal tobacco, which Alec trailed everywhere he went, clogged the air.

Like his tiny home at Pitlobar, Alec himself formed a part of all our Blarosnich lives. For twenty years he had looked the same age. By my fifteenth birthday Alec must have been in his late fifties, yet passing years made no visible impressions on him. He was ageless and solid like the mountains. We all went to him for comfort and advice.

Alec could not read or write but he was a poet nonetheless and often recited his verses to himself, or occasionally to a privileged person like Herself. When I think of school I remember the long hours of 'repetition', by which older and younger children alike committed large portions of poetry and Scripture to memory. Without necessarily digesting the passages' meaning, prose and poetry were repeated aloud, a line at a time, over and over until some nirvana-like stupefaction was induced. There was no virtue in this educational system except that our Highland mods and ceilidhs were full of people who could recite excellently.

People like Herself and Alec found comfort in quoting the Gaelic poets to themselves when there was nobody to talk to. My grandmother regretted innovations which killed the old ways, and she had no liking for the gramophone and the wireless which modern children listened to. Herself scorned city books of shameless romances which children read while refusing to listen to the superior tales their elders had to tell. Gone were the winters when every township could boast story-tellers who required three nights or more to relate heroic tales or sacred poems, a skill not at all the same as the pathetic five-minute verses of the modern mod.

Alec embodied Herself's chief link with the past. He knew all the poets and Gaelic tradition. She consulted him about the cures which herbs could effect and about shepherding traditions. Yet everybody knew that Alec would never die under the main Blarosnich roof. He would probably meet his end out in the bothie if not over at Pitlobar, for the close friend was also held in the greatest distrust by my grandmother because of his connection with 'the other side'.

Perhaps I should not have been so indignant when Aunt Jessie refused Joe the baker's roundsman admission to her smart Kensington flat. I knew perfectly well that at Blarosnich not a soul from the Big House gate-lodge would be allowed past our front or back door. They too were 'of the other side'. Practising Roman Catholics brought the Scarlet Woman of the Seven Hills into the very midst of our community when the travelling priest came to say Mass in their parlour.

I could never find out why Herself was so bigoted in this way. Two of the last families on Eilean a'Cathmara had been Catholics. An ancient feud was carried on between them and Herself, who kept it going to such an extent that Alec was not allowed to sleep in the house at Blarosnich. Herself bitterly hated association of any kind with the Roman church. She regarded Alec's age-old superstitions and obsessions with the Evil Eye as part and parcel of the same religion. Let him cure the red water in cattle with the Lord's herbs from the hill, but let him not allow the Catholic woodmen to come up after a charm to cure their sprains.

Alec was not a Roman Catholic but he was the son of Mongrel Maggie, and this, for all practical purposes, amounted to the same thing. His mother from Eriskay had been born a Roman Catholic though her family turned from it when she was quite young. But nobody around Blarosnich was allowed to forget this early connection: had not a hen crowed like a cock on the night Maggie died, an omen of weird significance which not even manse folk could deny?

Pitlobar—Croft of the Leper's Portion—may well have been named after this social outcast. Though she was buried in the same graveyard as The Captain, she had bequeathed her popish superstitions to her son Alec. He reverenced these in spite of regular attendance at the kirk and a love of having the Good Book read to him.

Nevertheless, although fear and prejudice existed, Herself's relations with Alec were no less diplomatic than those with Florence of Arabia. My grandmother was well aware that nobody would come to replace the shepherd on the far shore. His presence was worth the sacrifice of a few tart remarks about his connection with Mongrel Maggie. It was hidden from none of us that her friendship with Alec went as far as the borders of religion and no further. We could not help noticing on Saturday night ceilidhs that Herself never played and sang the 'Eriskay Love Lilt' voluntarily. Alec had to ask.

On the other hand, Alec kept his old Highland lore away from the farmhouse, apart from its herbal associations, and then he could give sound Protestant names without reference to the Virgin Mary or the saints. Because his secret charms and cures were taboo in our home I became as interested as I was in the tea-cup readings by Black Fergus's mother over at Sallachie. It was like the forbidden swimming in Stag's Pool and I would go silently up to the bothie and listen to Alec's stories. Without the lucky piece of juniper on a string round my neck it was unlikely I would have swum at all in Stag's Pool. Black Fergus wore his good luck charm openly, but then, as Herself said, what could you expect of a heathen boy whose own mother read tea-leaves.

There was a great domestic quarrel when Herself found a piece of *achlasan Chaluimchille* on the left armpit of my vest. I had the St John's wort—the armpit package of St Columba—on recovering from measles. Alec had taught me the old poem to recite on picking the powerful flower:

> *Armpit package of Columba, kindly*
> *Unsought by me, unlooked for!*
> *I shall not be spirited away in sleep*
> *Nor shall I be thrust upon iron.*

> *I will gather the sacred plant*
> *Ordained by Christ Himself,*
> *That it will keep my milk from souring*
> *And make my bullocks fat.*

> *Better the feel of it under my arm*
> *Than a byre of springing heifers;*
> *Better the reward of its power*
> *Than a herd of Lord Lovat's cattle.*

Going to Eilean a'Cathmara with the shepherd after seal oil always led to an adventure. I used to think that magic, black or white, brought us safely over the kyle and through the hidden skerries where my great-grandfather had perished so many decades ago. Our little open boat seemed to bow helplessly before the surging strength of the sea-swell, and then would emerge opposite the low southern cliffs as though Alec plied an enchanted oar.

Whether on the fairest May afternoon or a tranquil autumn morning the mood of Eilean a'Cathmara's waters was always unpredictable. The swells that hollowed out its caves and climbed the highest northern cliffs were never far away. They roamed around the island from one side to the other, so that what seemed from the southern side to be a quiet landing could suddenly change within an hour to a fury which crept around from the island's northern side.

No landings could be made on the north coast, although the

seals used it as a playground where they came in surf-riding on angry foam-crested waves. As we rode up and down in Alec's boat, shipping too much water for my comfort, the seals came alongside with friendly, inquisitive faces. Alec assured me that the seals recognized his boat. I was always amazed at their tameness. I expected some kind of instinct to warn them we were dangerous. Thousands of seals must have perished over the centuries so that Eilean a'Cathmara's township could have oil for its lamps and seal-meat for its tables. Alec regarded the seals as more than animals. He could not rid his mind of the haunting idea that these friendly creatures with strangely human expressions on their faces had once been boys and girls, lured to the sea by the Evil Eye.

Because the island had been uninhabited for many years, the seals had taken over the whole place. They wandered among the remains of the old township like so many whiskered grandfathers. Large numbers of seals went to Eilean a'Cathmara for calving. They climbed right up the cliffs and cried in high voices which reminded me of Aunt Jessie's husband talking to the budgerigars.

Alec and I would have been content to spend a week or more watching the fights among the old bulls or looking into the nurseries which at this time of the year were full of fluffy white calves. Fortunately for us, but unfortunately for the seals, Cathmara did not provide the best breeding grounds. The island's cliffs were treacherous. The seals were daring and inquisitive. The two together led to many accidents. I used to think that our dogs frightened the seals so that they fell over the high cliffs to death on the rocks below.

Later I discovered that most of these casualties happened through the seals' own efforts. The bulls thoughtlessly fought each other on the cliff edge, or those in playful mood took flying leaps, forgetting that the tide was out. Fat calves often met untimely deaths as they were dragged about by currents in the surf during gales. Alec did not need his gun. His friends among the seals died naturally in sufficient numbers to yield all the oil he needed.

Some of the old bulls were huge creatures, often hideously

scarred with battle wounds and still ready to bare their teeth and snarl at potential rivals. Alec had names for many of the seals and would go very near them indeed as they dozed on the beach. Some of the old warriors had grown up from calves under his watchful eye, and in their babyhood he may well have tickled them under the belly or have rescued them from the skerries.

I loved Eilean a'Cathmara's serenity during seal-breeding. The cry of young calves calling their mothers from the sea had a haunting human sound, uncannily like children's voices. The cow, proud of her young, would scramble at once out of the sea and crawl over the rocks to give suck the moment the heart-rending cries went up.

When I watched the cows, full with milk, hurrying so clumsily across the jagged rocks I was always amazed that they did not tear the two milk-full teats on the sharp rock-edges. But I discovered that after the calf had finished its suckle the two breasts gradually retracted again to the level smoothness of the rounded belly.

Alec and I went to the island several times before the September seal calving. Each month had its own fascination, though for me this was due to Alec's presence. Old ruins lay crumbling beneath moss and brambles but Alec did not see them as the haunts of eerily whistling winds and nesting birds. He regarded the fallen stones as still being the homes of people, unknown to both of us, who had died in the last century. But Alec had a clear picture of these people, for oral tradition had passed on descriptions of them through his father, who had it from his grandfather, who had been an islander born on Eilean a'Cathmara in 1795. The old man's tales handed down to Alec were more real to the shepherd than my own accounts of London's underground trains and painted Jezebels.

To me, Alec's grandfather seemed as remote as the Prophet Isaiah. Yet Alec's notion of time differed from mine. Neither his father, nor his father before him, had married until their respective mothers died. And now that his own mother was dead, Alec also felt himself free to marry. When taxed upon this touchy subject he would brush the matter aside with assurances that there was no need for hurry. He had plenty of time. He would still be only sixty in another two years.

Alec would never have been so indelicate as to point out another factor in his marriage situation, one which in any case we all appreciated. Although now free himself the shepherd would not have dreamed of asking Mirren to forsake her own widowed mother. It was quite unthinkable to leave the old lady alone in the township croft while Mirren went over as a bride to the far shore of Pitlobar.

In an extraordinary way, Alec conveyed the impression that the old islanders had never died. He knew every gillie and crofter, every kiln-burner and shepherd who had ever come from Eilean a'Cathmara, through a century and a half. Herself, the last person born on the island, could not compare with Alec for expertise on island affairs. At any rate, even if Herself did know, she never spoke of the island characters. Although Herself took pleasure from the fact that she was an islander, she remembered the place mostly for its isolation and poverty. She found no virtue in dwelling on this aspect of the past. Her mind was bent on winning present harvests and on keeping the fox and hoodie at bay. My grandmother's only concession to recognizing her past was in asking Alec and me to gather herbs from the particular spots where she had plucked them in girlhood.

But Alec lived in the past. The silent little shepherd found speech in every windbreak tree and crumbled ruin of Eilean a'Cathmara. He was transformed from the glum man who sat on the bothie steps at Blarosnich washing his clothes on a Saturday afternoon. From silence he changed to a flow of talk when we stepped from his boat onto the island. He became a magnificent story-teller, and I felt so happy to be there sharing the tales with nobody but the Atlantic seals.

Alec's mind contained the whole history of the island crofters' loves and deaths, the story of their herds and pastures. This was part of the Highland tradition which had come down from father to son through centuries, a tradition which survived the printing press and the Reformation and the Clearances, to meet its extinction only in my own lifetime because of the Devil's Box—Alec's name for the radio.

The only authority on the topic of Eilean a'Cathmara was Alec. He neither forgot facts nor muddled them. If he said Finlay Maclean of the well croft had been the fourth son and had a great charm against the king's evil, there could be no doubt that this was so, though Finlay might have been dead a hundred years. By no chance could Alec make a mistake. Our little shepherd knew the ruined township of Cathmara as thoroughly as he knew the hill of his Pitlobar hirsel. The island stories of the windowless, roofless houses described a simple life, and were told against a background of famous gales and shipwrecks.

Roderick of the goose-green, brother-in-law of Finlay Maclean, featured in Alec's best story, an episode also told by Herself, who had it from her father. Roderick's place in fame rested with his horse which he sold to a farmer on the mainland. The farm which took the horse was not, like Pitlobar, across the narrow kyle, but was on the other side. Eight miles of dangerous water, where the broad loch mouth and the Atlantic met, separated the farm from the island. During the very night following its sale the horse swam the eight treacherous miles back to Eilean a'Cathmara. When Roderick went out in the morning there it stood, cropping the white clover pasture.

Alec's story of the swimming horse, told with impersonations of the long vanished voices, remained the favourite story of my whole boyhood. The treasure trove that was washed up around our shores from shipwrecks, or the adventures of Old Mother Reilly in the cinema were not to be compared.

Only one tale could compare with Roderick's horse and it happened when a youthful Alec acted as gillie to the Big House tenant of the day. Nobody present had been more surprised than the hunter when he shot an eider and found five little ducklings on the duck's back. Alec told me this many times over and made me long more each time to see an eider assemble the young on her back and fly off to sea with them in this way.

Such a wonder still remains one of my unfulfilled ambitions, though I watched the ducks and their chicks during many a June day as they sported in high seas off north Cathmara. I did see young dabchicks riding their father's and mother's backs in the water, like other grebe, which they did until half-grown, when their weight almost submerged the parents.

The time when I reached years of discretion enough to watch dabchicks was a time when nothing was left on Eilean a'Cathmara of Roderick's goose-green and little enough of white clover. But though heather and sedge had long claimed a monopoly of the herbage floor, geese could still be found grazing the island's abundant chickweed and dog-tansy.

The nasal gabbling and honking alarm belonged to grey-lag geese. Flocks composed of several scores of grey-lag would come and share the winter pasture with the puckle of hoggs we put ashore. By then the seal calves had changed the silky white hair of babyhood and, following the cows and bulls, had gone to sea in sumptuous blue coats.

When the winter sea-swells rode high, making it impossible to cross to Eilean a'Cathmara, I could still hear the geese from Pitlobar. Alec would go to the door and listen to the cries coming distantly but distinctly from the island. The geese cries often sounded curiously like barking dogs, as though Florence of Arabia's three pomeranians were announcing Alec's arrival at the Big House with the evening milk. But by the time the birds came to us to escape the fierce northern winter, the yapping Knight, Frank and Rutley were safely away in London and the barking visitors to Eilean a'Cathmara were barnacle geese. And with the coming of the first snows Alec had moved over to winter quarters in the Blarosnich bothie.

The barnacles were not the wierdest cries heard on the island. Some years previous to my first crossing of the kyle with Alec, two public schoolboys, spending their summer holiday at the Big House, had gone over to the island hoping to find archaeological curios. Besides its ruined houses, the island boasted a larger ruin called St Mungo's Cell.

Alec rowed the youths across the narrow water to Eilean a'Cathmara and on the way advised them not to interfere with the Cell. The soil, Alec said, should only be disturbed when a small sample was taken as an ingredient for the cure against ring-worm.

Next morning the boys were on Alec's doorstep, having got back to the mainland as quickly as they could by hailing a fishing boat. Both had taken more than enough of the Island of the Sea-fight, and neither had slept at all that night. A non-stop sepulchral crooning kept them awake, until at dawn they waved their shirts at the fishing boats. The boys had been considerably frightened, for they had not thought that digging St Mungo's Cell would have such supernatural results.

The haunting sounds were natural enough, however, for I heard them myself many times afterwards. They were not the reward of sacrilege as the boys supposed. But Alec maintained nevertheless that the responsible Manx shearwaters were the returned souls of shipwrecked sailors. The seals' human faces, the storm petrels' staccato laughter and the shearwaters' screaming confirmed him in his belief that people could fall under the Evil Eye and be snatched away and transformed by spells.

Neither Florence of Arabia nor her sister went to any of the three islands whose sporting rights they held in addition to those of Blarosnich and Sallachie. Consequently, the snipe went un-molested among the rushy marshes around the Cathmara lochan. Coots and waterhens shared the aquatic plants and there was a friendliness in their metallic notes and guttural squawks. Alec could remember the day when the red-throated diver nested there, where the fishing was good. But no fisher of the reedy lochan could match the noble heron, now supreme fisher of all. His majestic figure stood slender and motionless in the shallows. He did not confine his diet to fish and frogs. The gulls lost many chicks to the heron's long, snaky neck.

Eilean a'Cathmara became a beautiful place by the time the herring gulls crammed into their nests on the sea-pink ledges and the puffins had gone into the cliff-top burrows to lay. A thousand golden hawkbit eyes burned brightly at every turn and caterpillars were drawn to the equally brilliant ragwort as though the weed were indeed the sun. A wealth of wild thyme grew there as it had in my grandmother's girlhood when she used it for a night-cap against bad dreams. Wood-sorrel flourished on the island too and from this plasters were once made against the king's evil. Speedwell spun a web round the earth dykes from whose tops love-links and foxgloves looked out to sea in the not unlikely hope of seeing a finback whale or a basking shark. Whales provided even better oil for fly-struck sheep but were not so easily got as young seals.

I often wondered if the Manx shearwaters were lured back to the island year after year by the cool sorrel. The shearwaters' burrows lay very close to Herself's old house in which Alec and I slept when we crossed to Eilean a'Cathmara. Although I spent many hours in the deserted house I could not begin to catch Alec's feeling that the past was not past, and the dead were not dead. Which corner of the stone house, I wondered, had the puffins been preserved in, and where had the sea-pig—porpoise meat—been salted down against the winter? Was it here, on this hearth that limpets were boiled in ewe's milk and fed to my great-grandfather for his first solid food?

I had learnt so much from Alec about the old island ways. But they would not come alive for me. I could not picture my sealskin-shod forebears settling down to an evening of story-telling, the women keeping strictly to the left hand side of the fireplace and the men to the right. Perhaps the ghosts would not come to life because the fireplace had long ago lost its soul of fire and could no longer be the soul of the house. Besides, the bare bones of the house told me nothing of the past and breathed out an unwholesomeness of decay, and of unconditional surrender to winds that carried salt on their lips from waves far below the cliffs.

I could well understand the two schoolboys from the Big House being frightened during their one lonely night. When dusk fell the wailing and weird cooing started, as the shearwaters returned from the sea. Husky screaming and hysterical laughter rang out from their nesting catacombs as though from mediaeval torture chambers. Alec had many rhymes to match bird songs, but he could not put words to the shearwaters' wailings. I found it difficult not to believe, as he did, that these were the demented spirits of drowned sailors.

The shearwaters were frightening. I preferred the secretive

corncrake in the night meadow and his rasping crek song which Alec translated as,

> O Lord of the day
> Put slugs in the hay,
> O Lord of the night
> Bring worms with the light.

Fishermen from townships along the mainland coast often passed through Eilean a'Cathmara's waters. Sometimes they called at the island on egg-stealing expeditions or, having laid their lobster creels, went ashore simply to laze in the sun. If these fishermen saw Alec they would bring presents of lobsters and crabs. Many of them came from the outer islands and so we had news of doings from places even more isolated than Pitlobar. Should Alec not be on the island, the fishermen sometimes called at his croft.

Alec spent most of our short Highland summer over at the lonely cottage and only came back to Blarosnich for sheep handlings. Willows grew profusely near the Pitlobar croft and the fishermen cut and bundled them for use in making the following year's creels. The shepherd liked their company for they broke the monotony. He kept their pint mugs brimming with tea, running out to the cow if there was no milk, and filling the jug there and then on the foreshore.

During Alec's long summer absences from Blarosnich, Herself forgot her grudge against his unorthodox religious views. She worried about him so much that once a fortnight she filled my rucksack with fresh food and sent me off to the far shore. And because she missed his plodding steps around the steading, Herself went so far as to buy a bar of tobacco or an ounce of snuff. Normally she disapproved of the tobacco habit and this gift indicated the reality of her concern for the shepherd.

I enjoyed being with Alec and his company was more congenial to me than my father's. For reasons I could never fathom, I was always much more at ease with Alec. But unlike my grandmother's decaying home on the island, Alec's shore house attracted me. No matter what the weather was like, summer rain or winter storm, men were not allowed into our farm kitchen during the day. It was women's domain and we could only go in for midday dinner. Even if the rain drove us to abandon haymaking and we resorted to chopping wood in the shed across the yard, Mirren had to put on her waterboots and rainproof and carry the *strubag* out to us.

Big House visitors never went into the Blarosnich kitchen. Their place was in The Room. Their Roman Catholic employees in the gate-lodge were never allowed even to cross the doorstep. With the exception of Mirren and Duncan nobody from the township ever received an invitation to our Saturday ceilidhs. Dogs and cats remained strictly in the steading. Our kitchen commanded as much respect as the kirk.

But Pitlobar was different. Everybody was welcome to the big coronation mugs of black tea, dogs and gate-lodge folk and roaming tinkers alike. And in spite of the croft being so remote Alec had a great many callers. Township poachers made a point of going over to Pitlobar as much for the hospitality and companionship as to find out where the deer were running or the mallard feeding. At weekends after work, the Paddies walked over all the way from the Forestry, and many a fisherman filled a sack with bracken bedding and curled up in a corner for the night.

I often thought that Black Fergus invented many of his sprains as an excuse for stopping work early so that he could go away off to Pitlobar for the charm, perhaps simply to please Alec by asking for the cure. Our shepherd was never happier than going out to get three long hairs from his black garron's tail. He wound these round the sprain and recited the age-old charm:

Our Saviour rode into Jerusalem
Upon an ass that sprained its foot.
The Master got down from His seat
And found the swollen part,
And put marrow to marrow,
Bone to bone,
Tendon to tendon,
Vein to vein,
Flesh to flesh,
Fat to fat,
Skin to skin,
And as the King of the Jews

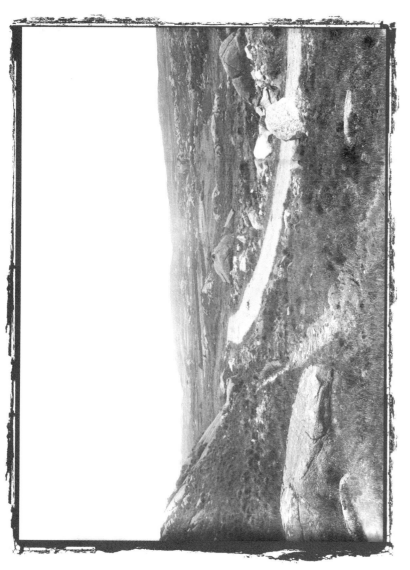

BETWEEN SANNA AND ACHNAHA, BY M E M DONALDSON

(INVERNESS MUSEUM AND ART GALLERY)

ABOVE.

SEAWARDS TOWARDS RUM, BY M E M DONALDSON

(INVERNESS MUSEUM AND ART GALLERY)

OPPOSITE TOP.

SANNA, BY M E M DONALDSON

(INVERNESS MUSEUM AND ART GALLERY)

OPPOSITE BOTTOM.

SANNA, BY M E M DONALDSON

(INVERNESS MUSEUM AND ART GALLERY)

OPPOSITE TOP
DULSE GATHERERS, SANNA, BY M E M DONALDSON
(INVERNESS MUSEUM AND ART GALLERY)

OPPOSITE BOTTOM
KILCHOAN, BY M E M DONALDSON
(INVERNESS MUSEUM AND ART GALLERY)

ABOVE
PORTVAIRK AND SANNA, BY M E M DONALDSON
(INVERNESS MUSEUM AND ART GALLERY)

ABOVE
KILCHOAN, BY M E M DONALDSON
(INVERNESS MUSEUM AND ART GALLERY)

OPPOSITE TOP
BETWEEN ACHNAHA AND SANNA, BY M E M DONALDSON
(INVERNESS MUSEUM AND ART GALLERY)

OPPOSITE BOTTOM
SANNA BHEAG, BY M E M DONALDSON
(INVERNESS MUSEUM AND ART GALLERY)

BELOW SANNA BHEAG, BY M E M DONALDSON

(INVERNESS MUSEUM AND ART GALLERY)

Made the ass whole
May I heal this.

Pitlobar exercised a fascination over Big House folk too. They often called at the croft while out stalking or fishing. When the sport had made them thirsty they asked for a drink from the deep spring well whose water had an icy-blue clarity like their decanters of gin at home. The first three mouthfuls the hunters took were certainly not drunk in the name of the Father, Son and Holy Ghost. In more youthful years Florence of Arabia and her sister used to walk as far as the Croft of the Leper's Portion and called in to admire the white dresser and its fine display of delft. Age crept on the two ladies despite their sunny winters in Egypt and now they could no longer visit Alec. But whenever they saw him they invariably enquired 'And how is beautiful Pitlobar and the dresser?'

One young man who never went hunting or fishing was Mr Edward. Compared with the Big House's normal visitors, he was most unusual. He came to Blarosnich and went into raptures about Herself's music, but did not endear himself to my grandmother. She took strong exception to his over-friendliness and was suspicious of the way he wanted everybody to call him Eddie. Such familiarity towards people of the Big House was not proper in Herself's view. But Mr Edward preached socialism and no better could be expected of him.

Herself would have been insulted to think that she held some of socialism's doctrines. This was so, however, for she praised the virtue and dignity of work. People in the newspapers, whose only work appeared to be the spending of money which they did not earn by their own sweat, roused her ire. The word 'cocktails' kindled the same fury as any mention of the Roman Catholic Church.

Quite acceptable, on the other hand, were the royal family and the nobility because God had ordained these. Herself strongly supported the Tories. Socialism for her meant no more than a dirty name invented by Glasgow workers who wanted more dole because they were too lazy to work. She would stop whatever she might be doing in order to entertain Florence of Arabia and

Miss Philippa up in The Room. But under no circumstance was Mr Edward going to be called 'Eddie' nor was he to wander into the kitchen.

But I liked the young man and found no difficulty in calling him Eddie. His flow of talk against the cruelties of hunting and Hitler, the government and class distinction, delighted me. He had a nice way too of mauling, verbally at least, the young bloods from the Big House who were also staying with the two sisters. Eddie hated their supercilious manner as much as I did. I told Eddie how for years I had dreaded meeting them on the moor because their grand London outfits showed up my own work-worn, work-torn clothes. Worse than that, I said, one of them only a few years my senior had once beckoned me with a fore-finger, called me 'Boy' and ordered me to carry a message for him. But though he sympathized, Eddie laughed at my embarrassment.

'Types like *those* won't *exist* much longer,' he prophesied ominously.

While other Big House visitors went out with rifles or butterfly nets, Eddie went visiting in the township to spread the glad socialist tidings or tried to lend a hand in the hayfield. Eddie was not built for the practicalities of hard physical labour and his effectiveness was doubtful. But he liked to think he helped us and nobody had the heart to disillusion the small young man with the smarmed-down straw hair and pale blue eyes whose sadness seemed expressive of all the world's injustice. Eddie's ambition lay in the theatre. He wanted to be an actor, but having no engagements at present he was glad to spend the summer cheaply in the Highlands.

Eddie talked more than anybody I had ever known, including Aunt Jessie in London. His flowery, unceasing chatter fascinated many people. They enjoyed his musical voice and the theatrical gestures of his delicate, effeminate hands whose corn-less palms had never known a day's hard work. Not many took his socialist ideas seriously. They regarded him as yet another joke from the Big House, to be laughed at along with the poor, leaky General and Susie's modesty belt.

Young Mr Edward inevitably fell a victim to Black Fergus's pranks, for Eddie was so ingenuous and Fergus so ingenious that a magnetic attraction forced them together. Black Fergus teased Eddie until it seemed that even the young man himself must see that his cherished ideals were being mocked. Herself asked my father to speak to Fergus and tell him not to be 'taking a hand' so perisistently against Mr Edward. Although Herself had finally announced her disapproval of the little blond actor, she could not afford to have her relationship with the Big House and Blarosnich strained.

Black Fergus had seen at once that Eddie was gullible and a good target for practical jokes. With his usual aptitude for making the most of a situation, Fergus had shortly dreamed up a series of outrageous feudal practices which, he assured Eddie with great solemnity, were imposed by the Big House on the township folk. There was, said Fergus in a sinister voice, a 'wee red book'.

Florence of Arabia and Miss Philippa kept the red book, Fergus insisted to an intrigued Eddie. Its pages contained an account of the crofters' debts going back many generations. Every man, woman and child had their name in the red book. Eddie's eyes narrowed under a frown of concentration. Black Fergus elaborated his theme. Only when Miss Florence killed a fowl with her motor car, he said, was its lowest market price deducted from their debt. As he warmed to his theme Fergus himself was carried away with indignation at the injustice of the Big House and its red book, so proving himself a better actor than Eddie.

Do you know, Fergus cried, that Postie supplies the Big House with free fish, because many years ago the sisters had taken his mother to the Glasgow Infirmary? Do you know, he went on, that our men had to act as gillies during the sporting season in the same corvée manner as their grandfathers built the stone dykes in the last century? When Black Fergus's enthusiasm threatened to give the joke away and Eddie looked sceptical, my friend accused the actor of not practising what he preached. He ought to get the red book and destroy it.

The two sisters were often mistaken for Jewesses because their bird-like faces were dominated by strong semitic beaks. Eddie himself, who was only a recent acquaintance of Florence's nephew, planted the red book in Fergus's mind by inquiring of my friend how the two ladies' fortunes were made. And now Eddie thought he had uncovered the secret.

We heard afterwards that he hurried back to the Big House and bombarded Miss Florence's silver ear-trumpet with indiscreet questions. Black Fergus understood by instinct that half-truths are more dangerous than outright lies. There was a little red book, though fortunately Eddie failed to find it. The book contained lists of fowl and mutton, milk and honey which we had supplied to the Big House, and for which we had received more money than the same goods would have fetched in Dingwall market.

Eddie's socialist activities showed a marked decline after the red book fiasco. Instead, he took to going over to Pitlobar. Although he regarded the Pope in the same light as Hitler and was outspoken against all forms of organized religion, Eddie found a friend in Alec. I never knew what to make of the actor. The jokes which Black Fergus and his woodmen friends played on Eddie amused me. Yet the sad expression in Eddie's blue eyes moved me. When he realized that people were mocking him and were failing to see their own good in his beliefs, the sadness became a kind of mute suffering. I did not like to see him put out in this way, and paradoxically wanted to protect him from the jokes I so enjoyed. Many of Eddie's arguments, to which I was then exposed for the first time, impressed me. Socialism seemed to contain not outrageous defiance of law, order, and godliness, but plain common sense of the kind Herself regarded as the highest virtue.

Over at Pitlobar one afternoon I was surprised to see Eddie sweeping the croft with a heather broom. He was angry because Alec had gone off, calmly obeying the gamekeeper's summons to act as gillie to the stalkers. Eddie said that it was wrong for a man like Alec to be at the beck and call of idlers like those who collected at the Big House. If socialism was like Eddie, I thought, then it must be a good thing.

I had gone over to give Alec a hand with his hay. Now the shepherd had disappeared for the day carrying a rifle for an overfed army officer or undergraduate. Eddie's arguments contained a lot of sense, though I failed to understand his literary quotations which supported them.

Oscar Wilde seemed to have the same importance to Eddie as Sir Duncan's poems had to Herself. Pausing between sweeps of his heather broom, Eddie quoted what at that time I thought must surely be the cleverest thing ever said. It was about the English country gentleman galloping after a fox, 'the unspeakable in full pursuit of the uneatable'.

That night, when Eddie had returned to the Big House for his grand dinner, and Alec was home from being a gillie, I asked the shepherd who was this Oscar Wilde I had heard so much about. But Alec had never heard of him. This was a pity because I much respected Alec's opinion. Instead, I had to content myself with repetitions of 'unspeakable in full pursuit of the uneatable' all the the way home to Blarosnich.

It was late when I got there, and I should have known better than to start questioning Herself at such an hour. But as she brought me a cup of thick cocoa I had to ask, 'Who was Oscar Wilde?'

Herself stopped where she stood, steaming cocoa poised in the air. She looked suspiciously at me as though I had asked for cock-tails instead of cocoa.

'Oscar Wilde?' she said, putting the cocoa on the table, 'he was a he who wasn't a he.'

7

Blighted summer

John the Baptist ate honey and locusts in the Judaean wilderness, and Alec insisted that the yellow rattle which flourished in our hay parks was the locusts. The biggest meadow at Blarosnich was itself a wilderness and the seeds rattling inside their dry cases overran it like a plague of locusts. Yet, for all their profusion, the cattle left them untouched.

There were occasions on which I enjoyed haymaking, particularly on fine, hot days when even the largest can of buttermilk failed to quench my thirst. It was also pleasant working in the long summer evenings when the humming beetle and rasping corn-crake grew restless with our invasion of their nocturnal reign of the meadows. These were sometimes rowdy nights when the Paddies came over from the Forestry to give us a hand with the hay. Apart from the spontaneous singing and joking, their enthusiasm for getting a field finished always impressed us. What weird silhouettes the woodmen made in the moonlight as they walked the parks under immense canopies of hay piled on their pitchforks.

The Paddies, alas, only came over when they were short of money to go out on the ferry and get drink from the steamer. We could not rely on their efforts. I never enjoyed working in the big park. After raking several swathes together I would be left with nothing but a puckle of yellow rattle stuck between the rake's wooden teeth. It seemed that the yellow rattle had been created to be useless and perverse. Sometimes, for weeks on end, the seed cases of this semi-parasite were the only dry thing in the hayfields.

Dry as this locust weed might be, the hay itself could seldom be cut and dried and gathered up without serious interruption from bad weather. Before there was time even for a good heart to develop in the meadows, the rains would sweep down again, forcing us into the shed where we chopped wood instead.

The rains and steamy mists brought prolific growth to the grasses and their attendant weeds. But there was seldom a break long enough for the sun to come out and wither up what we had already cut. During all my boyhood years not a single harvest was ideal when the horse mower went out, when the hay was cut and turned and raked and built into rucks, all within a few hot, dry days. Our hay always needed several turnings, or it had to be raked to keep it from rotting underneath where new grasses had already sprung up.

We resorted to lapping. Herself, at eighty years old, was not only still a great lapper in spite of her rheumatism but she firmly believed in the awful practice. Lapping was a back-breaking job and came near to killing my love for Blarosnich and farming. When the hay reached the half-dry stage but was still unfit for rucking and further rain threatened, we had to shake every ounce of many tons by hand. The lightly shaken piles were deftly scooped up into the lap and formed into loose balls. An air tunnel was left through them like a muff and then deposited in rows across the park facing the prevailing wind. Lapping was the only method we had in our rainy Western Highlands of saving the harvest.

I resented having to work on lapping, for it seemed too bad to slave so hard merely because we lived in a place cursed by a heavy rainfall. When I changed from a tall boy into a gangling youth, I hated bending over the damp hay for hours or days on end until my back threatened to snap in two. I was convinced in later life that my slightly stooping shoulders became rounded through spending my childhood summers on the wretched lapping. I was glad when the war brought silage into our lives. Compared with making hay laps, it was bliss to walk round and round the outside of the silo pit, like Biblical oxen on the threshing floor, to air lock the wet green grasses and molasses.

Superstitious anxiety gripped me when St Swithin's Day drew near. I could not help believing that if it rained on the ninth century saint's day then so it would for the following forty days.

Herself snorted at this belief and all similar ones. She defied every saint in the Roman Catholic calendar to do their worst. St Swithin got short shrift from my grandmother who quoted a Protestant rhyme:

> Better by far to rise betime
> To make hay while the sun doth shine
> Than to believe in tales and lies,
> Which Roman monks and friars devise!

The summer rain could not be allowed to hold up all work. When it kept us from the hay parks we turned to other tasks. My father and I went off to the woods sometimes, when enough fuel for the house had been chopped. Clad in oilskins against the fine but penetrating rain, we cut saplings down to make six-foot poles. We used these as tripods on which to build up the hay, for it never dried out sufficiently to be built into man-trampled haycocks on the ground. When the rain-caps of sacking had been tied down over the completed rucks, we opened up more air shafts in the sides, to let the wind blow through into the heart of the tripod, so drying the rucks out. The sighing winds of Blarosnich were our friends in a way the temperamental sun could never be.

On the other hand the sun could never be our enemy as the winds often were. Without warning a gentle, drying wind could veer and become a south-westerly gale. A park of good strong corn on the point of turning gold could be flattened by one blast of a south-westerly. Gales loved the Field of Sighing, and after such devastation my father's fine new tractor and the horse reaper were useless. I had to get my scythe down from its hook and hone the curving blade. Cutting out patches of fallen, wet corn was as bad as lapping hay. I usually liked swinging my scythe, opening up the sides of a park so that the tractor could enter, or going off to the braes and scything bracken to make bedding for the stables.

Rhythm and easy, flowing movements were the secrets of mowing a cornfield. The cutting of clean, neat swathes demanded perfect co-ordination and balance of the body, and an instinctive judgement for the lie of the land and a wide six-foot swing within which to operate. Alec made my scythe, specially suited to my long back and arms. If I used another scythe, Herself's or Alec's own, the total harmony of weight and counterweight was upset and the work again became as back breaking as lapping. But salvaging either corn or hay from the wind's and rain's vindictiveness never appealed to me as satisfying work.

We could rely on the winds either to do good or wreak damage. Yet, though the sun was fickle, our own moods as well as the crops' development depended upon its favourable appearance. I was an entirely different person on a golden afternoon as I stood in hot sunshine scything the standing corn from the bad-tempered youth who tried to rescue wind-pucked patchwork in clinging grey mists. My body was sensitive to touch and smell and I fell into sulky silences when the sun denied me its embrace, or a protracted absence made the burn too cold for bathing.

My father had long ago seen the wastefulness incurred by trying to harvest in the persistent rains of August and September. When he was my own age he had also rebelled against Herself's love of lapping. He continued to clear old rushy lands and to plough sour pasture so that he could sow the seed-hay which could be harvested by July before the rains came. But all too little of our hay came from these leas of waving timothy and rye grasses. The wild hay meadows eaten away by yellow rattle and black heads continued to be raked and lapped by hand for many years.

Herself disliked the ploughing even when she saw the results of the June-reaped leas. The broader acres of corn were grazed by rabbits when it was no more than tender green shoots. And when the corn was stooked, finches and crows came to ravish it. The still-wet stooks were carried into the barn in November, with green shoots sprouting from ears the birds had left. Herself stood by, shaking her head in silent but strong disapproval. But my father would not give in. He was made of the same granite stubbornness as Herself. He believed in the plough as she held to the lapping of old meadows and neither of them would give way to the other.

Yet there could be no mother more proud than that old lady of Blarosnich when she came out to stook corn on a fine day.

When the harvest was good she carried the last-cut sheaf into the house as the maid-of-honour. Herself shouted at the dogs if they became over excited about rabbits in the last standing islands of corn, and she nudged me and told me to use my ·22 rifle on the buzzards in the parks beyond. Nobody appreciated my father's efforts with the plough so much as the vole. The cornfields hid scores of their nests, neatly tunnelled under the sloping sheaf-butts. Even the short-eared owls would not wait until dusk before setting forth on the great vole-hunt which the buzzards took so seriously.

For a long time the self-binder held me with a curious fascination. The seven-foot wide mouth of vicious razor-sharp teeth reaping the corn onto the revolving canvas rollers and packers terrified me, together with the mysterious needle and knotter and cutter which tied the sheaf and then indignantly flung it onto the field like a giant spitting out victim's bones. Yet the whir of the binder's sails and my father's shouting at the horses who sometimes broke the machine-like rhythm by snatching mouthfuls of corn, had made friendly music for me in the harvest landscape. I loved the hairy binder string not only for tying sacks around my legs when thinning roots, but also to chew in winter when the last stems of grass lay under snow. The string had a taste and texture unlike anything else. My father also appeared to like it, for he held many strands of it in his mouth as he slit the sheaves open to feed the thresher.

For years we used an old second-hand binder. Three horses were needed to pull it and they seldom achieved any degree of harmony about pulling evenly. A tug-of-war took place between the old machine and the trio of horses. A well-earned rest usually came to the animals when the creaking and protesting binder broke down, which it did frequently. But when the new binder came and a tractor to pull it all day long without a mechanical hitch, my interest and fear of the machine went. I was no longer called in to lead the horses with the malicious reaper-blade working like a demented windmill behind me.

Because at first our tractor was the only one in the neighbourhood, a lot of outside work came up. Township crofters asked my father to plough or reap for them, as he did voluntarily for Mirren and her mother. The way that people took advantage of my father's goodwill was the real reason why Herself disliked the tractor, for in his generosity my father could refuse nobody. He would often set out after ten o'clock at night to oblige a neighbour rather than say no. When these jaunts became frequent, Herself grew very angry, for several of the families did not even pay the modest charge which my father made to cover running costs.

Herself demanded to know why the crofters could not use their own ponies, now growing as fat and lazy on the shore pasture as their owners. She could not forgive Mirren for starting this performance of outside work with the tractor. By asking for her mother's croft to be ploughed, and the cost of it to be taken out of her wages, Mirren had put ideas into the township's head. But Herself's anger, though much feared by township folk, did not stop the men from asking for the tractor. They would face my grandmother's displeasure rather than go through all the labour and trouble without the tractor. This required no little moral courage, as the women would testify who came up the lane with a bulling cow but without money for the fee. People who borrowed without intention of repaying ranked no higher in Herself's opinion than Roman Catholics or wine-bibbers.

Postie's brother once came up to the house looking for my father and the tractor. Herself saw him and knew at once what he wanted because of the season and the fine weather. She went out to meet him, brushing me aside as useless in the sphere of hard business. Postie's brother was a powerful man who divided his time between fishing and the Forestry nurseries. But he got short shrift from my grandmother. Her son, she said sharply, was about his rightful business on the hill. Nevertheless she would hate to see a man stuck with his crops for want of a beast to pull the reaper. She gave the crofter a rope-halter and personally conducted him to the horse park.

At that time we had a big gelding that looked more like a hunter than a plough horse. He was wilful and would never pull in a team. Because the horse was a harlequin with one milky-blue eye surrounded by baby-pink lids, Alec said it had the Evil Eye and did not care to work him. On the day Postie's brother came to us, the horse was caught with the aid of the dogs and the halter put on after a struggle.

When the crofter was on the point of going out of the steading, Herself gave the gelding a prod with her cromag. This made the horse buck before bolting back to the park. The big crofter refused any further suggestion of recapturing the horse. He only wanted to get away from the farm and the unruly gelding as quickly as he could, having learnt a lesson from 'Yonder Cailleach', as my grandmother was called in the township.

But the days only came rarely when the crofters or we could rely on the fair weather holding long enough to get the corn cut and stocked. The long tongues of sugar-laminaria seaweed, which hung in the farmhouse hall as the most reliable of barometers, seemed to be perpetually rubbery and damp like the yellow, rotting hay in the swathe. When these wet days set in, following each other monotonously as though the rain had come for ever, I grew tired of cleaning the potato and turnip ridges of weeds that gloried and sprang to massive size in the dankness.

Although I wore hobnailed boots or wellingtons, all day my feet got wet and the old tattered oilskins became as soggy as the sacks tied round my legs. I crawled up and down the turnip ridges on all fours, feeling as despised as the weeds I pressed into the muddy earth under my knees. I thought nothing in life was so good as when my father, with his superior hoe and calm face which seldom registered annoyance with the weather or the most obstinate sheep, called a halt to cleaning the roots.

We could not go into the house until milking time when I collected the enamel pails. Meanwhile we stayed in the woodshed between the barn and tractor house. My father loved this little wooden shack with its broken window stuffed with rags and cobwebs. The cats shared this love and gave birth to their kittens there amongst the plough-chains and lathes, the broken pieces of breeching and blinkers and the hundreds of oddments which my father treasured against the day when a certain horse-shoe or piece of driftwood would be wanted. The shed's woodworm-eaten walls were hung with animal skins being cured for carpeting or sporrans. And there were always a number of out-of-date seed merchants' calenders with kangaroo pouches bulging with string and snare-wire.

My father was happy enough to hum away to himself in the woodshed. Whereas I loved the byre with its smell of hay and breathing cattle, he preferred the smell of his shed. It exuded a strange incense of swallow droppings, sheep dip, wool-bags, tar barrels, row upon row of carpenter's tools, cats, sawdust, tractor oil and taxidermy. He was most happily contented when sharpening the reaper blades or oiling and setting the cross-cuts. He liked nothing better than to dismember a machine, clean and oil it, and then put it all together again. It was not so much necessity as personal satisfaction which led my father to spend hours perhaps soldering new teeth on a spike-harrow or to plug a leaky saucepan. He had both the craftsman's love of precision and the artist's love of his work.

I never had a sense of belonging to the world of the woodshed. Although I sometimes went in there to mend a broken tool-handle or do similar minor jobs, my efforts were not as neat as my father's. He seldom criticized my handiwork, but I knew he thought it poor, and I could tell he resented my interference in the workshop, especially if I used the tools or any of his bits and pieces and put them back in the wrong place, so disturbing the system of storing he carried in his orderly mind.

I rarely did anything in the shed other than saw logs and chop kindling wood. When my body had fallen into the rhythm of the sawing, I would try and lose myself in a day-dream, and stop longing for Mirren to come with the *strubag* or for Postie to come up the lane and set the dogs barking. But the more I wished time away the more conscious I became of the watch on my arm. I looked repeatedly at the slow-moving hands, sometimes taking the watch off and absentmindedly pressing the disc of sweat to my mouth as though in a kiss.

While I chopped or sawed, strange fantasies went through my mind. Like a stag lying down to cud, I chewed over past events. I reflected on my holiday in London and Aunt Jessie and her comfortable unhappy life. It seemed more mad than ever when seen now from the muddy fields and lanes of Blarosnich. I was not envious of London though I still remembered and grew excited by the atmosphere in the gritty streets of Camden Town. Aunt Jessie seemed to me like a prisoner, held behind bars of absurd snobbishness as strong to her as the chromium bars of the bird-cage were to her budgerigars. By comparison with my poor, strained aunt and the discontented Peter, I was as free as the rollicking chaffinches up in the Earl's Park.

I worried about Peter because he had made a bold attempt to fly from the gilded cage his mother kept him in. Herself felt very queer one day when she went to the front door at Blarosnich and was saluted by a policeman. Years had passed since the constable had last cycled the ten miles out to Blarosnich and then it had only been to collect a scalp of bees. But this time the constable brought the news that my cousin Peter had run away from home.

I was not surprised, and felt pleased when we were told that he was probably heading for the Highlands. For weeks afterwards I kept a lookout on the lane, hoping to see his friendly face and generous slanted eyes. But he did not show up and we did not hear until Christmas how his escape failed.

Before Christmas another event took precedence over Peter's disappearance and this was the coming of Dolly. She was Black Fergus's newest and greatest love. Engines were never to yield up their fullest secrets to me and though I could drive our tractor I found no pleasure in it. But Dolly was different, for this new motorbike of Fergus's enthralled me. She satisfied my adolescent unrest, from the first moment she roared up the lane. I stopped moaning at the flailing rain and no longer pined for the snug warmth of the cinemas I enjoyed in London with Peter. Every day now had its silver lining. Dolly would fling herself up the lane before I had bolted my supper. And Black Fergus would hardly wait until I was astride the pillion before taking off reck-lessly down the lane again and out to anywhere in the whole country which was ours to command.

With Dolly's advent the woodmen's camp up at the Forestry

became too tame for Black Fergus and me. The township palled also and the people tired of us tearing noisily up and down its one small street. We went far and we went wide, taking in a social or a dance or any other gathering of people. We did not particularly want to dance or listen to bands or chase girls. We wanted to be admired as riders of the new, powerful, flashing Dolly. Drawing attention to ourselves was the easiest thing in the world. Black Fergus revved up as noisily as he could, trying to make his motorbike appear superior to the most superior machine that ever sped along the twisting roads. Dolly did so much for me. She made me important and helped me to seem like a man big enough to match my oversized hands and feet and nose which seemed so incongruously adult compared with my still-boyish face.

Black Fergus and I had been supremely happy as schoolboys diving into the dangerous Stag's Pool, leaping our way through the Circassian circle at Saturday night ceilidhs and lighting camp fires in the hills. Now we were as dedicated to the thrills and potentials of the motorbike. We made many new friends, scattered over long distances from Blarosnich. Nothing would keep us at home, neither hail nor storm nor lashing, high-winded rain. The late return journey home was the climax of these innocent adventures. Precarious on the pillion, I clung to Black Fergus not only for warmth but also so that we could see with the same eyes the familiar places that took on a marvellous new quality from speed and the late starlight.

The powerful headlamp picked up the startled green eyes of roadside sheep and made them more mysterious than the spluttering Sirius above us. We always stopped several times on the way home, for this gave an extra edge to the sharp thrill of flying like the wind through the empty countryside. Flushed in spite of cold fingers and faces, we laughed and patterned the road with our urine. Black Fergus loved the stars. He had as many crazy theories about the seven Pleiades and all the celestial geography as Alec had about cures and charms.

Black Fergus and I thought that earth and heaven belonged to us and were made especially for us to fly through. More than

121

stars or streams we loved the Aurora Borealis and would seek out vantage points to see the brilliant and prodigal displays which sometimes lit our skies. The light on the waves and seawashed rocks as we fled alongside them would seem to be brighter than usual. Then glancing up we would see the sky filled with dazzling dancing light as though it had opened upon God's great white throne and the Spirit's seven lamps of fire. Fergus stopped the motorbike and switched off the lights and the engine. In the sudden silence the Aurora Borealis seemed even brighter, and uncanny in its own impressive silence. Vast aerial palaces scintillated above us, palaces of light that flashed and twisted and dashed like a thousand burns in spate over the crystal walls and towers.

The northern lights had frightened me the first time I saw a gigantic display. Nor was I with Black Fergus during the previous year when a fantastic display of the Aurora Borealis tore the night sky as though the Biblical four beasts full of eyes had indeed been unleashed from God's throne. This display of the lights was the most extraordinary and brilliant ever seen in the north of Scotland.

I stood at our front door with Herself who was quite convinced that the display heralded the Lord's return. Although she had seen northern lights throughout her life none had been as startling as this, and she was sure that by morning the Lord would have come again. Usually, the auroral display lasted only a few minutes. But that night's went on continuously for hours with constantly changing colours and shapes. The splendour was terrifying and while the bright flashings continued outside we sat round the kitchen table while my father read the entire Book of the Revelation.

The towering New Testament language matched the towering castles in the sky. As St John's angels and beasts passed before us in my father's quiet, clear voice so all the colours of the rainbow flashed outside, changing from red to green and white to yellow, lighting up the whole earth with a false dawn. The heavens flamed with burning tongues and froze with icy fountains, but still the Lord did not emerge from His throne. We climbed the stairs to bed and Alec, not a little afraid, crossed the yard to the bothie, taking out his false teeth which had been put in ready to greet his Maker.

I went to sleep wondering if I should still be alive when morning came, if indeed another morning there was to be. But there was and after the disappointment over the Lord's return, I took a rather more detached view of northern lights. I saw them afterwards on Black Fergus's motorbike, and knew the Aurora Borealis had more to do with electricity than with God directly, though my scientific bias did not destroy the wonder of this phenomenon which seemed at times near enough to reach up and touch, and at others to be a million miles away.

The northern lights were always eerie and too ethereal to be loved, as I could love the sea, heaving and vast and shining under the moon and stars. The Atlantic, surging with powerful forces, lunged at our coasts and even when calm it breathed like a sleeping mammoth. All the stars seemed to be scattered over the sea like we scattered grit on icy roads. Its shining expanses, as restless as my own heart, shone with the dust of stars.

As Black Fergus and I stood by the sea's foaming edge we thought its surface was a mirror that caught and shattered the image of the constellations we knew so well, the Milky Way and the belt of Orion, and the Great Bear. The midnight waves were phosphorescent as they flowed and gurgled amongst the rocks where the waders talked and chuckled in their sleep.

Just as he knew the stars Black Fergus could name the yellow glimmerings of townships and farms beyond the headlands. They were warm signals in the darkness, made for humans as the Aurora Borealis was not. Fergus would puzzle over other yellow pinpoints of light which moved slowly across the water, and try to work out which trawlers they were and to what watery grounds they were bound.

Our forays into the night and headlong dashings round the countryside were frowned upon by Herself. But I was growing up fast and considered myself to be on the verge of manhood. I rebelled against Herself's rule. I was delighted when Black Fergus took me up the Blarosnich lane after the ungodly hour of midnight. My fifteenth year had given me courage and I turned on Herself with impudence.

Then, as suddenly as she had come into our lives, Dolly went out of it. It was unaccountably sad, and I remembered a similar sadness from the time when Fergus had left school and so was unable to break the stillness of Stag's Pool with me in the late afternoons. The war with Hitler finished our wild careerings up and down the glens. Petrol rationing, the blackout, and identity cards took away our pleasant freedom. The whole neighbourhood became a defence area. Access to the coast was banned and travelling became difficult.

At first, unreasonably, I blamed Herself. It was as though she had personally arranged with Mr Chamberlain for him to make his September declaration of war simply to keep me at home at night. A score of times she had waited up to see me come home to Blarosnich drunk with the sweet, sharp night air and the rush of wind on the motorbike. 'I'll put an end to this,' she had prophesied over and over again. Now the end had come and Dolly sat sadly disused in a shed over at Sallachie most of the time, and I had to find other ways of rebellion.

Before my holiday in London, Postie's calls at Blarosnich held no particular interest for me. Our mail deliveries consisted of the *Glasgow Herald* and occasional letters from naturalists to my father. Herself answered these in curiously old-fashioned yet youthful handwriting, at dictation from my father while he did his cobbling and repairs by the fire at night. My father only liked writing when it was for the daily journal, although the naturalists' questions deeply interested him.

My soldier friend Colin on the train to London had infected me with his own letter-fever. My restlessness in the woodshed waiting for Mirren to come out with the tea was nothing compared with my anxiety now for a sight of Postie bringing the letters. Although I had written several times to Colin he had only replied once. But it was enough to whet my appetite. To receive mail seemed to me to be part of being adult, and I wrote to everybody I could think of, happy if only a postcard came in return. When the Paddies left the Forestry for Birmingham or Bedford they promised to write and did. They were the best of all for writing to me.

Familiar news and British stamps failed to satisfy me after a time, however, and the personal columns of magazines with appeals for pen-friends soon absorbed my free time. The world came to me through our letter-box with stamps as exotic as the departed dragonflies. I collected people of a strange variety—love-lorn secretaries out on the Canadian Prairies, soldiers in India, farmers in Iceland, nurses in Bangkok and coalminers in South Wales. But the friendships usually petered out suddenly, taking their brief brilliance with them like the dying dragonflies. The thrill of pen-friendships lay most in anticipation. To discover that the correspondent was too old or too young, or unacceptable in one way or another brought them to a mute, inglorious end. But where one died another was born.

The pen-friends I collected had not all inherited Herself's un-bending honesty as I had done. One particular postal vision in my mind was a young dusky beauty whose parents were both Mexican Indians. After many refusals she finally consented to send me a photograph. When it arrived I tore the envelope open and found myself looking at a bulky Ruby-on-the-train type of woman whose photograph was itself by no means recent.

Herself did not like my secrecy over this international corres-pondence which I would allow nobody to see. In the end, my father was reduced to giving me one of his very few serious talks. An extremely odd man arrived at the house one day while I was over at Pitlobar with Alec. In age and character the stranger closely resembled the type of Big House guest who seemed always to specialize in butterfly catching. He had, however, nothing to do with the Big House, but was one of my mysterious pen-friends, supposedly a young schoolmaster, though he was nearly bald and had a white moustache.

A tradition of rights to independence and privacy for each member of the family existed at Blarosnich in spite of our close physical proximity and the intimacy necessarily bred by our isolation from the outside world. My father, for instance, felt secure and happy at his carpenter's bench in the woodshed. We respected it as his and only went in there to chop wood. No one would have dreamed of going up the stone steps to disturb Alec's privacy in the bothie unless invited to do so. Herself dominated the warm kitchen and heaven help the mortal who dared to touch one of her tins of shortbread or shelves of herbs. And I too had to have a place peculiarly mine to which I could run with my precious letters, every one of which I kept for years just as my father kept every back number of the *Farmer and Stock-Breeder* magazine amongst the clippers and cocoa-tins full of nails and screws in the woodshed.

The byre did not provide enough privacy for the reading of my letters. Nor did the barn, for since the fire on the day of my mother's funeral another pair of doors had been built. They gave onto the stackyard and sheds on the side remote from the byre. Hay and straw for the animals was wheeled in a cart through the barn, and this was not a good place for clandestine letter-reading. The calf houses were low buildings and the manure in them awaiting spring cleaning often threatened to touch the roofs, so they were useless also. Dampness and the smell of decaying potatoes and mangels blue-bearded with rot made the root house impossible also.

But above the stables was the loft where we stored the wool before sending it to Glasgow. The horses underneath kept the loft warm in winter and light came dimly through two skylights. Besides these particular attractions, the wool loft held the huge cabin trunk which had come from the last sporting tenants of the Big House together with the *Encyclopaedia Britannica* and wine glasses.

As soon as it arrived, years before, I had claimed the enormous travelling box as my own. When still very young I put strangely beautiful pebbles and cushion stars from the beach in it, together with birds' feathers, chestnuts, old amulets and charms from Alec which had outlived an illness or a mood, and all the odd assortment of a country boy's secret treasure trove. With its domed lid and rows of rivets and faded remains of old labels the trunk had always captured me with its romance. Before the box became so full and my legs grew so long, I used to climb inside the trunk to bring the ships' cabins and the tropical hotels a little closer to me. The trunk had never been locked until my fourteenth birthday had come and gone and the pen-friends began to arrive thick and fast. Then, driven by an inordinate desire for secrecy I oiled the rusty lock and made the levers work once more. I kept the key always about my person, as closely guarded as the rhubarb rock in Herself's petticoat pocket.

Mr Edward turned out to be my most disappointing correspondent. When the Big House went south earlier on account of the war, Eddie had made elaborate promises to write to me. But not a single letter came from him. I did not know the terrible fate awaiting him because of his pacifist views. In ignorance, I blamed Herself for Eddie's failure to write. He must have hated our narrow-minded world of Blarosnich after his final reception at our house.

Herself had often threatened to use her massive wooden beetle, normally employed for mashing the hens' food, on any person who roused her whiggamore wrath. Like so many of her threats, this went unfulfilled until that September day when Eddie came to see us. Then Herself actually took up the wooden club as though to use it 'around the ear-hole' as she put it. Eddie had driven her too far. He had told all the township men not to join the silly war game, as he called it, and to Herself this was a traitor's work undermining all she held sacred. In addition, Eddie had also gone too far in infringing the propriety of relationship between the Big House and ourselves as tenant-farmers.

Eddie had insisted on my accepting his invitation to dinner at the Big House. It suited my mood to defy Herself over this unprecedented situation. The actual wording of the invitation strained my grandmother's temper beyond breaking point. She blamed Eddie for much of my adolescent discontent and disrespect for the Sabbath. Herself could not bear to hear the Good Book's words on the actor's tongue being used to support his socialist arguments. My invitation to the Big House was the coda to this symphony of horrors.

I sensed that Eddie's prolonged and farewell morning visit was making Herself seethe. The hay parks demanded every minute of

127

our time in salvaging the sodden swathes. Herself kept reminding me of the waiting work but I deliberately refused to take the hint and budge from the kitchen door.

Then Eddie said, 'Don't forget then. Seven-thirty down below for *the last supper!*'

He sounded as though he deliberately intended to goad the old woman. Eddie fled before the upraised beetle, and naturally I was not allowed to accept the invitation which Florence of Arabia would have thought as improper as Herself did.

When Eddie had finally gone and the war settled down as a permanent feature in our lives, a strange peace at last came over me. The restlessness and discontent had left as mysteriously as they had come. I no longer found fault with everything my grandmother said or did. The longing to roam the countryside after a hard day on the hill, left me also. And then the letter-writing began to lose its interest. I hated the idea of unknown censors and the destruction wrought by giggling girls in Glasgow whose scissors cut out whole passages of letters from my pen-friends in the forces.

Our experience of the war was a consciousness of it rather than direct experience. Although by law we could no longer kill our own lambs for home and Big House consumption and Herself disliked old meat from the town, we nevertheless always had a good table. During the handlings a gimmer or lamb occasionally met with an accident. Instead of leaving the injured beasts to die my father killed them in spite of Whitehall's edicts, which made no provision for such incidents.

With most of her visitors gone to the war and her gamekeeper unable to cover much of the hill, Florence of Arabia approved of my father helping himself to game on the understanding that half of the bag went down to the Big House. Herself preferred wildfowl to game birds because, coming from Eilean a'Cathmara, she had grown up with such food. We never lacked the poet's 'greasy victuals', especially mallard and teal.

Like the Saturday ceilidh it was a tradition in autumn and winter for Black Fergus's father and mine to go off shooting once a week. Fergus and I often hid and watched them go down the frosty shore where a flight of wigeon might be silhouetted in the moonlight, the sound of wing-strokes louder than our own heart-beats as we lay motionless trying to overhear the men's talk. We believed our fathers indulged in the same, only worse, bawdy stories as ourselves, and were disappointed when Sandy only complained about wool prices or a dirty load brought by the coal boat. My father's voice could not be easily picked up because he spoke too quietly. And in any case he would be listening to the shore cries rather than to Sandy. He had a habit of suddenly stopping whatever he might be doing in order to catch sounds, usually of birds, which his sharp ears detected and which nobody else heard until he drew attention to them.

Certain families in the township used the war as an excuse for wide-scale slaughter of gannets and puffins. Although once upon a time they had almost been Eilean a'Cathmara's staple diet, my father saw the danger of such a heavy toll and did not allow them at Blarosnich. On the other hand he was helpless to stop the game-keeper collecting plovers' and gulls' eggs for the Big House. Alec turned his skill to fishing because he never felt comfortable with a gun.

Again no doubt because of her island childhood, Herself loved fish from local waters and scorned the wood-smoky orange kippers from the travelling grocer which were a favourite with me. In all my life I never saw anybody enjoy eating in the way that my grandmother, even as a very old lady, relished a big cock crab. With eyes bright and her mouth moist with anticipation she broke open a strong claw and set to with enviable gusto. Black Fergus's cairns never descended a fox-den full of cubs with such ado as that hoary octogenarian cleared the last scrap of white meat from the crab shell.

A dish of oysters set her singing. After such a tasty morsel Herself might break out in a spontaneous bar or two of a song used by old fishermen as they trailed their dredging nets:

> The herring loves the merry moonlight
> The mackerel loves the wind,
> But the oyster loves the dredging song
> Because he comes of gentle kind.

Besides five score or more of hens we always kept ducks and turkeys and a big gaggle of geese for ourselves and for the Big House. But the meat which appeared most frequently on our wartime table was rabbit and venison. However irritated I may have been in my adolescence with Herself when she asked me to bring in herbs from the hill, nobody appreciated them more than I did when they were sewed up with stuffing in a young rabbit deliciously roasting in the oven. And as a family we had always preferred venison to beef. Our deer herds seemed to have grown larger perhaps simply because they were joined by those escaping the wholesale slaughter further along the coast.

Since the sound of Mirren churning could still be heard at Blarosnich we had our own butter and cheese. She washed and dressed the butter, moulded on top with patterns of harebells or a blackbird. Long before drowning in the hidden skerries off Eilean a'Cathmara, my great-grandfather made the two butter printers and the meal-ark out of driftwood. Decades of use had hardly worn the patterns away and I always admired the carver's skill in the flowers and the bird and their complicated designs round the borders. In company with a needlework picture of the twenty-third Psalm, the big wooden ark and butter moulds were the only things left from Herself's old home, except for the ruined house itself.

Although our orchard produced good apples and pears we preferred wild damsons from the far park hedge and thought these better than the plump cultivated plums. There were red and black currant bushes, gooseberries and raspberry canes whose fruit went in almost equal proportions, one half to us and the other to the birds in spite of scarecrows and Mirren's efforts at placing rattling pieces of tin to keep the pirates away. Responsibility for part of this daylight robbery could be laid at the door of our own domestic hens who concentrated their raids on the strawberry beds which my father specially cared for. What fruit remained went into jams and pickles. I cannot think of life at Blarosnich without remembering the preserving pans and spoonfuls of jam cooling on saucers so that Herself could taste them.

Old-fashioned jams like angelica and rhubarb, gooseberry and elderflower jelly, pear marmalade, marrow and ginger were my favourites. Herself sampled the sweet jams as she made them but preferred such savouries as gooseberry relish, apple and raisin chutney, sweet pickled onions, spiced crab-apples, red cabbage, and pickled nasturtium seeds.

Many of our visitors disliked going down the garden to the 'wee house' because six hives stood among the plum and apple trees. The bees belonged to Herself's province and she loved working with them as much as we enjoyed the honey. The dark, autumn sections were best, each waxy cell full of a harvest at whose secrets we could only guess. Herself's straw hat with its long black veil hanging from the brim lived in the hall next to The Captain's yachting cap and was no less sacred, for the bee-boater had once been his too.

Never once in my boyhood years had we to buy vegetables except for planting-bundles or occasionally a new brand of seed potatoes. Often we had more than enough for our own needs and sold the surplus to the township and the Big House. And more than half the jam made was given away or converted into hot drinks during winter. Surrounded by such proof of our Maker's bounty, we had little patience with ration books except for tea and sugar.

Sugar brought the war into Herself's awareness. Her secret fear was not like Mirren's of German paratroopers jumping out at her from the blackcurrant bushes as she made her way down to the 'wee house', but of the police coming to search her bedroom. Under the bed and under the stairs, on top of the wardrobe, in the old castle commode-chest and in a number of large biscuit tins, supplies of sugar lay concealed. A hoarder by nature, my grandmother had bought it all up before rationing began, thinking that no sugar would be obtainable at all. I think she lived with another fear that Teacher or Mirren would talk in the township about these hoards and that gossip would reach police ears. But since my grandmother never took sugar in her tea and a large part of the jam for which she saved the sugar went to the township anyway, her worry was probably groundless.

Herself did the actual preserving but Teacher and Mirren were responsible for much of the gathering. My father, in a kind of tradition, always brought the blaeberries home. Mirren could hardly be classed as a maid in our household because she principally worked out-of-doors with calves and fowl, gathering and washing eggs, and spent most of the fine weather in the hay parks. Teacher also took her turn in the meadows and on retiring from teaching she became a sort of unpaid but much loved housekeeper. We continued to call her Teacher.

Until I went to London, coffee for me meant a black syrup in a bottle whose label showed a soldier being served by an Indian servant. Camp coffee was never used at Blarosnich though we believed the township women drank nothing else. Aunt Jessie in London had superior ideas and her kitchen equipment included a coffee mill which ground up beans from Brazil. The results, I considered, did not taste so good as the coffee Herself produced from the dandelion roots she dug up in the autumn and dried at the back of the fireplace along with the rabbit skins and damp socks. But there could be no substitute in our house for real tea despite the numerous herbal brews Herself indulged in. The few ounces allowed each week were never enough and Mirren constantly engaged in bartering our homemade butter and jams to township people with large families of young children.

Except for these minor irritations, the war mostly passed us by. Its ragings seldom touched our isolated peninsula bordered on three sides by turbulent seas and rocky, inaccessible coasts. Even when billeting officers scoured the region looking at accommodation for evacuees from the bombed cities they went away without bothering to consider our desolate neighbourhood. Herself said little about this but I think she was disappointed when they ignored us. Perhaps a conflict went on inside her breast for we knew well enough the horror she expressed of everything to do with cities. She imagined our way of life being upset by gin-slogging mothers and bed-wetting, bug-ridden children. She gave my father strict instructions that at the first sign of evacuees arriving he was to take them at once to the fank for a thorough immersion in the sheep dipper. But none ever came. Our lane never saw the crocodiles of pathetic children. All the same we laughed at the stories about evacuees in other parts which entered every conversation. We liked to hear best of the outrages which took place in big castles like Balmoral or the Duke of Atholl's. We adored the plight of countesses and tweedy ladies like Florence of Arabia who were obliged to set up de-bugging stations and hang rows of mattresses to dry from their castle windows.

The war's comical inconveniences like drinking women from Glasgow and their bed-wetting offspring did not enter our lives. And even regulations such as the blackout did not bother us much. But there were moments when the war, even though far away, invaded our lives completely. Herself grew forgetful of feeding the hens. My father's hand lay on the tractor-wheel, his thoughts elsewhere. Alec became sad and never noticed that his pipe had gone out. No national tragedy affected us so much as the sinking of the *Royal Oak*. We recognized it as something profound in our lives, probably because it involved us in a personal loss.

Regularly every year my father announced that he intended going over to his cousin's farm in the Black Isle. He would take a holiday, he said, when the harvest was either finally gathered or finally abandoned and left to rot in the flooded fields. He never went. Something inevitably prevented him. I had never met the cousin's son who was only a few years my senior. When he went down on the *Royal Oak* I suddenly realized that not only had a family link been severed but what the war was meaning to lots of people every day.

When Herself came out to the barn and told my father the news she had just heard on the wireless an awful silence followed. My mother's death had not shrouded the Field of Sighing with such a sense of loss, though perhaps I had been too young to remember. Herself did not brood about her great-nephew's death only, but about all the sailors in the doomed ship. 'Puir lads. Puir lads,' she mumbled to herself for days afterwards. From the grave announcements on the wireless and afterwards in the papers we felt as if the great *Royal Oak* had been our only defence between the fox-like U-boats and our quiet Highland backwater. Now it had gone taking eight hundred lives with it in home waters just along the coast from where our hay still stood out in the wet parks.

We did not express our grief in words so much as in moods and in music. Although he practised on the chanter every week out in the woodshed, my father never played his pipes at a Saturday ceilidh when a pibroch master like the gamekeeper was there. But on the night we heard about the *Royal Oak* he finished work and marched slowly up and down the horse park playing laments, one after the other. The music blew sharply sad across the gathering darkness. I felt indescribably more miserable than at any other time I could remember. It seemed terrible to me that so many young men could all die at once. Our grief weighed oppressively and my father's pipes gave it voice. His laments wailed across Blarosnich for others besides the lost son of the Black Isle cousin. The reedy requiem rang out for all the hundreds of sailors, for all the shepherds and herders, young woodmen and old drovers who still had bad chests from being gassed in the First World War, the butcher boys from Plymouth and the window-cleaners from Birmingham, who had gone away to fight an enemy who, until now, had somehow seemed unreal to us. The outrages in Poland, the invasion of Russia, the fall of Paris, though terrible were distant and impersonal. But a feeling of insecurity and imminent danger came suddenly on us when we knew that a German submarine had slipped along our own Highland coast to torpedo the great battleship anchored at Scapa Flow. When the *Royal Oak* went down the war came closely home to the whitewashed walls of Blarosnich.

By the ceilidh on Saturday, Herself's melancholy had still not dispelled. She took up her harp more thoughtfully than usual. Then we heard once again the words the Lady of Clan Ranald used in the Caristone lament as she watched the homeward ship bearing a dead bride. We had heard the song so often before. But now new meaning and mournfulness imbued it. Overtones of my father's laments on the pipes ringing among the trees seemed to hover in Herself's song.

That night instead of getting straight into bed I took a pencil and paper. Somehow, I had to make my own lament for the terrible event which had cut so deeply into our peaceful round of life at Blarosnich. Without knowing how, I wrote a poem. That was the first of many and only odd lines of it come to me now out of that sad time.

Though I forgot most of my first poem, I never forgot the haunting vision in my mind of the great ship's decks crammed with faces like Black Fergus's, faces brown from hot suns and long starlit nights on watch. Pipes and harp could never be mine, and I turned to paper instead. Soon I began to write verse about Blarosnich and its changing seasons and about the long past which Alec's and Herself's tales had brought to life. I wrote about the wild animals and the birds on the hill. But none ever moved me like those first lines about the *Royal Oak*.

Alec eventually returned to the bothie after the lamb sales and became my constant companion in the field. The backbreaking work of lapping was finished for that war summer. We could look forward to autumn now with its pleasant tasks and good weather. Although it was late in the season, my father converted an outhouse into a silo and was busy filling it with luscious aftergrass which seemed an even heavier crop than the first cutting for hay.

By the end of September the sun returned and when I went out in the mornings to catch the harlequin gelding it had already dried up the dew. Not being yoked with one of the mares, the gelding worked well enough and seemed to enjoy using the ruckshifter as much as I did. This large platform on low wheels could be tilted to ground level and the haycocks moved bodily onto it by means of a winch. My new-found peace seemed particularly blissful when I sat on the loaded platform going across the grass parks to the hay-shed. Blarosnich was once again the most wonderful place in the world.

As September passed into October the willow warblers and redstarts began to desert the Earl's Park for the winter sun in Africa and the warm Mediterranean, while old and familiar friends from Iceland and Greenland arrived at the same time. New notes sounded among the juniper scrub and fir woods. Up on the high moors twittering flocks of snow buntings had come from the north for the weed-seed harvest.

The shore teemed with mixed flocks of waders, dunlins and sanderlings and ringed-plovers, and greenshanks amongst the red-shanks, and large flocks of knots sandworming with that sad minstrel of moor and mudflat—the curlew. Out on the seaweed-covered skerries the purple sandpiper joined the turnstones. I was always intrigued at the strength shown by turnstones in flicking over comparatively large pebbles to get at baby crabs. Three or four birds sometimes teamed together to overturn an outsize stone which promised a big feast of sandhoppers. The little stint was unmistakable with its thin legs daintily running along the shore. Although he was the smallest of waders, the stint was the most endearing of all the passing visitors to our coasts.

And beyond these, and the cormorants claiming every promontory as a pulpit, there were rafts of wigeon and eider and mallard. Up and down the whole coast auks and arctic terns, lesser and greater black-backed gulls, kept up a constant yelping and wailing, uncanny laughter and shrill chatter.

Autumn came on with the faintest hints of winter. Heather and harebells were hung with gossamer. Ragwort, buttercups, storksbill, wild sage, heart o' the earth, love links, midsummer men, stinking mayweed, all went on blooming until the first snows came and claimed everything. Even the brambles became beautiful in the frosty air and mellow sun. Herself's hands were stained with juice more than ever before from blackberrying in the Earl's Park where the last butterflies were held prisoner in dew-hung spiders' webs. The roebuck grazing the clearings had developed a redder tint than the brown velvet of reedmace.

The season was rich and restful. Pitchforking the hay and sheaves to Alec made warm, satisfying work. Despite the wind and rain and the efforts of gulls and crows, there was always sufficient corn for at least four stacks. Alec built these on straddles to keep them raised above damp and beyond the reach of rats. The shepherd took immense pride in building and dressing these pikes of corn that had to live out of doors until threshing in the New Year.

The rush thatching was carefully roped with hanging stones tied to the ends. When the stacks started to settle and shrink the weight of the hanging stones automatically adjusted the ropes. The damp sheaves had been placed around the barn to dry out. We did not thresh all at once but did a little each day, sufficient to meet the animals' demands.

At nine o'clock I went off to bed anxious to get my clothes off and shake them free of irritating hayseeds. Ideas of prancing into Herself's room in order to admire my body in the long mirror possessed me no more. The hooting owls and soughing rowans made a sweeter music for me than Black Fergus's motorbike. The nights never seemed long enough for all the sleep my body demanded. I had graduated from a candle to an oil lamp, and having dived quickly into bed I read until my eyelids would stay open no longer. The broken dream of Proud Alexander's 'lovely Greece', and the vision of bronze athletes in a land of burnished sun was now usurped by an older love—Iceland.

Perhaps the birds who came migrant to our shores, particularly the fabled great northern diver, had first drawn me to the land of the sagas. Or perhaps Iceland fascinated me because my father talked of it more than of any other country. Apart from his interest in birds he had frequently talked of going to Iceland to see how they won their harvests, for the Icelanders' rainfall was even greater than our own. Of course, he never went. To be away from Blarosnich even for the few days of the Dingwall market were as much as he could endure.

My father loved reading. And this involved him in a constant source of annoyance with Herself, for he kept his night light burning into the small hours. Herself had never forgotten the Big Burning on the day of my mother's funeral, and had a fear of fire which only subsided when every light in the house was extinguished. I grew to accept her nocturnal tappings on my father's door, as I accepted the dogs' restless rattlings on their chains down in the yard. I could sleep through Herself's indignant knockings, but I always woke at my father's hoots of laughter. He was just like Peter bellowing at Old Mother Reilly in the cinema. Sometimes, unable to bear my curiosity, I got out of bed and went to discover what made him laugh so much.

My father preferred to read the amusing passage aloud to me rather than explain it. I settled beside him in the big bed while he read in a soft voice from the sagas. Bersi the Wise, Worm Wallet-back, Kettle Longneck, Grim Hairy-cheek all had a familiar sound as though Alec had learnt of them from his own father. I realized that Alec would have been a success in Iceland nine centuries earlier.

The sagas also seemed familiar because they mentioned so many places along our coast and among the islands. But though my father's readings enthralled me, sleep often stole me away so that the last warrior rode off to Thingskala Thing unnoticed by me. Often on these occasions I would wake suddenly, startled to find that Herself was not knocking to tell my father to put out his lamp, but to light it for getting up. I had passed the night in oblivion in the bed where I was born fifteen years before.

I could never be sure whether the fifteen summers and fifteen winters that had passed since Rhona brought me into the world were a long time or a short time. For me, it encompassed my whole life. But what had those years meant to my father? I could not devine his inner thoughts. But he was never morbid about my mother and seldom mentioned her. He certainly would never have kept the bedroom as a museum for her clothes as Herself did with The Captain's. Nevertheless, I suspected that his love and grief were profound. And this presented me with a problem. Would I ever find somebody to love in this way, somebody to whom I could surrender everything?

8

Harvest of a quiet eye

After morning milking I drove the cows out to pasture. Nearly all of them were crosses and had no claims to pedigree. Piebalds of every colour could usually show some strains of Shorthorn or Angus, Galloway or Ayrshire. My father's zealously watched herd of Highlanders did not mix with our humble cows nor come into the old grass parks. These aristocrats roamed the woody slopes of lower Craigclamhan. They never came into the byre for milking and bore their calves amongst the heather.

I was attached to the score of old ladies and heifers which formed the permanent harem of John the Shorthorn. The bull was the most timid of creatures when he meandered down the old drove road in autumn. He had not only aged but was overfat. When I took his harem to and fro he always lagged behind, more nervous of the ladies' crumpled horns digging his meaty flanks than of slipping on the ice. With terrible cries I would jump on his back. John the Shorthorn was venerable and commanded a certain respect. Although I had wandered in and out of the narrow bullpen ever since I could walk and had no fear of bulls, I had never tried the leap which I knew from reproductions of Knossos frescoes. I did not care to trust my luck as the young Cretans did by somersaulting between the bull's horns.

When the cattle crossed the ford I was free to return for breakfast. But often I went searching for mushrooms. They were not hard to find, for in the Earl's Park they seemed to have favourite places to grow in. Sometimes I arrived back at the house with my beret half full. By the time we had finished our porridge they would be welling with their own sweet juice on top of the stove, ready for succulent eating.

Those mellow October mornings began with the taste of mushrooms and crispy bacon and the sweet tang of salt-sharp and wood-smoke air. And from the highest rocks of Craigclamhan, echoing among the mountain crevices, rolling down from peaks and crags and dying away among the wren's haunts in the Earl's Park, a roar sounded. We stopped whatever we were doing to listen. Even Herself paused for a moment as she went to gather the duck eggs up by the fank. The glen reverberated to the deep bass snarling. High on the lochan moor the anguished bellowing never stopped. The rut had started.

The red deer, usually such silent grazers of our herbage floor, now proclaimed their mating season with an unforgettable fanfare. The deer did not stoop to surreptitious caterwauling after dark, but day and night alike blazoned their royal proclamation from every hill where a stag claimed his followers, defying the roaming bulls to steal one mate.

Each October the rutting season aroused our excitement as though we had never experienced it before. Herself would remind us yet once more about a former Earl of Morton who died from an antler graze, such a wound being fatal at the time of the rut. Mirren had a repertoire of fantastic bull-fights, not one of which she had witnessed herself because she was much too nervous even to cross the yard if our own dogs were having a friendly scrap. When the noble creatures sent their cries down from the crowning rocks, my father forsook his tractor and went off to deer-watch.

For eleven months the stags had run together, taking no interest in the milk or maiden hinds or their own calves. But this mixed male company of young staggies and proud twelve-pointer royals broke up with the first frosts of autumn. They went in search of the hinds, each claiming a dozen or more for his seraglio. The guarding of these, as well as their calves from previous years, caused all the roaring. The stag went up to the hill-crest and lifted his head so high that the antlers were laid across his back. Then his neck swelled up and his throat distended as he roared.

Many of the hills had several families of deer and so the roar continued more or less uninterrupted. The stags in possession of hinds did not so much bellow at each other as at those stags unfortunate enough not to have claimed even a single mate. The roaring stags defied the wandering Don Juans to come within range of their menacing antlers. But the unlucky and despised bachelors did not give up. The great beam of the masters' antlers, and the muscular power in their necks, did not deter the Don Juans from trying to lure one of the hinds away from the closely guarded circle. The young stags had waited six years to reach maturity and they became impatient, wanting to taste the experience of age.

I lay watching these wanderers pace around the mating grounds, and felt annoyed with their tactics. When the master deserted his hinds to drive off a rival, the other loitering bachelors did not dash in and grab at least one hind, as I so hoped they would. Despite the awful warning of Lord Morton's fate, I put my services at the disposal of the wandering love-lorn stags and let off a few ·22 shots to get the herds on the move and the old masters off their guard.

Although Herself liked the juicy steaks and fried patties for breakfast, she did not take kindly to the deer. In winter they were forced by snow from their high summer grazings and invaded all the parks. We might go out and find the horse park full of stags or hinds, each company a hundred strong. Grass was in short supply even for our own cattle during the winter months and so we had to be ruthless in driving these deer back to the snowy hills. When big herds broke into the turnip field little would be left by morning.

Fortunately for us, the dogs gave good warning of such night raids. Their barking became furious and excited. Herself got out of bed and was downstairs within seconds, her blinding electric torch playing into the darkness and picking up score upon score of deer stampeding across the stone dyke, their lithe, dark forms flowing over the walls like a school of porpoises. It was a terrible thing to go out in the morning and see the whole season's potato crop smashed and ploughed into the ground after one of these lightning visits.

In spite of Blarosnich's considerable acreage and the amount of stock it carried, we were comparatively poor. When the war came, the government recognized the sheep-farmer's plight and presented him with a subsidy of eight shillings for every ewe he kept. This was very nearly the price for which we had been selling our lambs. For years my father had preached the gospel of the plough. But nobody listened seriously until Hitler's war dractically reduced imports. The township, once so independent and isolated, was plastered with government posters 'PLOUGH NOW BY DAY AND NIGHT'.

For every acre that was ploughed we received another subsidy of two pounds. But although cheques for these fantastic subsidies increased our budget, the Western Highlands still remained the poor relative of British farming. We did not complain, except when the government reduced the subsidies. Farmers in the mild and fertile south could well do without the money because they had suitable grazing and crops for fattening their lambs and cast ewes ready for the butchers, whereas we had to sell them to a middle man who fattened them and got the profit.

But Herself made sure that we never incurred debts. It was a moral issue with her. To owe was a cardinal sin. 'Never let your gear owergang ye,' she would warn my father when he looked at expensive new machinery in the farming journals.

Though stiffly corseted by principles, she unbent enough to allow Roman Catholics the use of our bull, and she hung a photograph of Mr Churchill in The Room even though he was holding a brandy glass. But Herself never forgave the borrower who had no intention of paying back. The township folk wanted my father's time with the tractor, or the horses or the bull services, seed potatoes, a sack of greens, a puckle of hay, old clothes, a setting of turkey eggs, the use of the harrow or a little corn to get the pullets laying. Even the minister came borrowing my father's Highland regalia to wear at a religious conference in America. A lot of this borrowing was done on the 'never-never'. But none of it drove Herself so wild as when the same people came up to get their batteries charged, free of cost, as well.

My father had been imaginative enough to construct a little water mill on one of the burn's waterfalls which we used for crushing our oats. A small generator was connected to it, powerful enough to recharge wet batteries. Mirren had hers done for nothing and because of this everybody in the township with batteries thought they had a right to free re-charging. They would not personally face the old lady of Blarosnich. Instead, they gave their batteries to Mirren, who concealed them in her basket, and smuggled them in to my father with a soulful plea that he take them to the mill. Herself often suspected that such things were going on and she would walk over to the mill to see it with her own eyes. Every day for a fortnight there might be rows with Mirren and my father over the batteries. My grandmother was not mean. She knew that the electricity cost us nothing. But she objected to the idleness of some of the township who thought themselves much too grand to come up and lend a hand with the gathering of the potatoes which they were not reluctant to 'borrow'. How could they possibly be doing their work properly, she demanded indignantly, if they were able to spend afternoons listening to wirelesses? The accusation was unanswerable, especially as Herself, in spite of being an octogenarian, only just finished her work in time for the nine o'clock news at night.

Older people in the township who remembered my grandparents as the ferryman and his croft wife resented the intimacy between the two Big House ladies and Herself. They used the battery charging as a weapon against us. They put poison in the sisters' ears. Being childless, Miss Florence and Miss Philippa loved their nephew, Captain John, second only to their dogs. I only saw Captain John twice in my life, for although we took it for granted that he would take over the Big House and the sporting rights one day, we knew he did not like the Highlands. He rarely came to Scotland, though friends of his such as Eddie sometimes did. In spite of his army service Captain John was not made for guns and hard walking in the mountain passes, for he was a musician.

This fact involved us with the township wireless batteries, because the ladies' nephew could occasionally be heard on the air. In their enthusiasm Captain John's two aunts made sure that everybody knew of his concerts and the reluctant audiences therefore thought they had the right to have their batteries charged for the occasion free at Blarosnich. We were a very small community and issues became magnified out of all proportion. If anybody failed to hear one of Captain John's performances they complained to Florence of Arabia that my grandmother's meanness over the batteries caused the omission.

The absurd thing in all this was that although the ladies blew fantastic fanfares about the concerts, Captain John's name never appeared in print or on the wireless announcement. He did not play solo but only orchestral continuo parts. I thought madness would come over me when I was summoned to The Room because the fond aunts had called on us, determined that we must all listen, and had the wireless on full volume for Florence's ear-trumpet. To me, no one sound seemed distinguishable from any other. I only knew when Captain John played because Miss Philippa would bare her horse teeth and give us her refrain, 'What a touch! What a lovely touch!'

Although Captain John rarely visited the Highlands we frequently used his name. When asking the Big House sisters about their dogs it was diplomatic to enquire about their nephew almost in the same breath. Such enquiries often brought interesting answers because things were always happening to the musician. From his aunts' reports it would seem that fashionable women from the world over spent their time running after him. At one moment an Irish countess would be involved and the next an American candy heiress, and always a score of debutantes in the newspapers, one and all head over heels in love with Captain John.

Ascot races and royal garden parties, Mediterranean cruises and the Parisian demi-monde came to us in the Highland wilds, until the war stopped them, by means of press cuttings and stories from Captain John's doting aunts. But what I recall of the musician, who was middle-aged with baby-pink complexion and silver hair, took more colour from Eddie's accounts. After the little actor's visit to the Big House nobody remained in doubt as to why neither the Irish countess nor the American toffee queen succeeding in seducing the musical nephew.

Herself had seldom been so outraged as when a suggestion arose that Captain John should arrange for her to play the harp on the wireless. She only saw the idea as yet another reason for the township to demand more free re-charging of their batteries and as a wickedness for keeping Christian souls from their work.

I knew Herself was extremely generous to people stricken by genuine misfortune. But towards those who begged, borrowed, or stole because they were too lazy to work, she had no sympathy. And this may have been one of the reasons why Herself held Duncan son of Colin as the greatest of poets and heroes, quite apart from his personal connection with Blarosnich.

My grandmother went on and on at poor Mirren in the language of the ancient poet in the same way as she plagued her Maker on a Sunday morning about the foxes. The Maker, however, was only besieged one day in seven whereas Mirren had it every day. The Good Knight's words became as familiar as my father's grace prayers before and after food.

> *Who asks for little purses?*
> *Who calls for needles*
> *And a bad coin without a stamp?*
> *Who borrows neck-cloths and peacock's wings*
> *And old hats of shag?*
> *Who wants his dinner in the morning*
> *And seeks gleanings of rye?*
> *Who steals his lad's wages*
> *And asks for old carding-combs?*
> *Who seeks rennet that has lost its strength*
> *And desires greasy victuals?*
> *Who pleads young wines for his dogs and ferrets*
> *And takes the hinderlins of the oats?*
> *Who is sick when he is well*
> *And always wants butter on porridge?*

Herself's extreme care with management was an instinct, and not one which my father always admired in her. He called it meanness. Often when he wanted to buy more equipment for the farm, Herself would not let him have the money from her personal funds. If my father wanted a new plough or harrow for his beloved tractor, my grandmother would let it be known that throwing money away on such new-fangled things was displeasing not only to her but, by implication, to her Maker also.

Since we sold quite a number of eggs every week to the travelling grocer we knew that Herself's private funds existed. She also claimed all the money raised by produce sold to the Big House. At night Herself could be heard rattling about in The Captain's sea-chest putting the cash away—or so we thought. It was not until Herself died and my father went to the sea-chest for money to cover funeral expenses that we discovered the truth about Herself's meanness. Instead of finding the sea-chest deep in silver coins and banknotes, only a few shillings lay at the bottom. All the rest had gone long ago in gifts to township people. The noises of a miser counting money we had heard for years had been Herself at the sea-chest getting out the latest egg funds for Teacher to give to someone in the township on the following day.

Herself's reverence for money was not for money's own sake but for its usefulness. Her idolatry could therefore be excused to some extent. But her zealous belief in the virtue of thrift needed a strong constitution in her audience and I for one could not stand long sessions of her moralizings. On many occasions I felt thankful to be denied the warmth of our kitchen during the day. At least I did not suffer Herself's preachings as poor Mirren did. Yet Herself applied the same unyielding demand for rectitude to her own behaviour as she did to other people's. I knew she would never kneel on the bedside sealskin rug at night to pray if guilt weighed on her conscience. Before praying she would go to my father or to me, even when I was very young, and apologize if she had been unjust or angry with us. One of the many texts around the house reminded us of St Paul's admonition, 'Let not the sun go down upon your wrath.'

Herself loved Mirren as if she were her daughter. She gave her so many presents, and sent her mother a hot dinner every day, that the other township women undoubtedly looked with jealousy on Mirren's good fortune. It may well have been this jealousy which made the township women determined to squeeze all they could out of the Blarosnich cailleach.

I could also see, however, why the township folk thought of Herself as being hard and un-Christianlike. On many occasions I would willingly have stormed out of the house for ever.

146

Herself's old, leathery face was easy to read. Moods and tempers fled across its usual sunny countenance like thunderstorms. Over-brightness could, to the inexperienced, be misleading, like 'whirl-winds of the south', as Herself so frequently quoted the Prophet Zachariah.

This smile turned itself on me one night at supper. Herself could hardly wait for my father to finish grace before she spoke.

'You'll be glad to know your Bolshevik friend is in his rightful place.'

This puzzled me though I knew she referred to Eddie. The Big House sisters had taken up residence again and had been up to Blarosnich that afternoon.

I asked Herself what Eddie's 'rightful place' might be, wonder-ing if the little actor had at last got a break in the theatre.

'The house of correction,' she assured me with righteousness spilling over her face in a nod of Christian approval.

Eddie in prison! At first, I could not accept it. Then when the fact began to sink in, I was horrified. All I could see was Eddie's pale, unhealthy face and the intense blue eyes that became like a lost dog's when he was hurt. Eddie had been no more than a joke amongst us. His socialist teachings had made no more impression on traditional Highland beliefs and prejudices than five minutes of wan sun made on Craigclamhan's mid-winter snows.

'Lions,' said Herself with a note of triumph, 'are not frightened by cats.'

But to me, now that he had stuck by his pacifist opinions, Eddie *was* a lion, as brave, in his own funny way, as the sailors who drowned in the *Royal Oak*. He may have been a runt physically, far too delicate to stand our hard Highland life for long. But he had a lion's heart. I looked across the supper table at my grand-mother, wondering if with all her high morals and ideals she would have been prepared to leave Blarosnich and go to prison because of her principles. I knew she would not. She would have found some loop-hole in the Good Book to support a change of heart. I had always been sceptical of the Bible's bland ability to contradict itself.

Because he objected to helping in the war slaughter, Eddie was in prison. No wonder, now, I thought, that none of his promised letters had come. The terrible news humiliated me. I felt guilty also, for not taking him seriously enough. His talk of pacifism and politics had not all been clear to me and that I could not help. But at times I had joined with others in laughing at the comic manners of the tiny dandy. Now I understood his sincerity and how good a friend he had been to me.

That night I lay in bed trying to picture Eddie's grim surroundings. What was his prisoner's number? How long was his sentence? What did the cramped cell smell like at night? The little knowledge I had of prisons had come from Eddie. When he went away. I started to read Oscar Wilde. *The Ballad of Reading Gaol* haunted me with its starkness and lingering sadness.

> *that little tent of blue*
> *Which prisoners call the sky.*

Then my reverie was broken, for Herself stood at my door. The smug smile of the supper table had gone. In its place was a puckered concern, a look she often wore near bedtime as she was examining her conscience before addressing her Maker.

'We are supposed to pray for the prisoners too,' she said uncertainly. 'Och the puir wee man, I wonder if he has anyone to love him.'

Sympathy had taken the earlier harshness from Herself's voice and I forgave her.

The war seemed a long way from us once again. We rarely saw anything but its lighter side, and then usually in connection with the Big House. Florence of Arabia and her sister had returned for the duration, having found Sussex too near London for their liking. German bombers passing overhead and the daily likelihood of invasion were not the sisters' main source of irritation. Florence and Philippa desperately wanted to help the war-effort. But the south had so many helpers that the two ladies were taken for granted. Nobody made enough fuss, nor were they invited to positions of high responsibility in the women's war. Keen gardener though Miss Philippa was, not one County Herb Committee had invited her to lecture. Piqued, they packed up and left Sussex for the Big House. At least in the Highlands, they said, their work would be *appreciated*.

Their main work concerned wool. In common with thousands of people in Britain, the two sisters started to collect wool caught in hedges and fences over the hills. The wool was then washed and spun and converted into comforts for the troops. But Florence of Arabia did not stop there. She loitered around our fank asking for the awful clats which were cut from the hind quarters of scouring ewes. These too were washed and spun and farmed out to crofts for knitting.

Rallying to their new-found importance, Florence and Philippa devoted themselves wholeheartedly to their war-effort. The Big House drawing-room, symbol of ease in the midst of struggle, was turned into a collecting depot. Petrol rationing put their great open car out of action for all but the most urgent of journeys. But the sisters became more of a menace on the roads than ever before. They both rode three-wheeler bicycles with large sagging baskets suspended from handlebars and slung from the saddle. These baskets were crammed with rabbit skins for making gloves, wool gleanings and sacks of herbs. The sisters clambered about the off-shore rocks completely rejuvenated as they collected seaweed for the important agar-agar which was used in the development of penicillin.

The importing of herbs for medical purposes had practically stopped, and the government paid handsomely for foxglove seed and coltsfoot, clover heads and poppy petals, plantain leaves and dandelion roots, male fern and yarrow, meadowsweet and even ragwort, as well as the poisonous deadly nightshade and henbane.

Our sphagnum moss, which Sir Duncan and his men had used to cover their battle wounds on Flodden's Field, was now said not only to be as good a dressing as cotton-wool, but also able to absorb nearly twenty times as much moisture as manufactured dressings. Herself delighted to collect an apronful of the mossy hummocks and dry it on the front door steps.

For the two old ladies from the Big House there was moderation in nothing. They could seldom see over the handlebars piled high with herbs and wool, and often collided with each other or went head over heels into the ditch. Naturally, they accepted no money for themselves from the sale of the herbs which they organized the township children into collecting, and the proceeds went for comforts or Red Cross funds.

Florence and Philippa, panting up our long lane on their tricycles, came to Blarosnich nearly every day to consult Herself about herbs. If the circumstances prevented them from coming personally they sent letters by hand of the gamekeeper. Even the shortest note ended with 'God save the King.'

Herself had previously regarded the two sisters as a cross to be borne. But now her attitude changed. She gave full approval to the way that British people were coming to their senses and recognizing the value in the fruits of the Lord's creation, not only for medicine but for use at the table also. Dandelion fritters and yarrow purée would do their livers a sight more good than the tinned food which Herself believed all city people lived on exclusively.

In addition to the activities of their knitting comforts and herb campaign, Florence and Philippa took up another duty which high birth and privilege demanded of them. For a long time they had been seized by spy-fever. The sisters went down to meet the ferry in order to make sure that no spies came among us. Perfectly innocent strangers disembarking at the pier were considerably disconcerted by the fierce scrutiny to which the two odd-looking ladies with tricycles subjected them.

The sisters' own return to the Highlands had, ironically, trailed rumour with it. When little girls the ladies had been subjected to a German governess, as we all knew. Due either to this or to some unusual impediment of speech, they spoke in a way which, to a suspicious person, might suggest a Teutonic accent. Other factions maintained that the ladies' semitic features and curious trick of speech were signs of their East European parentage. Clearly they were foreigners and not to be trusted.

Once begun, the rumours persisted. It was not altogether surprising. The number and size of boxes and trunks which composed the sisters' entourage when travelling had always caused comment. On their return to the Big House from the south for the rest of the war, the number of boxes was doubled. In normal times, their big car had been able to transport it. But now my father and I had to go down with the tractor and meet them and help with the vast mountain of crated pictures and valuables being evacuated from their southern home.

It was not until later that we discovered some of the crates contained the dogs' luggage, or rather the dogs' gas-masks. Because the dogs had vomited when fitted with ordinary gas-masks, special gas-proof kennels had been built for them with valves operated by the animals' breathing. And we had to take a dozen of these boxes by tractor up to the Big House. Knight, Frank and Rutley had not returned alone to the Highlands but brought with them a number of their little pedigree friends from the south also, evacuated to avoid the German bombs.

The General had also come back along with the dogs and their special kennels. But the old man was quite unable to get up to Blarosnich without the car. Instead, he spent most of his time at 'H.Q.'. This was not, as might be expected, the ladies' drawing-room headquarters used as a clearing house for wool and for packing Red Cross parcels and for drying herbs. The General's H.Q. was a hide-out built in the big tree at the side of the house. Whenever the General could hold himself together, he passed hours in the hide-out trying to spot enemy planes or ships.

The sisters were never without field-glasses either. And after Rudolf Hess landed in Scotland they went armed up on the moors to look for German paratroopers. They never explained precisely what they would do if they discovered a moor full of Germans. No doubt they would have been as frightened as I was by something I saw near the lochan one morning. Mists threatened to settle for the day. Through my telescope I saw what appeared to be gigantic great-black-backed gulls tearing at a ewe's carcass. My dogs rushed madly to the unusual sight. Instead of taking wing as gulls usually did, the outsize species turned on the dogs. They were revealed as Florence of Arabia and Miss Philippa in their gas-masks clipping wool from a dead and decomposing sheep.

Neither of the ladies had suffered any hardships in their lives greater than the inconvenience of wartime shortages. These minor disadvantages no doubt loomed large to them, so that their wartime behaviour did them credit. They might easily have moped, and sat about in their large house complaining bitterly because they could no longer winter in Egypt or invite shooting parties. Instead they flung themselves with surprising energy and courage into their chosen war tasks. They were both old and frail and yet had spent at least two hours going up to the moor where the dead ewe lay. It would take them longer still to get home again laden with a few pounds of wool collected under the most filthy conditions from the dead sheep. In a sense, as far as they were able, they shared the hard work of the soldiers and sailors to whom their wool would go as balaclavas, scarves and mittens.

We were amused when the sisters took their wretched little lapdogs to their childless bosoms, but everyone had respect for their war-efforts. Herself felt ashamed to be caught still in bed one morning at six o'clock when Miss Philippa called to give us another photograph of Mr Churchill before going on up the hill for wool gleanings.

Nothing so dramatic as the changes at the Big House touched us at Blarosnich. The farm's everyday life involved us as much as it had always done, though I often brought a knapsack of herbs for the ladies when I came home from the hill. First frosts brought a long winter routine into my own life. The cattle stayed in the sheds and byre at night. Stars and moon would still be out when I opened the back door in the early morning and found my way through half-sleep and snow to the byre door.

The cows turned their brown mild eyes when I entered, wondering at my intrusion into their snug, dark world with the amber flood of light from a hurricane lamp. They went on cudding, lying relaxed in the untidy beds of bracken. Despite the heat built up during the night from the score of heavily breathing cows, their wide nostrils worked like pistons exhaling steam jets. The animals rose awkwardly and reluctantly from their comfortable postures when I started mucking them out. The midden outside was at a lower level than the byre itself. But by January the pile of manure had already risen higher than the floor of the byre. And as I passed day by day, week by week from one two-sided stall to the next, the heap of dung grew bigger. Herself delighted in this for she regarded a big dung-hill as a more reliable sign of wealth than pieces of paper called cheques.

Shovelling the dung out at seven o'clock every morning was hard work, but not so exasperating as the foddering. The long hay-barrow's sides were five feet high to keep the loose hay and straw from blowing away. But since it only had two wheels the winds roaring about Blarosnich often tumbled the whole thing over the moment I emerged from the hay-shed. It may have been good as fire prevention to build the new stackyard so far from the byre, but wheeling the precariously balanced hay-barrow through gales and snow often put me in a thoroughly bad temper.

I much preferred to carry a load of hay on a rope across my shoulders when I went to the outwintering bullocks on the lower braes, for this was easier than manoeuvring the heavy barrow. By the time I had cleaned the stables too, and given the horses a feed of oats, a spluttering noise came from the barn, a hard and mechanical noise out of harmony in our snow-silenced landscape.

The threshing machine's chugging began an hour's work which soon turned the draughty barn into a tropical hothouse. Lit only by the oil lamp the thresher's drum spun with demoniac force while my father fed it with sheaves. Showers of chaff and dust clogged the air like a sandstorm. While dunging the byres and stable I had peeled off my various layers of jerseys, but now shirt and vest came off also as I tried to clear the straw and shovel the corn into sacks. Ears, nose, mouth, trousers, boots and hair were filled with the pestilence of chaff and weed seeds and dry dust. Going back across the freezing yard afterwards to fetch the milking pails was like a taste of paradise.

I loved milking and found it relaxing compared with the other morning chores. Most of the cows were suckled by their calves in the fields during the summer months and had already run dry. Only half a dozen were hand-milked for our own needs and those of the Big House. Herself had given up milking and the cows had to be content instead with my tuneless singing.

Although they had been fed, the cows were often restless, some going down on their forelegs to steal a puckle of hay from a slow-

153

eating neighbour. Others tossed the hay with their horns in contempt because it contained more meadowsweet and yellow rattle than good grass. Any special feed to a particularly delicate beast caused jealousy among the others. It astonished me to see how their chained neighbours could contort their necks and stretch their tongues to get at the bran buckets.

As soon as I began to milk, the soft sound of the hot milk jets purring into the frothy bucket made its own soothing music. But I went through my limited repertoire of hymns and songs nevertheless, partly for the cows' sake and partly for my own. I liked singing despite an inability to stay in key. Hymns were easier for me than songs. The Maker in the sky, with His nightshirt and a face that turned sour at every human weakness, did not appeal to me, but I liked Jesus Christ and saw much to admire in His earthly life. So I sang my hymns to the Son rather than the cross old Father, spacing them out with such cradle and boating songs as I could manage.

The cattle showed no preference for sacred or profane, and there was a strong possibility that my voice left them unaware that they were being sung to. However, the quiet hour's milking induced a state of well-being in me and I looked forward to it quite as much as getting into bed with an interesting book.

Alec joined me in the byre to milk Minnie, his black Galloway, accompanied by the dozens of cats from all over the steading who shared most of Minnie's milk. I could never be certain how strongly Herself objected to Alec milking the house cows. Because of his heathen charms, she somehow suspected him of infecting the milk with pagan nonsense. And also, Alec was a 'wet' milker. He continually dipped his finger into the froth to keep the teats moist. None of us ever had an infection from either source, that I ever knew of, in spite of Minnie's generous udder being dedicated to:

> The teat of Mary
> The teat of Paul
> The teat of John the Beloved,
> The teat of God.
> Let flow your milk

From clover pasture
Water of three burns
Summer grasses, winter hay,
The music of the byre,
The voice of your Maker.

Minnie herself was a real besom and undoubtedly bewitched. Although old and hornless and forced to take sedate steps on account of her vast udder, she would toss the liveliest heifer that got in her way while she went down the steep, dangerous bank to cross the ford. Minnie could be relied upon to break into any field of corn or to spend a winter morning secretly munching mangels in the root house. Minnie was the worst blackmailer in the byre. When Alec departed for the lamb sales I had to milk her. Tying her legs to stop the kicking did not help to produce milk. Minnie held on to her supply until I brought her a bucket of bran, a luxury, of course, which she had never had from Alec.

Herself did not like the black Galloway and Minnie was well aware of this. She took revenge on Herself by sneaking into the orchard and devouring one of my grandmother's nightdresses or shifts from the clothesline as though it were the choicest rye grass. Minnie ruined my bicycle saddle in this way, obviously because I had shown her an unkindness. I shared Herself's enthusiasm when summer came and Alec packed up for Pitlobar taking Minnie out of our lives for a few months.

Although Alec moved into the bothie soon after the lamb sales he went back to Pitlobar for odd days and sometimes weeks until the snows came and made it impossible. Black Fergus and I often joined him in these far shore visits which usually involved tracking down fox-dens. Minnie, however, did not come and we always arrived back at Blarosnich to hear of the cow's outrageous behaviour from poor Mirren, who had to do the milking during our absence.

But the shepherd loved his cow and talked to her by the hour in Gaelic. Minnie was a strong link with Alec's past, for his mother reared her as a winter-dropped calf by the fireside at Pitlobar. And whether it was magic or no, sometimes Minnie would turn her large soft eyes on Alec and they would have a strange human expression as though she were fondly answering his Gaelic. When he packed up in spring with the white Aylesbury ducks in the horse panniers, Alec had no need to put a halter on Minnie. She followed the shepherd as though taught to heel like the sheepdogs, and knew the track through the mountains as well as the black garron.

In defiance of the cats wailing for Minnie's milk, I often found a robin on top of the midden when I came out of the byre with my full buckets. Full daylight had almost come by this time and after feeding the ferrets and driving the cattle out to pasture I was glad to go back to the house for breakfast.

I ate voraciously, hardly able to believe in my own hunger. Herself stood by, watching the enormous quantities of food disappearing like an avalanche, and looking for any tell-tale signs of decline in my appetite. There could not be much wrong with me, she said, if I kept up such a 'grand packed craw', one of her favourite expressions.

When I could take no more, in spite of protests from Herself, I called in at the barn for a half-boll sack of the corn we had threshed earlier in the morning. I carried the corn on my shoulder through the grass parks to the little mill which stood beside the pounding waters of the burn. Ordinary machinery had no appeal for me but I loved working the water-wheel. Opening up the channel and waiting for the great wheel's grinding, tumbling noise, slow and painful at first, then creaking louder as it gathered speed, gave me a strange thrill. I could understand that, somehow, the power in rushing wind or in flowing water could be made to turn wheels. I often wondered why my father did not get a wind generator for electricity like the one Miss Florence put in at the Big House.

Before the arrival of Dolly resplendent in shiny black enamel, Fergus had owned a bicycle as I did, in common with nearly everyone in the neighbourhood. But Black Fergus's model in no way resembled my rusty, upright machine inherited from my father, complete with carbide lamp and broad seat. Fergus's was a sports bike and it suited him. My grandmother thought his bike frivolous and even indecent. Perhaps she took exception to the way Fergus's bottom was up in the air while his broad shoulders and strong arms were bent low over the sensuous curves of the dropped handlebars. His saddle was very narrow with a long taper like a miniature goose in flight. The bike shone with chromium and had narrow red tyres, and suggested speed and elegance as though made specially for contact with his powerful young body. It was in every way another thing from my own heavy old warhorse.

But then everything about Black Fergus had a special quality. The hair oil he used on Saturday always seemed redolent of exciting places and associations. His clothes appeared to have a superior cut because his bright personality, his sharp, quick wit and his warm charm transformed them. Even ordinary wellingtons became romantic when he turned them down at the top like a buccaneer's boots.

As he flashed about the countryside on his sports bike, Fergus seemed like some black-haired angel speeding on celestial business. The occasions, however, on which Black Fergus's business was celestial were rare. But at night his bike had supernatural power because of its lamp and this fascinated me more than anything else, for it was a dynamo lamp and had a strong beam. One of the first birthday presents I could remember getting when I was a small boy was an electric torch. I took it to bed so that I could see the red glow from my cheeks when I put the torch inside my mouth or under my fingers.

Although such a torch was a modern thing, I could understand somehow that the cold light came from the batteries inside like the wick in the lamp drinking up oil below in the kitchen. The magic of the dynamo was not so readily understood. Black Fergus never let anyone use his sports bike except me. And I never tired of riding the gleaming machine and knowing that the efforts of my legs produced the fierce searchlight beam from the lamp, just as the plodding waters of the Labharag burn turned the wheel for our corn.

When I returned from the mill, leaving my half-boll of corn to be crushed during the day, the morning had changed from its earlier, indefinite half-night, half-day feeling. Now the full day colour had crept into moor and hill and sky, even if clouds were lowering and no slits of sunshine sped like wraiths across the lochan and mountainsides.

Those sunless days were often nothing but tones of grey in varying intensities, all of which dimmed as the day wore on and declined slowly to the impenetrable colours of night. One such day would follow another in grey monotony when the tuneless squelch of our boots blended with the melancholy dripping trees, the cough of ewe from the dank mists and the harsh complaint of geese trying to draw Mirren's attention about food. All day long the pewter-plated sea ran in and out of the rocky coast with thunderings and sinister suctions like a giant sucking a rotten tooth. But whatever the weather no respite would interrupt the work of a hill-farm.

Alec and my father went off after breakfast, perhaps to drain the new parks or plough the leas. Much of the land at Blarosnich which was reclaimed from bracken and swamp had only become sour and waterlogged for want of proper draining. I often worked alongside the two men digging out clumps of rushes or making a herring-bone pattern of feeders leading into main drains. My father derived an immense sense of achievement in restoring this land to use. It was as much his own province as the woodshed workshop. When time allowed, he spent hours patiently fighting the years of neglect by the previous, aged tenant.

Alec and I left him and set about our own work in the woods on either side of Stag's Pool. Unlike the Earl's Park, a wilderness which was never intended to be a wood at all, the burn slopes were old and solemn forest, pillared with oak and sycamore, hung with pine and spruce and lofty larch with straight, tapering trunks. Beeches dominated this mixture of trees, their massive boles and wide-spreading branches making cathedral aisles whose piers and ribs were not stone but smooth, grey bark. The rich harvest of beaten-gold leaves from the beeches provided a sumptuous carpet, and here almost no weeds sprang up. Even the shapeless juniper failed to get a footing under the dense foliage. Along the banks of Labharag burn alder grew well in the rich humus washed down from the hanging woods. And there was ash enough and birch to keep the willow-warblers happy.

The tiny warbler was already far away in Africa when Alec and I resorted to the forest on mid-winter afternoons to fell timber. The unbroken frosts seemed to have checked all growth although a sinister life bloomed on decaying trees. Huge beef-steak fungi flourished on the oaks. Row upon pulpy row of dryad's saddle climbed the sycamores. Sulphur tuft sucked the last vestige of life out of rotting stumps.

The tracks were still fresh where deer had come to rummage for lichen. Now that the rut was over the stags came down together, for higher up the moors of blaeberry and sedge were covered with snow. The stags made the beech cathedral aisles into a monastery at night. Standing like silent, brown robed monks, the deer waited in the lower braes for the ring of the axes to end and for us to leave. Then, in slow procession they moved into the woods again.

Alec and I made a good woodcutting team, as we cross-cut a gale-felled birch or the withered arms of an oak struck by lightning in a summer storm. Alec had many stories about lightning striking men and animals, and above all oaks. He would never shelter near one in bad weather, although I never saw lightning actually strike the heart of a great oak, causing it to explode. Of all the trees in the forest, the oak undoubtedly seemed to attract lightning the most. From a single flash the whole side of an indomitable old tree could be wrenched open and laid bare to rot until some later gale finally brought it down.

We used a horse to drag the five-foot lengths of timber home. Often, as Alec and I left the wood, we would see that the moon was up again. We still had work to do. By New Year, when the tups were home from the ewes, we had opened up the silo. The cattle went into a frenzy of delight over the new war diet of silage, especially the matured stuff near the bottom which for texture and strength resembled Alec's plug tobacco. The silage was fed to the cows in the byre before the evening milking.

Often, as I came down with my barrow from the silo, I would suddenly see Minnie in the moonlight. She not only looked at me with disdain, as though to tell me they had been due in from the frosty park half an hour before, but she ran her milk on the cobbles to prove it. Minnie had opened the gate and headed the homeward herd. Not even John the Shorthorn dared to step in front of that Galloway lady as she dashed into the byre to devour more than her ration of rich silage before being chained for milking.

The second milking was more enjoyable for me than the morning session. We took it easily and sang many hymns and songs, for a long, dark evening stretched in front of us offering little to do. With my head leaning against the cow's flank and the milk flowing smoothly and the warmth of the animals' breathing mixed with the clean smell of freshly strewn bracken, I would not have wanted to rush off to Black Fergus's motorbike even if he had got petrol to make it possible.

After the last pail of milk had been strained, and the dogs and cats were fed, we took a bucket of hot water to wash ourselves in the lean-to store-house before supper. Herself liked Alec to linger by the kitchen fire as long as possible after we had eaten. But the shepherd preferred his own hearth in the bothie and the company of his dogs from which he was only separated when he came into our house and the kirk.

I always made a round of the calf-sheds and stables last thing at night, and looked into the byre to make sure that no thieving cows had strangled themselves on their chains. Then I went up the bothie's outside steps. Alec seldom lit his lamp because he liked to sit in front of the log fire where the dogs stretched and yawned, blinking and winking in the field of flames. This bare room of whitewashed stone walls, containing nothing but a bed, a chair, a small table, seemed wonderful to me. A magnificent patchwork quilt made by Alec's mother covered the iron bed and grouped around the fireplace were many illustrations of Bible stories.

Now that the Big House was in residence all the year round and required winter milk, we tried to have several cows calving late. On these occasions I spent the night, and probably the early hours of the next morning also, over at the bothie, because I would not then miss the sound of the labouring. Alec ranked these as red-letter occasions too. Although we had worked side by side all day in the fields and woods, our midnight sessions together had a special atmosphere. I would read to him. We might take up the Icelandic sagas for an hour before turning to the local newspaper. Alec wanted the deaths and marriages, the appointments of new ministers, the coming of soldiers home on leave. He also listened avidly to all the advertisements of grazing to let, the sale of pullets on the point of laying, wool prices, ferry sailings, and the contents of gentlemen's residences up for auction.

Then there would be a comforting silence in the room as the Field of Sighing gathered its winter strength and the winds lifted the draught-proof sack from the bottom of the door and flung it across the bothie. We would sit close to the fire enjoying the hush within and the storm without. Then Alec would recognize a particular log burning that had given us trouble in the forest or one which had been washed up as driftwood on the spring tides. Perhaps a piece of damp holly sizzled there which had been a torture to cut and even now dribbled a frothy protest on the hearth. It might remind the shepherd of the she-holly that once stood before the priest's house in Eriskay, though the tree had been cut down many years before he was born. A century had passed since Alec's grandfather was a young man and carved a cup out of the Eriskay holly wood.

'A vessel of she-holly is a power in the land,' the shepherd would say fondly as he got up to find the wooden cup to give his dogs a drink of milk out of it to save them from various ills, though the proper use of the cup was for children to sup goat's milk to cure whooping-cough.

Sometimes Alec talked of death and the manner of dying. He recalled that his mother had a grand passing despite the hen crowing like a cock. Old Maggie had died with a smile on her face having recognized her husband and his dogs waiting for her beyond the river flowing by the Throne of God. Alec never doubted that the dogs scratching themselves before the hearth now would also be sniffing after his white robe in heaven. Perhaps

Charlotte Mew wrote *The Old Shepherd's Prayer* with somebody like Alec in mind:

Heavenly master, I wud like to wake to they same green places
Where I be know'd for breakin' dogs and follerin' sheep.
And if I may not walk in th' old ways and look on th' old faces
I wud sooner sleep.

Those nights, unpredictable in duration, exciting in their atmosphere of suspense, gave me some of my richest hours at Blarosnich. Sometimes a knock louder than the windbreaks being flailed on the roof would announce Black Fergus's arrival. He always knew when one of our cows was springing. Fergus loved the night as I loved the sun. Petrol rationing had not brought his night roaming to an end. When no petrol could be spared for his motorbike, he resorted to the neglected sports bike, and if the snow was too deep for its thin red tyres, he walked. Fergus went from one croft to another until the last door was bolted against him and the people went to bed. Then he would go down to the coastguard station for another hour.

When I sat up in the bothie on those nights waiting for a calving, Black Fergus never appeared before midnight. And although we had only seen each other a few hours before evening milking he would already have something new to tell Alec and me. Like everyone else, Alec enjoyed Fergus's company even so late at night. If the birth was over by the time he called, Fergus lingered by the bothie fire just the same, and often spent the rest of the night sleeping in the chair. Before his parents were up and about, Fergus would be away off over the snowy hills to Sallachie. Neither Sandy nor Violet were early risers, a fault which Herself regarded as sinful as Violet's reading of tea-leaves.

All the time, above the shift and crack of logs in the fire, and the groanings and grumblings of the dogs in their sleep, and the striking of hooves on the stable cobbles by a restless horse, and above the winds' lament and the sound of my own voice reading the sagas aloud, or Black Fergus's jokes, we would be listening for movements from the byre. When they came, I lit the hurricane lamp and led the way down. The dogs came too, for like all

Alec's animals they were psychic and knew when a cow was calving. They knew also that if they hung around the proceedings with their tongues lolling out, they would eventually be rewarded with the first milking of the rich yellow beestings.

When a heifer calved, it was sometimes necessary for both Alec and me to pull on the soft emerging hooves. After wiping the helpless calf dry with hay, a bucket of warm gruel was brought for the cow. To an accompaniment of soothing, gentle words Alec rubbed the swollen udder and eased the warty teats before taking the thick, creamy colostrum.

No matter what the hour or mood of the night, I could be certain that Herself would be up, as anxious for news of the new calf as the dogs were for the beestings. A shawl covered her flowing nightdress and pulling it closer against the sharp night air she hobbled over to the byre door. She did not speak or interfere, but stood by in case of difficulties.

When my grandmother was very old, I tried to spare her this dangerous exposure to the night air. As soon as the new calf was safely delivered I dashed over to the house and announced the sex of the new animal, for this was of major interest.

'A fine bull calf,' I would shout excitedly, running up the stairs.

But it made no difference. Not until she had put on outdoor boots over her bed-socks, and clambered over snow, or navigated a yard treacherous with ice, and had seen the calf with her own two eyes was the old lady of Blarosnich happy.

9

Different destinies

All at once it seemed as if the war was exacting too heavy a toll from Florence of Arabia and Miss Philippa. Both ladies sank visibly away, leaving us more amazed than ever that so little flesh on so brittle bones could be capable of such strenuous war-effort. Why the south-west gales simply did not lift them bodily off their tricycles and carry them across the Atlantic, we could not tell. The sisters shrunk so that they resembled the fragile Dresden figurines in the Big House.

Everybody remarked upon the two ladies' sudden change in appearance and many forecast their imminent decease. The facts explained everything, as I saw one afternoon when Miss Florence came struggling into Blarosnich with a hefty log of beechwood. The Timber Controller had declared it unpatriotic for women to wear high heels. Florence and Philippa had always appeared to be walking on stilts. Even their outdoor shoes for the moors consisted of solid, built-up platforms like well-made surgical shoes.

This gain in stature was declared to be an unnecessary luxury. The timber for the satisfaction of female vanity in the form of high heels involved seamen's lives. To the sisters, however, it was not a frivolous vanity, for the height given them by their Maker was considerably below normal. To boost the Maker's gift of less than five feet and to put them on some sort of level with other people they wore absurd shoes which gave them at least another two or three inches. Accordingly, when proper built-up shoes became unpatriotic, nothing daunted they brought the beech log to my father and asked him to convert it for their purpose.

Odd requests had become familiar, and this one was no more odd than many previous ones. The sisters' enthusiasm never died. With an extraordinary fecundity of imagination they always had some new scheme for helping Mr Churchill or buying Spitfires for Lord Beaverbrook. The number of visits up our lane was probably exceeded by the flood of letters to the Minister of Food containing instructions as to how he should keep the nation's larder full on Britain's own home produce.

In those days the Minister of Food, Lord Woolton, was nationally known as 'Uncle Fred'. Big House conversation was often started by 'Uncle Fred has got a big surprise coming to him', as though the ladies had decided to disinherit Captain John in favour of Lord Woolton.

Once, in the middle of working a hay park, Miss Philippa burst upon us in a fever of excitement. She handed spoons round and we had to taste the hot dish with which she had tricycled all the way from the Big House. Flapping her broomstick arms at the surrounding hills, Miss Philippa promised all sorts of incredible riches in a very short period. A factory would be built immediately and food from the great sea of bracken would shortly be gracing every table in the kingdom, while Uncle Fred himself would be invited up to open the great enterprise. What we had been given to sample from the dish was none other than Miss Philippa's discovery—new to her but certainly not to my grandmother. Alas, in spite of the young bracken tips being substituted for asparagus at the Big House, nothing came of the scheme and Blarosnich went without its factory. We had enough to do trying to win our own harvest without running after the sisters on bracken-cutting expeditions. Nevertheless, my father did endeavour to remount Florence and Philippa on beechwood stilts and everyone was full of unfeigned enthusiasm for Party Day.

The crew from one of the naval ships which patrolled our part of the coast was to be entertained in the Big House grounds. Florence of Arabia and her sister went about for weeks beforehand instructing us in the art of being cheerful and kind to the sailors. Preparations included barons of venison, and the roasting and casseroling of game and poultry. Herself caught the mood of excitement and spent days baking shortbread, quite in ignorance of the two sisters' intention that it should be washed down by copious draughts of burgundies and clarets from their own cellars. My grandmother would not go beyond the farm marches of course, and was possibly the only soul in the whole district who did not attend the party. Even the gamekeeper's Wee Free wife, who was a much more rigorous religious extremist than my grandmother and kept the Sunday silence when nobody in the house might speak, deemed it a national duty to attend and be 'jolly'.

If the party turned out to be nothing like the intention, it certainly did not represent the sailors' idea of shore leave. Miss Florence's and Miss Philippa's interpretation of being cheerful was to paint their faces like glowing suns and clutter themselves with every jewel they possessed. Their few remnants of hair were given an over-generous rinse of bright ginger that clashed violently with the masks of red make-up. Even for the local people, accustomed to Big House eccentricities, the sight of the two ladies in party dress was staggering.

As part of her war-effort Miss Philippa organized various meetings in the schoolhouse with visiting lecturers who came to tell us how to help win the war. Only one point of these lectures seemed to have penetrated Florence of Arabia's silver ear-trumpet. Servicemen on leave should be offered hospitality, especially hot baths.

Florence therefore caused not a little astonishment on Party Day when, looking like a painted bird on a Red Indian totem pole, she invited every sailor to go upstairs for a nice hot bath.

Psychologically it was wrong. The sailors were not offended as I had been in London when Aunt Jessie suggested I needed a change on my arrival. They merely wrote off Miss Florence as crackers. The party must presumably be as crackers as the old girl, they thought, and this proved to be true when the sisters asked them to join in the games. The sort we played at township socials were no good to boisterous sailors fresh from the sea. They wanted girls. We had none, at least only a few as young as Mirren, and even then worse-looking than our maid who was not exactly a sailor's pin-up.

Florence of Arabia and Miss Philippa twittered and fluttered among their guests like two exotic cockatoos, oblivious of the fact that the party was a desperate failure. The young men soon grew bored with our rustic entertainments and the day was only saved from total collapse when the poor General was obliged to desert his post at the bar and the sailors helped themselves in a free-for-all.

The alcohol soon dispelled the sailors' gloom and broke down the barriers between them and us. By the time the fancy dress parade was announced the Big House lawn buzzed with talking and laughing and singing. Everybody felt ready to do the parade justice. It consisted of children except for two women who, horror upon horror, were garishly dressed in imitation of poor Miss Florence and her sister. They looked as brawny as the Big House ladies were thin. The situation became comic and tragic all at once, a monumental error of taste. I knew immediately from Miss Florence's face that she had received a mortal wound.

One of the two garish, coarse women was Black Fergus dressed up. The other one was a sailor. Black Fergus had taken him back to Sallachie as soon as he saw the two sisters' party get-up and knew there was to be a fancy dress parade. They dressed up in Violet's clothes and rushed back to the Big House again. The effect was devastating, the laughter loud and pitiless. Even Duncan's religious wife cried with laughter at the two pantomime dames who carried cairns with make-shift modesty belts. Black Fergus had always been a clever mimic of voice as well as manner. As he walked round with the parade, he talked to the dogs in Miss Philippa's Teutonic-tinted voice and the spectators went into fresh paroxysms. With a cry the watching sailors flung themselves on Black Fergus and his navy friend and would have stripped them completely.

Later, after more drinking and ragging, the crew returned to the ship in high spirits. It had, after all, been a good party and they went away saying that although the old birds were crackers they certainly knew how to lay the liquor on.

When it was all over I went back to the Big House with my father to take the benches back to the schoolhouse on the tractor. The garden was uncannily still and silent. Only the white feathers from Fergus's burst bosom pillow blew across the grass. Neither of the sisters appeared and the housekeeper looked as if she had been to a funeral instead of the merriest party in local history. And from the lady housekeeper we learnt of the sisters' mortification at Black Fergus's and the sailor's impersonations. They were humiliated, not only on their own acount but because their dogs had also been mocked. In one moment, like Belshazzar at the feast, Florence and Philippa realized how the township really regarded them. They did not mind being made fun of, but they knew in spite of all their work and generosity that the local people neither loved nor wanted them.

From that day, Florence and her sister withdrew. The Big House seemed to shutter its windows against intruders. The gates of its drives seemed to be closed inhospitably. Miss Florence's tricycle never appeared on the roads again nor was Miss Philippa's cracked voice heard singing one line behind everybody else in kirk. They gave up first aid classes. Spy hunts on the hills were called off and the sisters led no more teams of jam-makers on fruit-picking expeditions. The ladies' sudden withdrawal left a curious and unexpected gap in local life, as if they were dead. All we knew of their war-effort now was through the housekeeper who was sent out to collect wool and distribute knitting.

Nobody could have guessed that the two old ladies would be so susceptible. During the previous winter, the first they had ever spent in residence at the Big House, they had asked Black Fergus to dress up as Father Christmas at a party they gave for the township children. And at Hogmanay the sisters invited Fergus to perform the first footing, to be the first person over their doorstep on New Year because of his black hair. But the raven hair had not brought them a lucky year.

Fergus's debonair charm and irresponsibility usually healed any wound he caused by youthful excess. But the balm of his smile did not reach the Big House ladies. Wounded they were and wounded they remained, right through the rest of the war, until shortly after V.E. Day when they moved away from the Highlands for ever.

Yet nobody blamed Black Fergus. His impersonation of the

sisters at the fancy dress parade had only been a joke, and crude though it was, no particular insult or malice had been intended. The long-term effects could not possibly have been foreseen. Afterwards we all felt partly responsible, as we had done when Niall the Ferry rifled Susie's grave. None of us could be described as a dog-lover in the ladies' usage of the term. Neither the crofters nor the tenant-farmers would have indulged in lap-dog worship which the sisters understood as kindness to animals. Their genteel ideas did not fit in with working people who had working dogs. Now that rapport with the Big House was broken, looking back, we were amazed that it had lasted so long.

Herself was upset and very angry with Black Fergus. My grandmother had never been able to understand how two educated women could devote their lives to lap-dogs. She resented the sisters bringing their spoilt animals into The Room. She considered it wicked of Miss Philippa to preach about saving food because of the war, when, as everybody knew, a dozen lap-dogs at the Big House were having better fare than people in the township. On many occasions Herself almost dropped her diplomacy to tell the two tiny women what she thought of them.

Their private war on wood-pigeons brought Herself to boiling point. Florence of Arabia would come panting up the Blarosnich lane and announce triumphantly that the gamekeeper had shot another pigeon. With immense self-satisfaction Florence would say that 749 corn seeds had been counted in its craw. It annoyed Herself that Miss Florence had time to waste in counting corn seeds in every pigeon shot while my grandmother still had to work fourteen hours a day. But worse was the irritation of listening to Florence's claims about saving the nation's corn by shooting pigeons, when, down at the Big House, pounds of good meat were being consumed by Knight, Frank and Rutley and their horde of friends. Herself ground her teeth and muttered when Miss Florence began to talk her nonsense about wood-pigeons. But she never muttered loud enough for the words to penetrate the silver ear-trumpet.

Nevertheless, Herself was extremely angry with Black Fergus, for Miss Florence and her sister were to be pitied rather than mocked in public. Herself dismissed the whole party as the work of the Devil, with Florence and Philippa as much at fault as Black Fergus. They had provided the alcohol which not only made Fergus lose respect for his elders but for himself also.

Herself admired Black Fergus as a wonder and genius at routing the fox and a fast clipper at shearing-time. But she remained suspicious of his character, especially after the fancy dress fiasco. Nothing goaded her quite so much as the fruity 'Amen' which Black Fergus still gave at the end of grace. She felt sure that Fergus was mocking her and her religion as he had done the Big House ladies and their dogs. The innocent delight of a Saturday ceilidh would be broken if Herself heard Mirren scream because Black Fergus had pinched her bottom.

Fergus was almost a man now, and I too had changed. But though I preferred early bed and a book to late night jaunts on the motorbike, Black Fergus remained my best friend. Both my father and Herself frowned on any activity which interfered with work on the farm, so Fergus and I kept our daytime meetings secret. We could not always invent fox troubles or an afternoon's ferreting that would take us away from woodcutting or mending the long, rutty lanes to our homes.

We did not so much conspire against our families as seek each other's company because we belonged to the same generation. Alec's tales of old porpoise hunters and of cows that calved years before I was born, always pleased me. I derived a warm sense of well-being when my father read the sagas to me in bed while all the winds of Blarosnich battled at the windows. Yet I could not talk to them as I did with Black Fergus. He understood why I wanted to escape the monotonous hay park and plunge into the burn. Only he could tell me where the young coastguards had laid the Big House maids.

Going back to the mill after dinner to collect the sack of oats which would be crushed by then, I looked out for signs of Black Fergus. He might be curled up in one of the empty tar barrels we used for storage, hiding like Ali Baba, to jump out and frighten me. Or he might be lying on his stomach, chin propped in hands, legs idly waving in the air, completely lost in a sexy novelette the coastguards had given him. Considering the extraordinary schemes we contrived in order to meet every day there was little of importance we could talk about.

I would report on any gossip Postie brought us and say what callers had been to Mirren's croft. And this sounded dull compared with Black Fergus's news, for he prowled around the countryside at night visiting the camps as well as the crofts. Did Teacher know, he would ask me, that a couple of drunk soldiers had slept in the schoolhouse shed and made themselves cocktails with methylated spirits?

I must go down, he would say, to the pier station and see the new coastguard who took size thirteen in boots. Black Fergus had an unshakeable faith in the theory that boot sizes were indicative of virility, the larger the boot the greater the virility. When challenged, Fergus would cite the minister's boots which were tiny.

'It goes to prove it,' Fergus said confronting me with this irrefutable evidence. The new coastguard's boots filled Black Fergus with a restless, envious awe as though his own chances with the local girls were gone for ever. But it would take more than boots to depress Fergus, and soon he was talking about the twelve-pound lythe landed by the ferryman or a fight between his cairn bitch and a wild cat. And there was always some erotic dream which took him an hour to tell and left me wondering if it had not been myself wandering through those gilded halls of wantonness.

Black Fergus and I always exchanged our night dreams, but I well knew that my friend had a recurrent day dream which was only hinted at. It stood between us like a gulf. My father's tractor and Dolly the motorbike still held his interest. Fergus lived in a world I was not only ignorant of but also indifferent to. Planes and tanks fascinated Fergus, but more than anything, he wanted to go to sea. Submarines had become his secret love.

And so, inexorably, our lives took on their different destinies. I knew nothing would stop Black Fergus from joining the war. The happy and carefree sailors at the Big House party had only unsettled Fergus. He was envious of their tight-fitting uniform, symbol of the manhood denied him on the rocky, deserted hills of

Sallachie. Fergus had not meant to hurt the old ladies by dressing up. He had always been on good terms with them in spite of poaching their game birds. At the party, Fergus drank too much wine in order to keep pace with the hardened sailors and had dressed up to win their applause and prove his own bravado.

When an old shepherd was found to take his place, Black Fergus went off leaving us with numb feelings. The navy accepted him and long letters began to arrive at Blarosnich. They made it clear that Fergus had found the life he wanted. Nothing my friend had done was ever dull or sordid and never could be, even if his doings had not always been kirk-blessed. I missed Black Fergus in a way I had not dreamt possible, and I felt alone, especially as midwinter set in with iron fastnesses of ice that held the earth in its bitter grip.

Neither spade nor harrow made the slightest impression on the hollow-sounding fields. Our cows made the noise of glass being shattered as they carefully put their hooves through potholes glazed with ice on the drove road out to pasture. Even Minnie the Galloway took no chances in the familiar and treacherous holes which, by the next morning, would again be covered by panes of brittle ice. The season of laying drains and watching gulls wheel and turn in the wake of the plough would not come round again for a long time.

The sky grew daily more leaden and heavy. Waking up one morning to a new light I found the Field of Sighing changed. The well-known leas and grass parks, hills and valleys, moors and mountains emerged in a sparkling radiance. A new, brilliant white world captured the sunlight in its billions of crystals and glowed in a pink ambience. Woods and hedgerows bloomed with crisp snow which would have shamed the whitest of June's guelder-roses. Muddy lanes and soiled fields, deer skulls on the hill and pools of tractor oil in the yard lay hidden beneath the pristine perfection of the snow's planes and deep wind-sculptured curves heaped and scooped like shining ploughshares.

Craigclamhan and Craighar were clothed anew in grandeur, seeming to rise higher than before the snow fell, to command a new nobility. Hills that yesterday had been dim beneath the heavy sky now took on clear-cut forms in the prismatic light. Last memories of lapping in the soggy meadows and the rites of harvest were blotted from the fields. Snow covered the yellow tracks marked by swathes of rotting hay.

But already these pure plains bore hieroglyphic messages of life. Printed across the smooth mounds and hollows, delicately incised in the dazzling marble of the drifts, was a network of spoors. We could tell at a glance whether wild cat or fox had made the first visitation to the hen house, or both. The neat, four-toed footprint of the fox and its grey droppings sent Herself into new wailing and quoting from The Tailor's poetry. The wild cat escaped more luckily from my grandmother's invective, because this wily animal often received praise for its hunting prowess after voles and mice in the grass parks. The stoat turned pure white also and left his track down to the warm twilight amongst the cornstack straddles to put the rats to battle.

As I cleared a way through the drift against the back door and across the yard to the byre, a sense of discovery possessed me, like archaeologists bursting into a tomb-chamber sealed for centuries. Writings in the snow told where blackbird and robin, chaffinch and sparrow had been. And later, when Mirren scattered food for the hens and turkeys, the sharp but frail footprints would be joined by those of bramblings and redwings.

That first day of snow surprised us year after year as though we had never seen its all-pervading splendour, as though its ermine pall burying the marked stains of the past was something we did not know how to comprehend. We knew only too well that now had begun the cruellest period in our calendar. The cows in the byre failed noticeably as the short days and long silent nights became weeks and the first Christmas snows merged into an arctic February. Although the cattle could not get at the grazing under the unrelenting blanket, at least they had hay and silage and warm bedding indoors. But stags and hinds and their young calves got very little even after they dug through the hard snows and reached the mosses and withered grass underneath. Driven by desperation they attacked farm stocks, for these were the only oases in the limitless white desert.

Our sheep were not so resourceful. They could sense a coming storm and get to shelter by a bog bank or dry side of a dyke, but snow defeated them. As hunger overtook them, and they tried to get over drifts, the snow caught and balled in their long fleeces. So once more the shepherd returned to the hill perhaps to find a puckle of ewes keeping themselves alive in icy caves between the drifts which their warm breath kept from collapsing on them, or he would discern a smudge out on the moor and recognize it as a gimmer balling badly.

Going through these heavy snows, with a pair of dogs at heel, was not easy, though it did not compare with the wild lambing days of spring. Once more, the wind rather than the sun befriended us. Admittedly the raw, slicing winds blew the first snowfalls into treacherous drifts, but the same blasts also carved out pathways and helped to cement the sleuch underfoot. Huge icicles like aeons-old stalactites hung in the burns and sometimes broke off with alarming tinkling sounds.

And just as we could trace robbers' spoors to the hen house, so I could tell which way Alec and my father had gone, because all three of us used a common path up to the fank parks and lower braes beyond. Even as a boy I was never told by my father where and when to go to the hill. Instinct was our governing impulse as well as the animals'. If I was reluctant to get out of bed Herself hammered on the door and announced that the cattle were waiting, or 'There's heavy plodding to A'Mhin-choiseachd.' Up on the wide open moor it was The Easy Walking. Not so were the heathery braes which supported tufts and hummocks and deep snow and made the going arduous.

At no time in the year did I dwell so much on Alec's stories as during my snow rescue expeditions. From time immemorial there had been bad winters in the neighbourhood. Since the days when sheep were first introduced on a large scale some had perished in drifts every winter. All my life I had seen wood-pigeons robbing the garden greens and deer invading the parks. Alec's more sombre stories told of other shepherds foundering in snows of long ago, or of Victorian travellers losing their way, of drunks overcome by the drugging snow-sleep and sad accounts of children who never returned home from winter school. Best known of the winter tales concerned Long Sammy of the Coach and Pair. Gambling debts and debauchery ruined this proprietor and one night, as he forced his horses along the shore road, they plunged into a drift and went over a cliff high enough to kill both horses and sever Long Sammy's leg. That place is still known today as The Fall of the White Mares. Sammy's own memorial became as famous a landmark in the district as the peak of Craigclamhan. The tall obelisk which Sammy left behind him posed for me the problem of his nickname 'Long'. I never knew whether it referred to his own height or that of his graveyard stone.

When first built the obelisk was taller than today and a part of it is missing. A jagged scar like a lightning-blasted oak branch marks the top. Two different stories were told about the broken obelisk. According to Alec, when Sammy's soldier son returned to inherit the estate he found so many creditors that the lands had to be sold. On seeing the splendid mausoleum Sammy had erected for himself at great cost, the son brought a sledge-hammer and a ladder. He went up and with a single powerful blow knocked the top off and also broke his own arm. A divine punishment, Alec would add, for desecrating his father's grave, extravagant though that grave may have been.

Herself's version of the event was that after Sammy's death the architect who designed the monument returned with other creditors and demanded his fee. When turned away by Sammy's son, the architect then struck the obelisk saying 'He had only a stump of a leg himself in any case.' Herself dismissed this with 'There's nowt sae queer as folks', usually meaning the wealthy. If some of the local stories of the gentry in bygone days were true, Florence of Arabia's eccentricities were normal by comparison.

Perhaps the obelisk's top was felled during some other incident, but whatever the truth of the matter, the stone served as a landmark and we could forecast the weather from its visibility and its appearance of being near or far. Long Sammy's obelisk had associations with ghosts too. Many of Alec's stories began 'It was a night of stars and the Devil could be seen from as far as Ferryman's Park sitting on top of Long Sammy.'

As I wandered over the hills of winter I always stopped at the braes before going across the moor. In sunlight the snows became rose-coloured and our sheep, which in summer looked as white as clouds, now were dirty against the brightness of the unsullied snow. There was no need to use my glass in order to see the top of Long Sammy. Although the snow brought a profound silence to the white-pink world, there were some weird noises which enhanced the void. Perhaps long ago those noises may have been interpreted as the Devil shouting from the broken tip of Long Sammy. But I recognized only too well the uncanny scream of a vixen desiring her mate and the disyllabic note of red-breasted merganser. All around the coast the extraordinary courtship of ducks had begun. Such displays of passion in the middle of the coldest weather always seemed as unlikely to me as did the coming of the snow itself. Yet both happened and could not be denied. Weird though the drake's serenade might be, gracefulness informed the aquatic dance. In contrast was the fierce battle which took place when the powerful muscles of a large eel were fixed, writhing, in the merganser's beak.

Certain corners of the woods and moors remained curiously free of snow. Here the vermilion dog-hips glowed like hot embers and mother's heart already had white flowers on top of the rows of seed cases like ancient shepherds' purses. In such places as these I would sit down to eat my piece. The warmest of these sheltered corners always seemed to be near the whin bushes which, besides having a nutty fragrance, were ablaze with yellow blossom, even in early February. Sheltered as best as possible, I set out my piece, making something of a ceremony from this break in the long trek. And the climax of the ceremony was to re-read the latest letter from Black Fergus. I would already have read it the previous evening if Postie had succeeded in getting it up to us. I only skimmed it then, waiting to be alone with yellowhammers among the whins before I carefully digested each statement.

At first Black Fergus wrote long and full letters and they came often. But as the winter weeks went by his letters grew shorter and came less frequently. I sensed my friend's difficulty in finding new things to say each time, though this did not assuage my disappointment when gradually the trickle of letters stopped altogether. For news of Black Fergus then we had to rely on his correspondence home to Sallachie where I was included in his 'regards to all at Blarosnich'.

Relentlessly the snows covered the familiar patterns of the fields and hills. Yet by equally powerful forces, hidden, it seemed, within the earth itself, the winter vice was forced at last. My father's new drains gurgled and sang when the great thaw set in. By the time the last flanks of Craigclamhan had lost their white livery I had got over the hurt of Black Fergus's leaving. Shortly afterwards our world was shaken by the arrival of someone who was to change several of our lives, including my own—completely.

10

The Holy Bough

Our lives changed because of Betty. Those who said Black Fergus had deserted from the navy and had come back permanently disguised as a woman had much to support their claim. The shepherdess of the Sallachie hill never wore skirts, though the sight of her broad bottom comfortably, if ungracefully, accommodated in khaki trousers was not the least objection which Herself had to Betty.

Sandy had taken on three elderly men in quick succession as replacements for Black Fergus, and had reached the point of selling half his ewes when the Women's Land Army came to the rescue. The marches of Sallachie were not easily walked. Despite its name—the Place of Willows—the farm was a place of massive rock, although there was no rising to a peak or climax comparing with the remote nobility of our Craigclamhan.

Unlike Blarosnich, which the sea almost surrounded though not within sight or earshot of the house, our neighbours had only a little coastline on the far Pitlobar side, further along from Alec's croft. Blarosnich acted as a windbreak for Sallachie, shielding it from the moody Atlantic. But the snows around Black Fergus's home always seemed deeper and more treacherous than ours, perhaps because the winds which whipped Blarosnich did not ravage the sheltered Sallachie. The farm had only two small grass parks and hardly enough moor. In our neighbourhood it was recognized as a hard hill to work and the dogs, flinging themselves among the brittle rocks, were short-lived. Sallachie was a place of stones, not willows.

Yet despite the steepness of the scree braes and labyrinths of rocky outcrops, which made ideal fox-dens and wedging traps for lambs, until Black Fergus went away the hill had carried eighty score of ewes. Then, after a year or so, when the future lay heavily in the balance, Betty came along, in the big woolly green sweater and thick khaki trousers of the Women's Land Army. Sandy and Violet were delighted, Herself outraged and my father sceptical. Soon everybody was talking about Betty. Her likes and dislikes swept the countryside. She had Black Fergus's daring and disdain for convention. But she had a woman's guile as well.

Betty came from London and expressed considerable pride in the fact that she had been born within sound of the now silent Bow Bells. The shepherdess could take the roughest flanks of Sallachie in her stride and proved to be a master with plough and harrow. But surprisingly she had the most dainty little hands and a tiny red mouth glowing in all seasons like winter dog-hips in the soft pink face which never saw paint or powder. Before coming to Sallachie Betty had not experienced sheep or hill farming, but she soon became a fast shearer and clever dog handler. Her Land Army days had mostly been spent on tractor work in the mild south, and she impressed my father with her superior knowledge of farm machinery. A score of bed-wetting evacuees from the bombed cities would not have given rise to so much local gossip. And by the time Violet brought her over to the first Saturday ceilidh we had been regaled by Mirren and Postie with reports of Betty's fantastic energy and revolutionary ideas for working a poor hill-farm.

What particularly pleased us at Blarosnich was that Sandy had at last found somebody who satisfactorily took Black Fergus's place. We could not help feeling suspicious of this Londoner when talk turned from the desperate remedy of selling Sallachie's ewes to optimistic ideas about increasing their number. And Betty did not wait for the second grace after Saturday supper before getting up from the table to go out and examine my father's tractor. Not in Black Fergus's wildest moments had we ever seen such enthusiasm.

Herself did not know where she stood in relation to this ebullient newcomer. While Betty bounced about the place, my grandmother remained as aloof as Craigclamhan. But I could see that the old lady definitely disapproved of the trousers and the cheeky way Betty dug her little hands into the pockets. Her Cockney friendliness conflicted sharply with Highland reserve and straight-laced modesty. During a pause in the dancing later in the evening the gamekeeper broke wind. We all tried to talk and divert attention. Not so Betty, who turned to old Duncan and said 'God love you.'

This remark, both timely and untimely, made Herself feel as uncomfortable as when Black Fergus gave his too-loud 'Amen' at grace. Before the ceilidh finished I could see Herself had decided on final and conclusive disapproval of Betty. Almost at once our relationship with Sallachie became strained and after a few weeks the knell of the Saturday ceilidhs was tolled. Sitting in the house waiting for our guests, we heard the once-familiar roar of Black Fergus's motorbike disturb the deep Highland night. In a moment of excitement I thought Black Fergus had come home on leave. I rushed to the door and found Betty there, with Violet riding on the pillion.

Herself had never approved of Violet reading tea-leaves, an activity which was classed with Alec's pagan charms and cures. Nor had my grandmother liked the way that Violet and her son laughed and joked together. These small irritations could not be allowed to become sources of discord in a farming community like ours where united effort was essential in sheep handlings. Minor grievances were one thing, but to Herself the sight of the two Sallachie women on the motorbike was quite another. She went to her room complaining of pains in her back. We had no dancing that night nor did the motorbike appear in the lane the following Saturday evening. I knew that the long tradition of the Saturday gatherings, which even heavy snows and thunderstorms had seldom interrupted, was at an end.

Herself, however, was not the Almighty, and although she successfully registered objection to Betty's brassy ways and cut our social intercourse, we still saw a lot of the Sallachie folk both in the fank and at the clippings. My father made no secret of being pleased when Betty took over his tractor to do much of the township ploughing and reaping in addition to Sallachie's. This extra work had always made a big claim on his time and was a permanent source of annoyance to Herself. Although I grew accustomed to Betty's presence and learnt to admire the sturdy character hiding behind the London cockiness, I never felt really at ease in her company. Invariably she greeted me with, 'Hullo my old fruit', which made the others laugh and confused me. Somehow I sensed that she felt no particular passion for shepherding or farming and that our Highland way of life exercised no very special fascination over her.

Betty belonged to that group of persons whose drive and energy allowed them to master any situation if it became necessary. If Betty had been milking water-buffaloes in India, packing herrings in Iceland, or leading Communist guerillas in the Chinese mountains she would have done so in the same wholehearted way as she ploughed the township parks and climbed the barren wastes of Sallachie in wild lambing weather. I did not like acknowledging to myself, let alone to anyone else, that her zeal and tirelessness and her mechanical skill made me jealous.

I also resented the way she monopolized Black Fergus when he came home on leave. Too suddenly and too irrevocably, it seemed to me, Fergus had changed into a man. He laughed and joked as he always did and in some ways looked unchanged. A radiant healthiness hung about him. He loved the navy and the roving life of excitement where anything could, and probably did, seeing that this was Black Fergus, happen at any time. But when I looked closely at him, I saw that he had become thick-set and heavy and though his movements were powerful, they lacked the quicksilver lightness I had known.

More lines scored his face than I remembered and sometimes, when he was unaware of being observed, all the brightness would drain from his eyes and be replaced by a faraway look. I could not imagine all that had happened to Black Fergus to bring these changes about. Nobody but me appeared to notice. A barrier stood between us and I felt both sorry and glad that his call over to Blarosnich was only a brief one.

He cut it short in a hearty way and showed not the slightest sign that anything differed at all from the old days. He had to get back, he said, because he had promised to take Betty on the motorbike up the coast to see another Land Girl. After Black Fergus had gone Herself observed that he would have stayed a while longer had it not been for 'that city besom', meaning Betty. Alec surprised us by calling Betty 'great' and defending her even in front of my grandmother.

Black Fergus did not come over again during that short leave. And when he had gone back to join his ship the ritual of spring came on us once more with its miracles of rebirth. Long hours on the lochan shore combing the pre-dawn darkness for difficult births and rescuing orphan lambs took all my strength of mind and body as similar hirsels kept Betty occupied and people like us on every hill-farm. Alec had gone back to Pitlobar for the lambing so that we could not argue over the rights and wrongs of Betty's actions.

Such things as trouser-wearing, motorbike-driving women did not claim our attention now that winter dropped rapidly away. Male arguments of another kind about females began again as the skies gradually lightened and the snows withdrew. Hares rose up on hind legs to battle each other like boxers in a ring. Partridges turned the high ground of the grazing parks into a cockpit and feathers flew before the aggressive males spotted me and started up on whirring wings.

My father and I got in each other's way and were irritable. Not even during the most strained period of my adolescence had there been so much rudeness on my part and curt withdrawal on his. I began to wonder if my adolescence was lingering on, long after it should have left me. Sometimes I wished I could be away from it all like Black Fergus, having my fling in a carefree life.

I could only be happy away from the house. Spring made me delirious. The green waves of new growth flowed around me. I swam in them. As I lay prostrate in the warming sun I imagined I could hear the fescue and bent grasses growing under my head. Happenings in the off-shore gannetry or the relics of lambs outside a fox-den, or birds' heads by an otter's lair interested me more than the curtain-lectures Herself was giving poor Mirren in the kitchen. Piping redshanks made sweeter music for me than the best-played pibroch. I looked forward more to the willow warblers' coming to the Earl's Park than to a social in aid of the Red Cross in the schoolroom where I invariably felt out of place. Rather than wanting to possess this lovely earth reborn each morning, I longed for it to possess me, to make me a full denizen of the moor like the nesting plover and dwarf willows.

I was old enough now to understand that my dissatisfaction came from within myself and was not particularly provoked by a quarrel with Herself or the kirk or my father and his idea of what manliness should be. The men in the township, the smart young coastguards on the pier station which always smelt of manly sweat and old socks, were equally alien to my secret world of the lochan shore. These men climbed through the heather braes to poach deer and shoot wildfowl. When I went off to the remote hirsel, the others supposed that I had merely gone to shepherd there. And so I had, but much more besides. I went to worship rain and sun where singing lark and wheeling gull lived magically.

Black Fergus had been closest to me throughout my whole life, yet he had never plumbed the depths of my real feelings for the moor. Before joining the navy Fergus had been a great wildfowler and master of precision with the gun which rather frightened me. My father had presented me with a ·22 rifle on my thirteenth birthday and for him this had been an essential part of my initiation into manhood. He had no idea that the rifle held no interest for me and I learnt to handle it well enough so that he should not suspect my indifference. Rather than involve myself in complicated explanations which none of the others would have understood, I feigned pride in seeing the ferrets bolt terrified rabbits into the waiting nets. Nobody would have believed that I felt sick each time I took the warm bundle of fur out of the net and, suspending the rabbit in my left hand, brought my right hand down heavily on the back of the pathetic head. This had been one of my first lessons as a small boy. I could not reveal now that I loathed it. I could not possibly tell my grandmother that I admired the fox who came in broad daylight and made off with three ducklings in its mouth, paying not the slightest attention to Herself's screams nor to the wooden beetle flung after him. My family and friends would have thought me mad if I let fall hints of fancies that filled my mind, such as my feeling that I would like to be a young rabbit sampling the sweet grasses of spring or a badger cub playing in the moonlight.

I now had a fine working pair of collies to myself, but I did not always take them with me to A'Mhin-choiseachd despite their excitement and the lolling tongues greeting me as I crossed the yard with my cromag which told the dogs at once that I was off to the hill. Up there, the young hares feared the dogs' approach more than the pouncing golden eagle, the lapwings rightly mistrusted the barking more than the egg-robbers' laughter. Even the sheep were never happy with a dog in sight.

Unlike the other men, I tried not to go up to the moor as its enemy or as a menace to its hundreds of fascinating creatures. I wanted to be one with the covey of red grouse, the basking lizard, the roe and the heron, the tender life emerging from the wheatear's pale turquoise-blue eggs in the deserted rabbit hole, the hardy old stags running together in the summer grazing of high corries. I wanted the moor to accept me as belonging to itself.

When I stripped off my shirt now, it was not merely to let the sun rouse sensation in my body but also that I might feel the breathing earth. Sometimes a kind of bliss came over me, in which my body's sensuality seemed to be only a part of the whole sensuousness of nature. I did not think of these things in high flights of poetry or philosophy. My feelings expressed themselves in simple ways, such as my wish that a hind might come and breathe her sweet breath over my naked chest. More often than not this romantic desire met with no greater fulfilment than an emperor-moth caterpillar could give as it walked with its tiny feet down the valley between the muscles of my chest.

At one period, much to my surprise, religion became a preoccupation. It was a dreamy, un-kirk-like religion, half pagan and vaguely associated with my earlier discoveries of Classical Greece and the gods. I wondered if Jesus Christ communicated with the animals up on our moors just as He had walked on the sea and commanded the winds and the waves. From the first time I heard the story I had been impressed by the way St Peter went on his

Master's behalf and found the tribute money in the mouth of a fish. And although I had several times counted the seventy-six gall-stones Teacher so proudly kept as a souvenir from her operation (at school it had been a sign of approval to be allowed to count them) I still hoped to open a pike from the lochan and find something more interesting than the remains of a gosling.

Alec's folklore stories appealed much more strongly to me than the Gospels. I loved the idea of the waders covering Our Lord with seaweed when the Roman soldiers came to arrest Him. But though I lay silent and motionless for hours on the shore, the oystercatchers and sandpipers never lost their suspicion of me. Occasionally a dunlin, suffering from exhaustion on its long migratory flight, would allow me to smell its streaked chestnut plumage. And even the friendly seals would not let me indulge in more than a surreptitious scratch of their basking sides.

When quite a small boy I kept pet jackdaws and owls, rabbits and squirrels and even a fox. But later I could only see them as unhappy captives and let them go. Poor Roger the fox managed to free himself, but the chain around his neck caught in a hedge and he was hung. My cock pheasant gave me the greatest joy of these tame animals. In the morning he would fly off to freedom in the woods. At nightfall, I rattled corn in a bucket and called out to him. Then, with a startling loud crow he would come back and land on my shoulder.

Lying out on the moors, I so wanted the creatures to come to me as my pets had done. I did not want to use my superior human force by robbing their young and keeping them as sad prisoners. And the ancient Greeks, I felt sure, experienced nature as I was trying to do. Certainly, for me, they got nearer to natural things than Jesus Christ's disciples did. Although I had come home from London with my dreams shattered about heroes on old stone friezes and white gods on the lawns of Attica, the picture of Pan frolicking in the woods among animals to whom he half belonged was my idea of a deity. But the Arcadian gods, like Christ's disciples, did not help me to win friendships on the lochan shore. Hermes did not come for my offerings of marjoram and hyacinth.

Why did not the harmony the ancient Greeks felt for their surrounding natural world come to me now, as I lay hypnotized by mist and sea-roar? I asked myself this question and could never find the answer. True, those days of spring had moments when I felt my body passing into unity with the newly resurrected land. The lake accepted me as though I were a water-shrew swimming with an air-locked fur. Winds dried me. Sun warmed me. Lapwings warned me of intruders. And the mountain springs which gave drink to otter and deer quenched my thirst also. Yet there were limits beyond which I could not pass. The roe did not beckon me, nor did the curlew trust its four buffish eggs to my love. Human nature may have been a part of all nature, but human behaviour, however well intentioned, was not.

Mystical union with nature failed. Putting religion on one side I was then moved to become a vegetarian. Apart from the extra strain this imposed on my already overworked grandmother, there was another way of regarding the situation. As usual, Herself was blunt. 'Who,' she demanded, 'listened to the death pangs of the bluebell in your button-hole?'

I had no answer. Herself, seeing that her question silenced me, went on with an eloquence which emulated Giolla Criost The Tailor. Finally, when she came to the end of her harangue, I felt life would be easier, after all, in *not* being a vegetarian. I could find nothing to counter my grandmother's insistence on wanting to know who could stop a stag in its cudding and obtain justice for the mangled grasses, or prevent the sheep-rot's sticky leaves from closing over and crushing the unwary insects they devoured.

Nevertheless, these arguments, though apparently unanswerable, did nothing to quell my unquiet love for natural things. Herself was a practical woman, trained in the hard school of her childhood island of Eilean a'Cathmara. But kindness also lay in her. Any orphan lamb which did not respond to the bottle went forthwith into a tasty dish. Yet, sometimes at night I would hear Teacher getting annoyed in their big bed in the next room because my grandmother had swatted a fly and was scrabbling about under the bed to make certain she had killed the fly properly. Just as she ranted against township folk who borrowed, and then gave them her precious egg-money, so she attacked my refusal to eat meat.

Unknown to myself in those formative years, my grandmother influenced my life more than anyone else, more even than Black Fergus or Alec. However much I resented them at the time, Herself's values were the ones I carried into later years, regretting then only the fact that I had not inherited her fine ear for music. Alec knew interesting stories but told them badly. Herself made poetry out of them. And if only she had not preached the gospel of lapping so loudly and persistently, I would have enjoyed her company out in the summer parks.

Astonishingly, however, even Herself seemed to be learning a lesson from the war which was now looking as though it might go on for ever. Our silage had been such a success with the cattle that a second and larger pit was built. Herself was out, walking round and round the outside, air-locking the succulent grasses, skirts tucked up as though she were a priest encircling the walls of Jericho with a ram's horn. Indeed, my grandmother called the big pit Jericho—the Place of Fragrance. The sumptuous smell of this rich mixture of clover and rape and black molasses sent the cattle into raptures when we placed it in the winter cribs.

Only when both silos had been filled and sealed with boulders until winter, did I realize that for once I was not the cause of the friction between my father and me. While in the house, he had been snappy and moody with the others also. Mirren said that his teeth must be bad. The reason lay hidden from me. But when the potato gathering came round, I found out what was happening.

Going about lost in my dream world on the hill, trying to make tangible contacts with the natural world around me, I had misunderstood my father's moods. And as I crept into the steep forest by Stag's Pool one day I saw something which shocked and astonished me as much as Pan himself would have done had he been there among the beech leaves. But my reaction was not so startling as my father's as he uncoiled himself from Betty's embrace.

Betty's efforts to put me at my ease were much more disturbing than the actual discovery in the woods. She knew by now the delicate threads of past and present that wove the fabric of life at Blarosnich, how the dead often seemed more powerful than the living, the ghosts of The Captain and Our Rhona shadowing the chairs we sat on, the cups we drank out of. Betty realized my father's difficulty in communicating with me, or indeed with anyone since his wife's death. And now Betty's breezy friendliness and joking remarks to cover up the incident under the trees made things much worse. They confused me and made me feel so naïve because I had been unaware of the friendship maturing over the months.

Three months later the kirk-supper was eaten in the garlanded barn and Betty became mistress of Blarosnich. Two score and more dancers filled the Field of Sighing with boisterous laughter. The music of jig and reel carried far over the still, frosty night, as people told us afterwards. But this was like a fanfare of trumpets heralding a new reign at Blarosnich.

Undoubtedly the most extraordinary aspect of the whole romantic story came from Herself's attitude towards having Betty as a daughter-in-law. She had bitterly resented the Cockney Land Girl in trousers who not only drove a motorbike but went off on the Lord's Day to shoot rabbits on the hill. But my grandmother had aged considerably in the past year. Rheumatism made it almost impossible for her to go even as far as the hen house to gather eggs.

Faced with being a cripple, the old lady knew that Blarosnich had to have a woman in the house, a sound and practical woman who would not be beaten by the long hours of work and the unceasing fight against the weather while trying to win harvests or save sheep. Most of the women in our own and neighbouring townships seemed set against the drudgery of a farm kitchen. Their older children nowadays came to potato gatherings only reluctantly and talked about the rate of pay per hour they expected.

For the woman who ruled the Blarosnich hearth there could be expectancy of neither wages nor thanks. Nobody would consider her worth a tinker's curse if she failed to be at the kitchen stove when the men left for lambing in the bitter pre-dawn of spring. And she would be lucky if her boots were off when the moon rose up over the harvest fields.

Although Herself had been helped for years now by both Teacher and Mirren, neither of these two were able to take responsibilities and make the decisions which occurred each day. Also, Teacher was no longer young, though she was a victim not so much of senility as overweight. Mirren was too scatterbrained to be left on her own for long. Fear afflicted her as rheumatism did Herself. She feared the bull in the yard and darkness on the way home to the township. Poor Mirren could not have been left alone while the men were over at Pitlobar. My grandmother faced the reality of our situation and acknowledged the fact that a strong and fearless woman was needed.

Herself had obviously turned these matters over in her mind and come to the only possible conclusion. Despite Betty's city origins and occasional dropping of phrases which outraged whig-gamore taste she was the only woman we had known who had an identical calibre of spirit with my grandmother. Although these two differed widely in outlook and manner, they both had granite characters. To give Herself credit, she quickly recognized this quality behind the offending façade of green jersey and khaki trousers.

Forgetting Sir Duncan's verse and The Tailor's eloquence, my grandmother returned to the Good Book. 'Jehovah-jireh,' she could be heard mumbling for months after the marriage—God had provided once again as faithfully as He had given a substitute sacrifice to Abraham. Herself tried hard not to notice Betty's remarks, and this was the old lady's way of showing gratitude to her Maker who had made provision against the day, which could not now be so far away, when she herself would bake the last griddle of dropped scones. And even if Betty did sometimes take the Lord's name in vain, she also had the language of the hill and the music of the byre.

This peaceful co-existence could not have come about at Blarosnich without Betty's own determination that it should. Her very first deed on becoming my step-mother impressed us all, especially Herself. As the harvest had already long been in, my father thought that a week or ten days snatched, at long last, with his cousin in the Black Isle, would be an ideal way to spend a honeymoon. Betty did not think this right. Alec had come back again to the Blarosnich bothie and Betty suggested they spend the week over at Pitlobar.

Another recruit from the Women's Land Army, Gladys, was herding the Sallachie marches, and an entirely new atmosphere surrounded the hill-farming community. These city girls not only cheerfully did jobs which the township women despised, but they also made the men ashamed to grumble so constantly about the weather and market prices. The Land Girls brought merriment into the dreariest routine. They made us think it a pleasure to work in the summer hayfields, and they sang happily as they drove tractors well into the night. Betty stayed out cutting bracken long after I had taken my socks off and hung them to dry near the kitchen fire.

The most piercing of the winds about Blarosnich had no effect on Betty. Her innate cheerfulness defied even the long days of drizzle which turned frequently into revengeful rain. When its knife-like slashings threatened to cut any human face exposed to the sky, Betty came into the woodshed. 'Lovely weather for ducks,' she would say in innocent heartiness. The rain trickling from her hair and down the red cheeks played no part as stage props to sham heroics. Rainstorms left Betty as happy as a hare snug in its forme of summer grasses.

By late spring I could see that Betty had overcome the last of my grandmother's resistance. On going into the house for the milking pails I heard Herself mumbling away in Gaelic as she stood gazing from the window. The old lady was watching Betty putting bar-frames on a beehive. Herself had given the care of the bees to Betty. This had been significant enough. But my grandmother had crowned her new daughter-in-law with a sacred relic of The Captain's—the straw boater with black veil which I had never been allowed to touch.

Domestic bliss hung over Blarosnich like a summer midday sun and another harvest was gathered into the stackyard. Herself had not been able to tread the silo pits but nevertheless, bent over two sticks, hobbled out to smell the fragrance of Jericho. The high season rushed on into autumn and before the snows came Black Fergus was home again, this time radiant with a new glory. He had become a fully-fledged officer. Gold gleamed on his uniform cuffs and his eyes shone with pride. He seemed impossibly healthier than before.

When he came bounding into the house, as he had always done, like a big black shaggy dog, though now impeccably groomed, Herself nearly dropped her two sticks in surprise and delight. She had thought highly of Fergus as a boy out foxing in the hills, but she had always equally resented his cheeky familiarity and the way he pinched female bottoms and teased the unwary like Alec and the gamekeeper. One Christmas he had even desecrated Herself's private altar by putting cottonwool moustaches and beard on the glass of The Captain's photograph over the fireplace. But now all this was forgiven, even the fruity 'Amen' that had made the old lady wince after so many meals. Black Fergus had gone away under a cloud when he joined the navy because of his dressing-up at the Big House party while under the influence of strong drink. But that disgrace too was forgotten when Herself surveyed the radiance of his new uniform.

Black Fergus had made good. Henceforth he was called *The* Lieutenant. Herself had his photograph framed and put on the mantlepiece beside the tea caddy, just a little below the faded portrait of The Captain which Fergus had dared to mock with Father Christmas whiskers. Just as Don the Ferry had 'got on in life' and become master of a great yacht, so it appeared that Black Fergus had kept his 'neb at the grunstane' and returned to claim our respect and admiration.

After my father's marriage the restlessness in me grew to a climax. I felt that I got in the newly-weds' way. I imagined that had I been elsewhere Betty's laughter in the night would have been louder. I thought my father's glances at me when she kissed him in the middle of the fank meant that he wished me gone. Betty behaved in an open and spontaneous way, whereas my father remained the most shy and retiring of men. He blushed when perhaps he would not have done had I been away. And now that Black Fergus had reached such outstanding achievements and Herself could not knit him socks and comforts quickly enough, eyes turned expectantly in my direction. Nobody needed to say anything. I knew they thought I should join up as well.

Gladys and Betty took the war far more seriously than we did. They spoke with bitterness whenever Hitler's name was mentioned as if they had personal grievances against him. How she would just love to be a man, Gladys repeated often, just so that she could 'get a crack at him'. Perhaps her outbursts were never intended as hints to me, but increasingly I regarded them in this light.

With my seventeenth birthday behind me, I would shortly be old enough for conscription. My father had never doubted I would be exempted from call-up because of my indispensable work on the hill. But Betty's contribution made mine no longer indispensable. Within a very short period she was able to manage a lot of my shepherding apart from the lion's share of the ploughing and tractor work. There was already talk of another girl coming to run a large-scale poultry business. The Women's Land Army proved its worth in a way that farming people never suspected it would. Young men like me could easily be done without on many farms.

Being remote as we were from the realities of the war, we all regarded it in a romantic way. Black Fergus's triumphant return was seen as an affair of honour. Herself's idea of war came largely from the Gaelic stories of long ago, and she saw it as my duty to go out and do battle. My grandmother expected me to prove my manhood like The Captain and The Lieutenant. Before Betty became mistress of Blarosnich, any suggestion of my leaving would have been treason. Now I would not be forsaking my rightful place on the hill but merely handing it over to someone just as competent as myself.

A trial of my faith began. My true nature was being forced into the open. I remembered that other occasion on which the truth stole upon me unawares, when Aunt Jessie found the whisky leaking through the cactus pot. I sat out on the hill brooding, recognizing myself as a coward at heart. Many of little Eddie's ideas about killing came to me again, but I neither knew whether they were right nor how to express them if they were. To have done so at Blarosnich would have produced an unexploded-bomb situation. Life would have been unbearable for everybody.

As I contemplated the war, I knew instinctively it was not an affair of shining glory as Herself pictured it. The hundreds of times I had taken rabbits from the ferreting nets to silence them with a single blow of my right hand seemed now to rise up with jeering accusation. Even when my grandmother told me to get my gun and bring something home for the pot, I had to deny myself and assume the convention of manliness which was demanded of the son of Blarosnich but which was alien to my true nature.

When I was only nine years old my father came into the kitchen one day with a small fox cub. He had brought it home as live bait for training young cairns. But as I heard the dogs being encouraged to attack the little cub which snarled with terror in a corner, I burst into tears and turned on my family. It was the biggest and most dramatic scene of my life. I cried and shouted, kicked and howled in protest. The baby fox did not appeal to me as a pet so much as a victim of what seemed a senselessly cruel and slow death. My family degraded itself in my eyes by abetting such a thing. But the screaming prevailed and I was given Roger. For two years I cared for him until the day he broke free and hung himself on his prisoner's chain in the hedge.

People thought me 'soft' for this. In order to avoid being laughed at in the way Eddie at the Big House had been, I purposely deceived them into thinking I was made of the same 'manly' fibre as themselves. While only nine I had won the battle for Roger's life. The battle of manhood had to be won by more subtle means than passions and tears.

Wandering up through the heather braes with a rifle to stalk deer the same conflicts weighed on me. Nothing would have been easier than to continue my present life of shepherding. Alec could easily have taken over the lochan hirsel and it would have been simple for me to go and live permanently over at Pitlobar. The life this would have brought about appealed to me. I was never afraid of being alone. It did not worry me to be sealed off from other people by snows and distance and inaccessibility.

I felt sure my father would fill in the conscription exemption papers if I asked him. Concealing my real feelings from family and friends and even Black Fergus had become a habit. None of them suspected the difference between the person who knelt before the nesting plover and the sham hunter who sickened when his finger touched the trigger.

Every day the strain grew. In a way, I despised that side of my character which could bear with so much duplicity. I wondered if my life had been degraded and had become nothing but one long effort at deception. Would I always have to put up a façade in order to be accepted? Had I sipped the hated whisky with my cousin in London only so that he would not regard me as a country bumpkin? Had I roused the Paddy woodmen's emotions with outrageous untruths about Ruby on the train only so that I could be one of them? Had I hidden my real thoughts from Black Fergus during a dozen years, and had I done things which repelled me, just to win his friendship?

Alec had always been easier to talk to about serious matters than anybody else I knew, but even he could not understand why I used to avoid the smart young stalkers from the Big House when I was a boy. Poor, nervous Mirren in the kitchen hated to drown kittens and pups down at her mother's croft. When the occasion arose, she would ask me to go down and do it for her, completely unaware that I shrank from stifling the animals' terrible cries and only did it so that others should not question my manliness. The hours I spent admiring my body in Herself's long mirror were only a fraction of those I spent making sure that others' ways and ideas were faithfully reflected in my own outward life. Teacher probably guessed at the conflict inside me. But although, when I asked her, she got the works of Oscar Wilde from the travelling library which came to the school and then smuggled them into the house, I could not go to her now.

I did not know what to do. There was nobody I could turn to for help. As soon as I entered the house I sensed that my sullen moods put a restraint on Betty's happy relations with my father, clouding the sunlight of their landscape. Something had to happen and in the end Black Fergus solved the problem.

I had resented his officer's uniform, thinking it raised an insurmountable wall between me and my old friend. But I was wrong. One morning when I went over to the water-mill I found Fergus waiting for me. He was wearing his old blue jersey and wellingtons and looked as if he had never been away, as though dressing up in the gold-braided uniform had been just another prank to frighten me. As soon as I saw him I guessed that he had something personal to tell me, something not meant for Postie to carry from farm to farm, nor for Gladys to laugh about with Betty. It was these confidences I missed more than anything else when Black Fergus had first gone away.

Fergus had never been one for beating about bushes. He came straight to the point. He did not talk about the war or about a girl as I thought he would, but about his own life when the war finished. Nobody liked to forecast when the end would come, but by this time it looked as if Hitler's New Order was not going to rule the world. Britain would eventually win. And what then, Black Fergus was asking. He certainly had no intention of coming home to Sallachie, as we all thought he would. The sea had got into him. He talked of tankers and the South American run, the Big Lizzie and the Far East tramps. In spite of the gold braid he had won, Black Fergus told me that he would leave the Royal Navy at once if they would let him join the merchant service, which was the silver lining of his tomorrow.

My friend's confession came in a troubled voice as we crouched in the dark shed which trembled with the deep rhythm of the falling wheel and trickling ears of corn. I hardly knew how to deal with his troubles as well as my own.

Black Fergus looked at me, 'We could go away together,' he said.

When the war ended, which might be soon, why didn't we pack up and go off together? We would see Rio de Janeiro, Hong Kong, San Francisco, the Nile, Bombay, the dolly dives of Naples, desert islands in the Pacific, the North, the South, eastern women and western oceans. I remembered how he had laid the world at my feet once before when he first got his motorbike. But it was a far more dazzling world Black Fergus offered now.

His leave ended, and resplendent once more in his officer's uniform Black Fergus went away. At our parting he shook my hand, gave me a broad, but solemn wink. 'Think about it,' he said.

I thought of nothing else. Black Fergus's idea had cleared a way through the tangle of my life. Also, I was filled with a buoyant happiness that in the end, after all his adventures and triumphs, Black Fergus had not replaced our solid, lifelong friendship with any of these things. Now that he had made this clear to me, I almost did not care what happened. In all my uncertainty, one thing was certain : Black Fergus and I would sail the Seven Seas together as we had roamed our own moors and hills.

It no longer gave me anguish to think that perhaps Black Fergus, whose voice we knew like that of the bantam cock which defied Herself's beetle and gained entry to the kitchen half a dozen times a day, might no longer go fishing when peace came and the herring fleet rode out in the darkness he loved. When Fergus had gone, my mind still seemed crushed by his powerful grip. His flashing dark eyes, winking at our newest secret, seemed to be laughing. Our words in the corn-mill still sounded in my ears.

However, it was not until a cold, wretched day some weeks later when I sat in the root house sorting seed potatoes that I made up my mind. Fergus's prophesy about the war ending soon did not look like coming true. The wireless and the newspapers were talking about new fronts. Even Herself was growing weary of solemnly listening to all the Allies' national anthems, like a victory parade that abruptly ended when the news bulletin announced more losses at sea, more blitzed towns and cities.

I made a decision. I could not wait for the war to outrun my eighteenth year. Wasting no time, I went immediately across to the house and found Herself in the kitchen. As far as I was concerned she was still head of the house, though she could hardly move from her chair beside the fire.

'I want to join the Merchant Navy.'

It burst from me. Now it was done. All the months of agony and tension were over. Even if the old lady did not give permission, I would go anyway. But her wrinkled face puckered in a broad smile of approval. She gave me the greatest blessing any suggestion could receive at Blarosnich. Looking up at the portrait of The Captain she spoke to it as though I were not there.

'Did you hear that, Donald Cameron? Your lad's got it in him.'

I told nobody what had passed between Black Fergus and myself in the corn-mill.

Now that my future was settled, my fears went. And I recalled that for years I had pictured myself packing up gladly and leaving Blarosnich for the sea. The place where I kept my secret letters and childhood trove was in the great sea-chest up in the loft. Even when I was seven or eight I would climb inside the trunk, close the domed lid and imagine myself as a stowaway waiting to be discovered by a ship's steward or a negro servant at one of the hotels whose labels still decorated the outside. I had loved the trunk because it had been to China and India and smelt of an exciting life in a score of exotic countries. Although it lived in the loft, the big trunk was the most noble piece of furniture at Blarosnich for me, because it was a veteran from the oceans and seaports of Black Fergus's plan. I had not corresponded for years with my pen-friends from magazine columns, yet I still kept the trunk locked in the loft with those mementoes of the past.

I had no difficulty in being accepted by the Merchant Navy. Only the date of my departure remained to be fixed. Meanwhile the wooden trunk in the loft needed attention because I had decided to get rid of its contents. If anything should prevent my coming back to Blarosnich, somebody else might discover my secret hoard.

I could not bear to think of other people reading the simple, frank letters from the Paddies or those from Canada and Mexico requesting photographs and enclosing others smothered in barbed-wire rows of kisses. And if Herself were ever to rifle the trunk she would be hurt to find the charms and amulets Alec had given me and which I had kept from my earliest days. She would certainly fall into a paroxysm if she discovered the rosary I found in London during my holiday and often looked at. The Christ on the crucifix was a young, tortured Jesus, like a Greek athlete impaled

197

on the gallows. It represented much more closely my own idea of a godhead, rather than the nightshirted Father of the kirk who threatened hell-fire to sinners exposing their limbs on holiday beaches and enjoying to the full the bodies He had made after His own likeness.

The rosary lay on top of my notebooks and scraps of paper with thoughts I had scribbled over the years. I had to get rid of these as well. Without meaning to be unkind Betty would laugh at the sentimental verses I had cut from newspapers or my own poetry written in moments of emotion, like the sinking of the *Royal Oak* or the pastoral poems about a winter morning spent watching the roe in the Earl's Park.

Discovery of these precious things could not be risked. I still wished to keep my real nature hidden from exposure. Betty may well have laughed at me, but I did not want to take a chance. Before I went away I discovered Betty shared feelings which were kindred to my own. One day when we were loading firewood near Stag's Pool she pointed to a noble beech.

'Hasn't she a lovely skin? You want to hug it.'

I too had often admired the broad-bellied trunk and felt compelled to put my lips against the smooth grey bark. Betty's habit of calling things 'him' and 'her' pleased me. It showed she appreciated that they had an individual identity, apart from every other thing, which was the way I thought of things.

Betty talked about trees and machines as if they were persons, just as my grandmother always referred to the kitchen stove as 'him'.

No melancholy attended my clearing out the bundles of letters from the trunk and the carrying of them up to the moor for burning. I was relieved to destroy their secrets, glad not to have betrayed the confidences of people on Mediterranean islands or from lonely farms on Icelandic fjords who had poured out their hearts to me on paper. I was also thankful that my family would gain neither amusement nor offence on finding them. This would have been as mortifying as if Herself had discovered me in front of her full-length mirror examining my lanky schoolboy body. As each letter burned and coiled into thin white wafers of ash, emotional fetters binding me to the past were broken. The burning freed me.

With the letters and poems gone and the rosary given to Alec, I left the key in the lock of the trunk, though it still contained odd pieces of junk which even at this late stage I was loathe to destroy. But they could be left unlocked. No intruder could possibly read the secrets behind the dried-up chestnut conkers that had split out of their fleshy green burrs a dozen years before. The razor shells and cockles had histories which most people would think the same as those of the curious stones and pieces of driftwood my father kept on his bedroom mantlepiece. Many might recall the fox-trots and ballads on the gramophone records in the trunk, but nobody except Black Fergus was left in the Highlands who had heard the ash logs crackle as the records were played over and over to the Irish woodmen up at the Forestry camp.

I put in my pocket the only thing from the trunk which I wanted to take away with me—the lucky piece of juniper. In our northern woods the juniper fared poorly and grew to little more than a straggling bush. But although the juniper never lifted its head high, the bush possessed all sorts of exalted powers which the lordly trees, whose undergrowth it formed, never achieved. Alec had told me to pluck a piece of juniper years before I ever thought of diving into Stag's Pool with Black Fergus. The shepherd saw me paddling in the shallows by the cattle crossing of Labharag. Alec had already impressed me with his tales of shipwrecks besides the drowning of my great-grandfather on the hidden skerries of Eilean a'Cathmara. Juniper, said Alec, was a powerful protection against drowning.

And so the juniper wood which I now took from the trunk in the loft was among the first things I had ever collected, a piece of wood against death at sea. I got it from the bushes around the pines on the tups' hill leading to Earl's Park, a favourite resort of my sun-bathing days. I wanted the piece of juniper with me when I went away from Blarosnich not so much as an amulet as a link with the past. Alec could not have guessed how the old Catholic custom inherited from his mother's girlhood home on Eriskay influenced me years later. Perhaps like the pleasure of the body, or swimming in Stag's Pool, staying out late and not reverencing the stern Highland Sabbath and other forbidden activities, Roman Catholic ideas intrigued me simply because they were taboo at Blarosnich.

The shepherd taught me some lines when I was a small boy. They were old and used long before Herself went out to gather spring nettles on Eilean a'Cathmara or Roderick of the goose-green sold his famous horse. Alec's concern for me, his undemonstrative love, reached out and helped me many times by means of the strange litany I learnt from him about juniper.

With the loft trunk almost cleared I held Alec's amulet and looked at it. Perhaps I had seized on this as my talisman because when Black Fergus was home on his last leave I noticed that he still wore his under the officer's gold braid. Then I remembered that I had only committed Alec's curious charm to memory because Black Fergus had done so. Though I was only seven I had to emulate my hero. Smiling to myself about the years behind us I said again,

I will gather this holy bough
By one fair rib of Jesus
In the name of Father, the Son and Spirit of humility,
Against fatigue in running, walking and lying down.

I will gather this holy bough
By three fair ribs of Jesus
In the name of Father, the Son and Spirit of wisdom,
Against a stony heart, pain of body and false friends.

I will gather this holy bough
By nine fair ribs of Jesus
In the name of Father, the Son and Spirit of compassion,
Against misfortune in travelling, against fire, against drowning.

Days of waiting to go for my sea training dragged into agonizing weeks. I longed for the new life to begin and grew weary in the battle of parting with the old. That way of life I had known so long would also change. The juniper might protect me from a stony heart and drowning. But nothing existed which could hold back the tides of change which must inevitably overwhelm the Blarosnich I was leaving. The steel hames of the bay mare would be exchanged for the steel gears of a more efficient tractor. A hydraulic loader would replace my simple muck fork with half a broken tine. Betty would give the Field of Sighing five sons, each of whom would tread the familiar sheep tracks through crowberry and deer's-hair grass. These fine lads would grow up to know a different Blarosnich, prosperous with a fleet of cars to whisk them off to agricultural colleges. They would see pink-tiled bathrooms in the township crofts and hear the genteel voices of retired couples going 'back to nature' in converted cottages crammed with Georgian furniture.

My portion of that inheritance was not the withered conkers and broken shells left behind in the loft trunk. As I set off at last one morning with my kitbag for Glasgow, I also went overburdened with all the riches Blarosnich had showered on me over the years. I was taking the whole place with me, a Blarosnich quite different from Herself's or my father's or Betty's sons'.

Craigclamhan's proud profile, the cliff of the peregrine falcon, the beds of yellow flags garlanding the Mother of the Little Loud One, the eyes of toads hypnotized by a hurricane lamp among the ruins of Eilean a'Cathmara, the black claws of slumbering seal bull upon the rocks, nights in the orchard when I waited to see if the hedgehog really carried apples impaled on its spines, days when laughter consecrated the waters of Stag's Pool—all these, sight, sound, and scent, went away with me. That I was losing Blarosnich was an illusion. Time was the deceiver. Living memories crowded my mind like city people crowded the city streets. My head was as tightly packed as my kitbag. Nobody could ask for more than that. It was a kitbag I would carry about for ever.